BEARS

An Outdoor Life Book

BEARS

A veteran outdoorsman's account of the most
fascinating and dangerous animals in North America

BEN EAST

Illustrated by
Tom Beecham

OUTDOOR LIFE
CROWN PUBLISHERS, INC.
NEW YORK

Library of Congress Catalog Card Number: 76-053205
ISBN: 0-517-53231X

Manufactured in the United States of America

I dedicate this book, with sincere thanks, to the many people who contributed to it in one way or another. Most of them are named in its pages. Some figure in the episodes and encounters, some supplied anecdotes, others added to my knowledge of bears and their ways. Without such help the book could not have been written, for there is vastly more here than one man could learn by himself in a lifetime. To all whose assistance made it possible, I acknowledge my obligation. Their help was given generously and graciously, and it is valued accordingly.

B. E.

Contents

Part II — THE GRIZZLY AND BROWN

Part III — THE POLAR BEAR

Introduction

Bears have fascinated me most of my adult life.

I met my first bear hunter more than fifty years ago. He was Ike Cooper, who for a number of years before and after the turn of the century had owned and operated a drugstore at Cheboygan, on Lake Huron some fifteen miles southeast of the Straits of Mackinac in northern Michigan. A twenty-four-hour lapse in insurance coverage, coupled with a freak bit of bad luck—a fire set by an arsonist—destroyed the store and its contents and left Cooper stripped of most of what he owned. He moved south to the auto-making city of Flint and took a job as production manager in one of the factories there. That was where I came to know him, when I went to work in the same office in 1918.

I was twenty at the time, a southern Michigan farm boy whose hunting had been limited to rabbits, squirrels, and now and then, without any conspicuous success, ruffed grouse. For me, Ike Cooper's stories of his encounters with bears in the north woods of the state were heady stuff.

In the years he had lived at Cheboygan, that area of northern Michigan was prime black-bear country. He teamed up with a partner, a peg-legged veteran of the Civil War named Littlefield, whom he always referred to as Cap. Together, they turned into what must have been two of the top bear hunters in the country. Before the heyday of their sport ended they had accounted for some 175 blacks.

Today that would be regarded as excessive and indefensible killing. But the logging era was coming to an end then in northern Michigan, settlers were moving in on the heels of the lumberjacks, and bears were proving trouble-making neighbors for farmers raising sheep or hogs.

There was no closed season on them and the standard way of holding down the bear population was by the use of heavy steel traps with toothed jaws. The idea of faulting Cooper and Littlefield for killing too many bears never crossed anybody's mind, including their own.

Introduction

They used the same technique that accounts for most of the black bears taken by hunters in the Midwest today, except those run with hounds. They did the bulk of their hunting in early spring, when the bears were coming hungry out of winter dens, and they relied on bait stations of one kind or another.

One of their favorite locations was a logging-camp slop hole, where the cook had discarded garbage and waste grease all winter. When the camp closed down in spring the bears of the neighborhood were quick to locate such dumps and pay nightly visits to clear up the scraps. Ike and Cap made many of their kills by standing watch in the door of a deserted cook shanty.

It often happened, too, that in the course of winter logging operations a horse suffered a broken leg or injured itself in some other way so severely that it had to be killed and left in the woods. Camp bosses were good about letting Cooper and Littlefield know about such incidents, and come spring a horse carcass was almost sure to attract bears.

Finally, if no ready-made bait station was at hand in the right place they arranged one of their own, usually by netting a bushel or two of suckers when the spring run was on in a nearby stream, and dumping them beside a used bear trail. Whatever the bait, the hunting was almost surefire.

Often a bear came in the black of night, when it was too dark to see the barrel of a rifle, much less the sights. The two hunters learned quickly how to deal with that. They knotted a handkerchief around the barrel near the muzzle, with the knot on top. That blob of white, against the shadowy shape of the bear, was all they needed. Many of their kills were made at ranges of ten to twenty feet.

It was hardly to be wondered at that I found Cooper's bear stories as exciting as anything I had ever listened to.

In the years since, I have come to know a great deal about black-bear behavior. Some of the lessons I learned firsthand. Others were gleaned from people who had had dealings with blackie.

I have hunted him with gun and camera. I have spent time with trappers and hunters, outdoorsmen to whom the pursuit of bears was almost a way of life. I have talked with homesteaders who had met bears under very lively circumstances; with timber cruisers and with conservation officers and government trappers who had gotten rid of nuisance bears; with game researchers who had live-trapped, tagged, and moved bears from one place to another, who had even fitted them with radio tracking collars. As a writer and staff editor on *Outdoor Life* magazine since 1946, I sought out and interviewed people in just about every part of North America who had had extraordinary bear adventures of one kind or another.

My files today hold close to half a hundred detailed and authenticated accounts of raiding bears, hostile encounters with them, bear hunts that had a surprise outcome, bear attacks provoked and unprovoked, even of bears that turned man-eater. That wealth of factual material is the stuff of which much of this book is made up.

Many years after Ike Cooper's bear stories first fired my imagination, I came to know, in much the same way although not as intimately, the traits and behavioral patterns of the other three bears of North America, the grizzly, Alaska brown, and polar.

Scientists today are in agreement that the grizzly and brown are no more than separate races of the same species. But because of the marked differences between them, in appearance and size, preferred habitat and food habits, and mostly because there is no other game animal on this continent as awesome as the huge Alaska brown, they will be treated here as different bears.

Saying there are four kinds of bears in North America brings to mind one of my favorite anecdotes about Bill Rae, the gifted editor of *Outdoor Life* for whom I wrote for more than twenty years, and under whose direction much of the material that makes up this book was gathered.

Bill had taken to lunch in New York one day an aspiring young writer who was keen to sell material to the magazine. He got on the subject of bears, and was holding forth at some length on the various races and color phases of the black bear; the cinnamon, Kermode, and glacier. Finally Bill headed him off.

"So far as *Outdoor Life* is concerned, there are just two kinds of bears in the world," he said firmly, "the exciting kind and the other kind."

Much as that reveals about Bill Rae's editorial viewpoint and acumen, I have wondered many times since whether he was altogether right. Is there really any such thing as an unexciting bear?

Of the four bears, the black is by far the best known to Americans in general as well as to sportsmen. Found over much of the United States and Canada, with a colorful history that goes back to the earliest days of settlement, he has played a major role at one time or another in the outdoors of almost every state and province.

Of the major carnivores that walk the wilderness trails of North America, three, the wolf, the mountain lion, and the bear, have cast an especially strong spell on human imagination and influenced substantially the lives of those who live where they are found. And of that somewhat mystifying trio, the bears have exercised by far the greatest influence.

There are sound reasons. It was the deer, the whitetail, mule, and blacktail, that made this a nation of riflemen. But it was the bears, from pioneer times up to the present, that went far to make it afraid of the dark.

A surprise encounter with a bear of any kind or size has always been a startling, and often a frightening, experience. There is no record of wolves attacking man anywhere on this continent, and mountain lion attacks are extremely rare. But the same cannot be said for bears. Not a year goes by but that they kill one or two humans, and attacks and maulings are almost commonplace.

Too, apart from the threat he poses to man himself the bear's propensity for making trouble, his raids and depredations and nocturnal visits, bring him forcibly to human attention and give him a dubious name just about everywhere he is found.

For the hunter he has another role. Hunting him, by whatever method, is a thrill-packed and exciting sport, and a good bear pelt of whatever kind is one of the finest of trophies. Many outdoorsmen rate the brown and the polar bear (the latter no longer legal game in the United States or Canada) close to the top of the world's trophy list, fully as beautiful and desirable as a lion, tiger, or leopard.

I am sure there will be those who will fault and resent this book for what they will see as undue emphasis on instances of bear attack and the danger to humans who venture into bear country. The charge will probably be made that I have tilted my story deliberately against bears, that I seek to arouse groundless fear and hostility toward them.

That is not the case. Nothing is farther from my mind than to imply that every bear is a fierce and terrible beast, the deadly foe of man. That is no more true of all bears than it is true of all lions or tigers or any other wild animal.

But there is one point that needs urgently to be made, in the interest of human safety. Bears, of all kinds, do attack and kill humans. More often than not the attack comes with little or no warning and for no apparent reason save that the bear and the man happened to be where they were at the moment.

This book is no scientific treatise about bears. It is, however, a factual account of their way of life, their behavior, of how they hunt and are hunted, and of how they sometimes strike back at the human who intrudes on them, whether or not he means them harm.

As for the instances of attack, I have set the record down as it stands. I would be doing my readers a disservice if I did otherwise. There is real need for people to be made aware of what bears are capable of.

I suppose there will always be the uninformed and the foolhardy who will continue, despite all warnings, to feed park panhandlers and garbage-dump bums from their hands or out of car windows; who will even attempt to seat a child astride a wild bear for the sake of a "cute" picture. Just as there will always be the misguided who believe that the Gentle Ben brand of TV hokum portrays the true character of bears.

Such mentality is beyond the reach of advice, and anyway, this book is not intended as a manual on correct human behavior in the presence of a bear. But the lessons are clear in its pages, and it is my earnest hope that it may give second thoughts to those who believe wild bears lovable and harmless playfellows.

PART ONE

THE BLACK BEAR

ONE

There's a Bear!

"There's a bear!"

To my own surprise, I said it out loud. I was talking to myself, for there was no one with me, and I hadn't known I was going to say anything until the words were out. I blurted them in a startled undertone, and suddenly I realized that my heart was pounding and chills were running up my back.

The time was early May. I was one of a party of trout fishermen who had gone by boat along the south shore of Lake Superior to the mouth of the Carp River, in the roadless wilderness of the Porcupine Mountains at the western end of Michigan's Upper Peninsula. We had hopes of intercepting the spring spawning run of big steelhead trout in the lower pools of the Carp.

After supper the first day I elected to go for a walk by myself. There was a flat bench along the shore of Superior, a hundred yards or so wide, formed by an ancient beach line, grown up with cedar and pine and hemlock and hardwood.

An old brush-grown wagon road, long unused, followed the bench at the foot of a steep bluff, and that was where I chose to hike. The spring wildflowers were out, new leaves were opening on the trees, I'd be likely to find morel mushrooms, and it was a pleasant place to be.

I was half a mile from camp when I heard a noise in a tangle of brush to my right. My first thought was that it was a deer skulking out, or maybe a bumbling porcupine. Then I turned to look, and a big black bear was staring at me over the top of the thicket, ten steps away. My heart shifted gears and it was then I made my surprise announcement to myself.

There had to be a reason for the bear to stand there on its hind feet and stare at me, close enough that I could have hit it with a slingshot. And whatever the reason was, I didn't like the situation.

I was not left long in the dark. I heard another noise, back at the foot of the bluff, and then two young cubs broke into sight, running full tilt up the steep slope. They were going so fast that they looked for all the world like little black footballs rolling end over end uphill.

If I had been startled before, I was really frightened now. A number of times, I had listened to hunters, trappers, or woodsmen who had gotten into bad trouble when they stumbled across the combination I was confronting, a sow bear with cubs. There was danger here, real danger. I knew it but there was nothing I could do about it.

The bear did not growl or pop her teeth. So far as I could see she didn't move a muscle. Neither did I. I didn't think I even blinked my eyes. We stood staring at one another until the cubs went out of sight over the crest of the bluff. Then the mother dropped to all fours with a woof that lifted me half out of my boots, and went crashing up the hill after them.

I aborted my hike and cut for camp. I didn't run. That didn't seem like a good idea. But I walked fast enough that it would have taken a Paul Bunyan with seven-league boots to keep up with me.

Any encounter between a man and a bear is very likely to be hair-raising, and fairly often it is actually dangerous. Rarely if ever is it dull. Since pioneer times this animal has had an extraordinary impact on the human nervous system.

I know nobody who has summed up the "man meets bear" situation better than Bud Livingston, a northern Michigan conservation officer.

"There are no words in the English language more startling than 'There's a bear!' " he told me once.

Bud has worked for upward of thirty years in the bear country of the Upper Peninsula, and has dealt with more bears than he can remember, mostly the problem kind.

He was five when he had his first encounter, but he remembers it as vividly as if it had happened yesterday. His family had moved from Minnesota to Michigan, where his father became a farmer and part-time logger, and also worked as a fire-tower lookout with the Michigan Conservation Department in summer for added income.

The family had a homestead, but in summer they lived in a house near the tower, about three miles from the homestead. One hot July day Bud and his brother Ben, who was a couple of years older, tired of doing small-boy chores and decided to walk to the homestead, something they had been told not to do.

They had covered about half the distance when a big black bear stepped out of the brush ahead, and planted himself in the middle of the dirt road. Ben saw him first and yelped, "There's a bear!"

"That was thirty-five years ago," Bud told me when he related the story. "Those three words had about as electrifying an effect on me as anything I have ever heard. If someone were to bark them at me today the result would be exactly the same."

Nothing really happened. Nothing needed to. One second the two boys were staring open-mouthed at the bear.

"He looked as big as a barn and as black as midnight," Bud remembers.

The next second two barefoot kids were flying down the road, back the way they had come. They never knew what the bear did or where he went.

Then I turned to look, and a big black bear was staring at me over the top of the thicket, ten steps away. There was danger here, real danger.

When their grandmother heard about the escapade she gave both of them the shellacking she thought they deserved.

"I still remember that licking," Bud admits, "but not half as vividly as I recall the sight of that big black bear standing there in the road staring at us."

There was one other time, years later, when Bud heard the same frightened announcement under circumstances he will never forget. He was working with a crew of men repairing a fire-tower phone line that time. The crew was eating lunch on the porch of the general store at the hamlet of Melstrand when a group of badly scared children came bolting around the corner sounding an urgent alarm. They were yelling "There's a bear!" in chorus.

Behind them, strolling down the middle of the little town's main street, came a tremendous black, sauntering along as if he owned the world. He walked past the store without turning his head, ignoring the knot of people watching from the porch, and at the far edge of town he disappeared in the brush.

It turned out that he had been feeding at the garbage dump of a nearby logging camp. The camp had closed and he was on the prowl for groceries. He no longer had any fear of humans, and he proceeded to make trouble.

He went on showing up in broad daylight, growing more and more arrogant, and the residents of Melstrand, fearful for their children and themselves, wanted him done away with. The job fell to Livingston.

That was before the day of tranquilizing dart guns. Bud tried livetraps. The bear wouldn't go near them. He tried a rifle but the bear eluded him. He tried steel traps but they were dug up and sprung. In the end he ambushed blackie in the vicinity of a baited pen and put an end to him. A huge bear, but thin and in poor condition, he weighed 389 pounds. In prime shape he would have exceeded 500. When he was skinned another reason for his surliness around people was discovered. He was carrying a charge of bird shot and several .22 bullets just under his hide. At some time in the past, small-game hunters or somebody at the logging camp had tried a very foolish thing with him.

Even a bear track is calculated to send shivers up the human spine. You stare at the footprints, printed big and deep in the sand of a woods road or the mud along a stream bank, and you say to yourself, "A bear walked here, in the black of night, cloaked in darkness, furtive and silent. On what bloody errand was he bent? What prey did he finally find? Did he surprise and brain a young deer? Sniff out a wild turkey on her nest? Raid a pigpen on some settler's brush-bordered farm? Or did he only tear a log apart for ants? What would have happened if I had met him face to face?"

You feel your pulse quicken with an ancient fear.

In his excellent book, *The Big Game Animals of North America*, published by Outdoor Life in 1961, Jack O'Connor, one of the most respected authorities in the country, said, "The chances of a hunter being mauled by a black bear are about the same as of being struck by a meteor. One whiff of human scent will generally send this bear off like a scared rabbit, and he'd always rather run than fight."

Jack was wrong in that last statement. Usually yes, but not *always*.

Apart from venomous snakes, bears are the most dangerous animals in North America, blacks as well as grizzlies. Wolves have scared a lot of people half to death but they have never attacked man anywhere on this continent. The mountain lion does make such attacks but they are so rare that the lion can almost be dismissed as a threat to humans. In contrast, bear attacks, provoked and unprovoked, occur too often to be counted. The danger lies in the bear's unpredictability.

Every year thousands of people come face to face with black bears in national parks, at campgrounds and garbage dumps, and no trouble develops. Fall after fall, hunters collect the makings of bearskin rugs almost as uneventfully as they take a trophy deer or elk. Bow-hunters make kills of black bears at frighteningly close range without the bear making any attempt to fight back.

But each year, too, newspaper headlines tell the other side of the story, of a man recovering from bear attack, of another dying, of campers mauled, of a backpacker attacked while asleep in his tent.

It happens often enough to justify human fright at the sudden appearance of a bear close by. The fright may be groundless but the man can never be sure.

Take Pat Furlong, for example. Pat was a district conservation officer stationed at Newberry, in the eastern end of Michigan's Upper Peninsula. Walking out of the woods from a timber cruising job one hot July day, following an abandoned railroad grade, he came to a clearing of five or six acres where a logging camp had once stood. At the far side, where the railroad had run through a shallow cut, he saw a bear standing on the old grade.

It stared at him for a minute, then scrambled up the bank and disappeared. Pat walked on. He had lived in bear country all his life, was not afraid of bears, was skeptical of reports of them molesting humans, and he gave this one no further thought. But when he was partway through the cut he heard a noise and looked up to see the bear on the bank almost beside him.

He backed up, as a matter of common sense, to make sure the bear knew he was a man. It jumped down into the cut and faced him at fifteen feet, and then started for him. Pat turned and ran, and the bear came pounding after him.

He was unarmed except for a jackknife. He made for a spruce tree in the center of the clearing but never reached it. When the bear was only a few steps away, he turned to face it and tried to drive it off by throwing chunks of wood and sod in its face.

The animal pressed in, closer and closer. Furlong pulled small wild-cherry seedlings up by the roots and whipped them in its face. He shouted and whistled and screamed, but it did no good.

The bear didn't growl or rear up on its hind legs, but it kept feinting at him, hardly more than arm's length away.

He finally found two pieces of dry board, left from the old camp, and by whacking them together he drove the bear back for the first time. He crowded it until it ran into the brush, threw the boards after it and started once more for the spruce tree. The bear returned to the attack instantly.

Pat never knew how long the strange battle lasted. He tried once to light a handful of dry grass to throw in the bear's face, but it didn't even give him time to find matches in a pocket.

The afternoon was almost gone when he stumbled over an old dishpan left from the camp cookhouse. He grabbed it and drummed on it with a stick, and in the face of that strange noise the bear retreated again.

Pat drove it out of the clearing, kept it at bay for a little while, and finally it disappeared. He went back to the railroad grade and hurried out to his car, carrying the dishpan just in case.

He returned the next day with another conservation officer, intending to kill the bear if they encountered it. But it was nowhere in sight.

If there was any real reason for the attack, Pat never knew it. Certainly he was not threatening or crowding the bear, and he saw no sign of a cub. Whatever triggered the encounter, the evidence indicated that bear and man had fought for hours, and woodsmen who knew bear ways believed Furlong's life had been in genuine danger. The bear had come after him exactly as it would have closed on a shoat or steer it meant to kill.

Pat believed that a loud hammering noise of the kind he made with the old dishpan is likely to drive off any quarrelsome wild animal, and I agree with him.

In addition to his own experiences, he knew an old timber cruiser who had once put an angry black bear to flight by whacking on the trunk of a dead tamarack tree with his cruiser's ax.

I have never tried it with a bear, but in the spring of 1936, when the Michigan Conservation Department was moving live-trapped adult moose from Isle Royale in Lake Superior to the mainland of the Upper Peninsula, a thoroughly enraged bull in the holding corral was driven to retreat when two or three men advanced on him drumming with sticks on empty syrup cans.

Clovis Delene probably had his dog to thank for his encounter with a quarrelsome bear, although he was never sure. At any rate, Delene knew as soon as the dog started making a fuss what the reason was.

"Bet you smell a bear, boy," he said with a grin.

Half a minute later his guess was confirmed in a fashion that was about the last thing he anticipated.

Delene had spent a lifetime in the woods of Michigan's Upper Peninsula. He had encountered at least a hundred bears and killed a dozen or so. All told, he had had entirely too much dealing with them to be worried by the fact that one was walking around in the brush within a stone's throw. He had no warning that anything out of the ordinary was about to happen this time.

A retired conservation officer, living at a place known locally as Bear Corners, near the hamlet of Covington in Baraga County, he had gone trout fishing that rainy July afternoon, heading for a brushy creek that ran into the Sturgeon River not far from his home. He had caught one nine-inch fish when the dog, a springer that accompanied him wherever he went, began to bark furiously, and then beat a sudden and fast retreat to the far side of the stream.

"That springer is a great bird dog but not much for bears," Clovis remarked afterward.

Maybe the fact that a 250-pound black had tried only a short time before to break into Delene's dog pen and get at the springer had something to do with that. Clovis shot that one in the dooryard when it paid a return visit just at dusk the next day, still intent on doing away with the dog. Anyway, spaniels are not supposed to be bear dogs.

Delene glanced behind him now, the way the springer was looking, just in time to see a big black bear walking out of the brush. It was a lean, gaunt-looking brute; its hair was standing up on the neck and shoulders; it was slobbering, and growling in a surly undertone. And to the man's astonishment it kept coming straight for him.

He waved his arms and yelled at the top of his voice, "Get out of here, you mangy so and so!"

The bear didn't pause. It kept padding in, and in spite of the racket the dog was making just across the creek the bear didn't even look in that direction.

"He had his sights set on me and he was coming to pick a fight," Clovis told friends later.

He had never seen a bear behave that way before, and he concluded something was wrong. Maybe this one was exceptionally hungry or full of porcupine quills. When he yelled again without stopping it, he splashed through the stream and he and the dog cleared out.

"I figured he wanted that fishing hole more than I did, and he was welcome to it," Delene explained.

A couple of hundred yards downstream, when he saw no more of the bear, he stopped and began fishing again. But within a minute or two the springer broke into an uproar of barking once more and when the man looked up the bear was coming for him a second time, only fifteen yards away.

It stopped at twenty feet and reared up on its hind legs. Its ears were laid back, and it was growling and chomping on its jaws like an angry hog. Again Delene tried yelling. It dropped down on all fours, but instead of backing off it took two or three more steps toward him and unreared again.

His pickup truck was parked on the road a quarter mile from the creek. A trail led out from the place where he had first seen the bear, and that trail seemed the safest route to the truck. But there was a hitch. The bear was in the way, and Clovis decided to try a shortcut through the timber.

He didn't run but he walked as fast as hip boots would allow. The dog stayed at his heels, cringing and whining, and watching over his shoulder Delene could see the bear following about two hundred feet behind. It came no closer, made no effort to overtake the man and dog, offered no further threat of attack. But it trailed them more than halfway to the road, and then disappeared in the brush. That was the last Clovis ever saw of it.

My old friend Ted Updike, who lives now at the hamlet of Love on the edge of settlements in northern Saskatchewan, but who was a bush trapper for many years, has lived among bears and dealt with them firsthand most of his life. He has some firm theories about those that challenge or threaten or even attack people.

To begin with, Ted rates any bear a potential powder keg.

"Every mature bear has a superiority complex," he told me once. "They are animals that have no enemies apart from man and in the right circumstances they soon lose their dread of him. A big one cuffs smaller bears around if they come near, and he gets to believing he is king of the woods. The instant something doesn't go his way he flies into a rage. He is definitely an animal to be avoided."

Updike believes two kinds are especially likely to be dangerous. One is the panhandler that hangs around a garbage dump or begs handouts in a park or at a campground, and becomes so familiar with humans that he has no fear of them. The other is the true wilderness bear, living back in remote bush, that has never run across a man and so has never learned to respect him.

"North of the settlements, where I trapped, there are no roads and the only human inhabitants are scattered Indians and an occasional trapper. I suspect that even today more than half of the bears there have never seen a human," he says. "That kind you have to watch out for."

It was Updike, incidentally, who told me about the only case I have ever known of a man coming out ahead in hand-to-hand combat with a black bear. It happened not far from Ted's home.

Four men driving a bush road saw a bear with two cubs cross ahead of them. The cubs scrambled up a tree, and because one of the men had never seen a bear before, a second, an old trapper named Madliner, proposed they walk to the tree for a better look.

They had no gun, but Madliner took an ax and led the way. The sow was watching, only a few yards from the tree, and as the quartet approached she reared up on her hind legs and walked toward them, snarling and muttering.

Madliner waited until she was within arm's length, growling and slobbering, standing almost as tall as the man. Then he brought the flat of the ax down on top of her head full force.

She dropped like a polled steer, got up, shook her head and fell down again. After a minute or two she regained her footing and kept it. But there was no fight left in her. She staggered away without looking back.

Not often, but now and then, a man-bear encounter is funny. One of that kind happened back in the 1930's at the hamlet of Seney, in Michigan's Upper Peninsula.

There was an old ramshackle hotel at Seney, a hangout of lumberjacks when the town was in its roaring heyday, later fallen stagnant and largely unused. I stayed there a couple of times of necessity, when my car broke down on the road late at night. Many of the bedrooms had no doors, and it was not an uncommon experience to have an inebriated stranger wander in in the small hours, looking for either female companionship or just a bed.

Rumor had it that Bob Hudson, who ran the place, was a refugee from a rum-running dispute in the Detroit area, who had decided that it would be safer to retire to the north woods. A friend of the chief conservation officer in the

Upper Peninsula, he had no difficulty getting the needed permit to keep a pet bear. He kept him chained to a post outside the hotel as a tourist attraction.

His current tame bear was a hefty adult, genial and interesting, that delighted visitors by panhandling for pop, sitting on its broad black rump, holding the bottle in both forepaws and guzzling the stuff down like a thirsty small boy.

Toward the end of summer one year the bear's collar, worn thin, finally broke and it escaped the chain. But it showed no intention to leave town and go back to the woods. Instead it prowled the streets and visited back doors, begging handouts. Especially it haunted the hotel, where Hudson rewarded it with doughnuts, candy bars, and other tidbits.

A wide screened porch ran across the entire front of the hotel, and Bob discovered that he could coax the bear onto the porch with an offering of food. The next step was to lure it into the big square lobby, where a pot-bellied stove was about the only furnishing. The bear's visits to the lobby became a regular performance.

As the days went by the residents of Seney became more and more concerned about the bear in their midst. School opened and the idea of a full-grown bear padding along behind children on the street was upsetting. But Bob laughed the fears off.

"That bear is tame," he told one and all. "It wouldn't hurt a fly."

The Duluth South Shore and Atlantic Railroad ran through Seney, and there came a frosty morning toward the end of October when Hudson unlocked the hotel to find a hobo huddled on the steps of the porch, shivering and blue with cold. Bob invited him in, and the stranger settled in a chair behind the big stove to thaw out.

In a few minutes there came a scratching at the door. Bob picked a candy bar out of the counter, let his erstwhile pet in and led it into the lobby.

The hobo stared in amazed silence for minutes. Finally he blurted, "So that's that damned bear."

"I don't know what you mean," Hudson told him. "It's a pet bear of mine that got loose a while back and is still hanging around."

"Well, I'll tell you what I mean," the man replied. "I rode the rods in here on a freight train about two o'clock this morning. I was just about froze to death, and when the train stopped to take water I climbed off and went looking for a place to bed down. I'd never been here before, but I finally found that old empty stable across the tracks, with clean straw in the stalls.

"I burrowed down in the straw and was just starting to get warm when I felt something sniffing around my feet. I sat up and struck a match, and there was the biggest damned bear in North America, standing right over me.

"I'll never know how the bear got out, but I can tell you how I got out. I went straight over the top of him. Then I came over here and sat on your steps to wait for daylight."

Sometimes it seems that a bear makes threatening moves for reasons of curiosity rather than hostility. In Montana a few years ago a girl college student, trapping mice for a research project, saw a bear walk out of the brush and head her way, as if coming to look her over.

Terrified, she climbed a tree. What happened next is hard to believe. The bear went up a nearby tree to her level and sat there, watching her.

She finally mustered enough courage to climb down, backed away carefully until she was out of sight, and then ran. The last she saw of the bear it was still perched in its tree, watching her.

That was the last time she went mouse trapping by herself.

There's a bear!

As an oldtimer in the southern mountains told me many years ago, "Ain't nothin' can put the fear of the Lord into a sinful man like meetin' up with a bear when you don't have a gun."

TWO

How Like a Man

Despite his common name, the black bear is frequently anything but black. That is the most common color phase in the eastern United States and eastern Canada, but these black individuals are almost unfailingly brown around the face and many of them have a white blaze on the chest or throat.

Farther west, the reddish-brown color commonly called the cinnamon bear is found frequently, and somewhat surprisingly black and cinnamon cubs are often born in the same litter. Hal Evarts, an outdoor writer of the early 1900s, reported that in the Yellowstone country he had seen not fewer than twenty she bears followed by twin cubs, one black and one cinnamon, regardless of the color of the sow.

Varying shades of dark brown also occur, and California has light brown and even a blond or yellow black bear. In the early days that same color phase was found in the foothill country of Montana and Wyoming, with fur of a light gold-taffee hue. The mountain men and fur traders called it the sun bear.

In Alaska a rich chocolate-brown phase is common, and Alaska also has, along the coast from Mt. St. Elias southeast to Mt. Fairweather or a little farther, the unique race known as the glacier bear, an exquisite silver-blue in color.

Jim Martin, a young Alaskan who killed a big glacier bear with a bow in 1972 (believed to be the first ever taken that way), called it the most beautiful animal he had ever seen.

Strangest of all is the Kermode bear found on a few big islands and along the coast of British Columbia south of Prince Rupert. The Kermode is a white color phase of black bear. Not an albino, for its eyes are the dark color of a normal black bear's.

In *Outdoor Life*, July 1965, Howard Shelley, Michigan hunter and wildlife photographer and lecturer, described a Kermode, killed by his hunting partner Art Hutchings on Princess Royal Island a year earlier, in these words:

"Color converted him into a magnificent freak like nothing I had ever expected to lay eyes on. He was milk-white on the sides and flanks but the white was washed with bright orange-yellow around the face and on the shoulders and feet. A broad band of the yellow also started between his ears, ran back over the shoulders and faded out on his rump. His nose, lips and the pads of his feet were light gray. There was no black on him anywhere, but his small beady eyes were dark, not pink.

"Plainly this was no albino, but a race apart. When we first saw him, against a background of green timber and the rushing water of a nameless river, he had looked like a ghost bear from another world. Studying him close up, we didn't wonder that local Indians had long held the Kermode in great reverence, as our guide had told us."

Many sportsmen consider this white bear the rarest trophy-game animal on the North American continent, but almost none have been taken under hunting licenses. In the old days a few skins taken by Indians found their way into the fur trade. Some have been shot under special permit for museum groups, and now and then one has been captured for a zoo. But they have enjoyed protection from hunting almost continuously since they became known to science shortly after 1900. Hutchings believed the one he took, in an open season that lasted only one year, may be the only such trophy ever collected by a hunter.

No other quadruped in North America displays as close a superficial resemblance to man himself as the black bear. A heavy-bodied animal with relatively short, thick legs, more than man-size, standing some six feet tall when he rears up on his hind legs, this bear is like a shaggy, burly man both in appearance and behavior. As a young cub, he romps and wrestles and rolls, and even whimpers and whines, much as human kids do. If he wants a better look at something or needs to test the wind, he stands erect. He does the same thing, from cubhood to old age, to play or even fight with another bear. Angered, he may rear up and walk into battle on two feet. If he screams in pain, the sound is so like that of a human that hunters who have heard it call it hollering.

No human is more expert at climbing into an apple tree and raking or shaking down the fruit. Attacking large prey, the bear is far more likely to kill with a blow of a forefoot than with his teeth. Like many people, especially in wild country, he prefers to lead a solitary life, keeping largely to himself. And the best of human mothers is no more solicitous, and no more of a strict disciplinarian, where her young are concerned, than the sow black bear.

Finally, whatever physical resemblance this bear may show to man when alive, walking around on four feet and covered with a dense and heavy fur pelt, that resemblance becomes far more striking once he is killed and the pelt removed. The skinned carcass of a bear is downright startling in its similarity to a stout, short-legged human body, although the legs are far thicker and more muscular, the neck bigger, the whole structure more sturdy.

That strange resemblance may well have been a major reason for the Indian attitude toward the black bear.

From the time whites first made contact with them, the woodland Indians showed strong feelings of kinship with and deep respect for this furred imitator of man. They hunted him, both for food and for his pelt, but when they killed him they apologized for the necessity. They believed his spirit went to the same Happy Hunting Grounds as their own, and they appeased him and courted his goodwill there by putting up strange icons in his memory. Finally, they believed he had supernatural understanding of human language.

Much of those attitudes still persists among remote and primitive Indian peoples. Take for example the case of Alexie Pitka, an Athapascan Indian from the village of Kaltag, on the Yukon in the interior of Alaska. Pitka wounded a big black bear and it turned on him savagely when he walked up to it.

As he lay beneath it, dreadfully mauled and torn, and fighting for his life by stabbing it in the belly with a short-bladed knife, he said quietly to the bear, "Go away. I won't hurt you any more if you go away." He lost consciousness, and when he "woke up," as he said, the bear was gone.

Relating the story later to Dorothy Fossman, a teacher for the U. S. Bureau of Indian Affairs, Pitka, old and permanently crippled from the attack, told her, "I cannot hunt or fish and I am not much good. I think it would have been better if I had talked to the bear the first time I saw him, half a mile away, and said, 'Go away. If you do not hurt me I will not hunt you.'"

To the aged Indian there was nothing illogical in his belief that when he spoke to the bear, even at a distance, it understood him as another human would have done.

Almost across the continent, in the roadless wilderness of Quebec on the east side of James Bay, the roving trapline Crees have kept alive the same beliefs. When Dave Jarden, a wilderness canoeist from Pennsylvania, led his party down the turbulent tumbling Eastmain River in the summer of 1953, he passed through the winter trapping country of the nomadic trading-post Crees.

Stone fire rings and the pole frames of wigwams marked the campsites of the Indian trappers. They were living as their ancestors had lived, by the trapline, the fishnet, and the gun. Many of them still do, although a huge power development sponsored by the Quebec government is altering both the face of that vast wilderness and the life ways of the Crees.

Frequently at the winter camps Jarden came on trees to which was fastened a bear skull or a birchbark box that held the shriveled remains of a bear's foreleg.

Trophies? Not in the sense whites use that word. Rather these relics had been put up to show respect for the dead bear and to let him know that the Indian was sorry he had had to kill him. They were evidence of an esteem that approached reverence.

Full grown and old enough to breed, this bear shows a surprising variation in weight, ranging from less than 150 pounds for young females up to a high of around 700 for an occasional exceptional male.

Astonishingly, the offspring of animals of this size enter life as the smallest, in relation to the size of the mother, of North American mammals, excepting only the opossum, a pouched marsupial that gives birth to half-developed embryonic young no bigger than a honey bee. They complete their growth suckling in the mother's pouch.

Nothing about the members of the bear family is stranger than their size when they come into the world. At birth, a black bear cub born to a 250-pound mother is no bigger than an adult red squirrel and weighs about eight ounces. By way of pointing up the contrast, a newborn porcupine may weigh from one to one and a quarter pounds, compared with a weight of 12 to 15 pounds for its mother.

The bear cubs are born in January or February, while the mother is in winter quarters. Especially in the north, where the denning period is longer than in the south, she may be in the torpor of hibernation, and some writers have even suggested that she is not aware she has given birth. That is a theory I cannot accept, although it is obvious that no one can say for sure.

The cubs, most commonly two in number although three and even four are not unusual, are born almost naked and with their eyes closed. Not until they are three or four weeks old do they see the light of day, and then, if the den is a cave under a stump or log, only dimly.

The performance of the mother for the first three months after the cubs are born is one of the most remarkable in the animal world. Without stirring from the den, and usually at least in semi-torpor, and without taking a bite of food or a drink of water for herself, she must provide sufficient milk to nourish the fast-growing family.

I know of no human who has sampled bear milk, but certainly it has to be a nutritious brew. For by April, when she leads her cubs away from the den, they have grown from the half pound they weighed at birth to an average of about four pounds, and although they are still toddlers, somewhat uncertain on their short little legs, they follow the sow without much difficulty and claw their way up a tree if the need arises. A month or so later, weighing maybe twice as much, they can run like little black streaks.

The first summer of their lives they are totally dependent on the sow. She keeps them close by, suckles them, teaches them to find food and to climb if danger threatens, and above all to obey orders. An unruly cub, or one that is laggard in obedience, gets a swat on the rump that often sends him rolling head over heels a dozen feet into the brush, or even sailing through the air. Rough play that turns into an argument is likely to bring the same kind of reprimand.

In late June or early July the breeding season of the bears arrives. But, for reasons not fully explained, the sow with young cubs has no interest in sex. The most logical explanation seems to be that because she is nursing offspring, she does not come in heat.

In any event, the prohibition is a necessary one. The cubs born back in the winter will go into hibernation with her again in the autumn. If she were pregnant, the new young would arrive while the whole family was still together in the den, and trouble if not actual cannibalism would almost certainly result. By breeding only every second year, the female bear is spared that problem.

It is commonly believed that bear cubs less than a year old do not know how to find a den if separated from their mother, and cannot survive their first winter. But in recent years studies have shown that to be untrue.

Deprived of the sow's care, cubs as young as five months have made out on their own. And Michigan game men settled the matter conclusively by releasing in late summer, on islands of the Beaver group at the north end of Lake Michigan, cubs born the previous January. The winters in that area are long and severe, but when spring came the young bears were still alive and in good condition. They must have spent the winter in a den of some kind.

By their second summer, the cubs weigh in the neighborhood of fifty pounds. In June or July the breeding season arrives again for their mother. They are weaned now and the sow is ready to come into heat and accept a boar. The time has come for the family to break up.

That driving off of the young when one or both of the parents are ready for a honeymoon is something that happens with a number of wild animals and birds. I have not witnessed it among bears, but woodsmen who have tell me that the cubs get rough treatment.

The sow turns on them angrily, slaps them around, and makes it abundantly clear that she no longer wants anything to do with them.

I have watched the same thing with wild geese many times, and it is an entertaining and highly amusing performance.

The young birds have lived with the parents since they were hatched. They flew south in the autumn as a family group, wintered together, and made the spring flight north in the same close association.

But now that the time has come for nesting and rearing another family, the old birds no longer want the young underfoot. The gander drives them off time after time, day after day.

The two old geese undertake to swim off by themselves in search of privacy. The young birds swim after them, determined to stay close. The old gander lifts from the water and flies at the youngsters with angry honking. They honk back, but take wing and retreat. He chases them for a short distance, drops down and starts to swim back to his mate. The young geese likewise drop back to the water and swim after him. When he is back where he started they are hardly more than fifty feet behind, and the whole thing starts over again.

It goes on at intervals all day long, but after a week or so of harassment the young geese finally get the idea and give up. They go their separate ways and the old pair is left to build a nest and bring up another family. A year from now those young will be driven off in turn.

In much the same way, the sow bear rids herself of last year's cubs, comes in heat and remains in that condition until she takes up with a boar and is bred. Once that is accomplished, in a brief honeymoon, the two separate and resume the solitary way of life that is characteristic of all bears.

Fierce fighting between rival boars for possession of a receptive female, while very rarely witnessed by humans, is far from rare. Old males killed by hunters are often scarred about the face and head or have torn ears or broken teeth, mute testimony to battles over a girl friend.

THE BLACK BEAR

2′ −3′

4½′ −6′

The black bear has a straight profile and hardly any shoulder hump, small eyes and well-rounded ears. Average males weigh from 250 to 400 pounds, but many specimens have been recorded that measured up to 9 feet in length and weighed over 600 pounds.

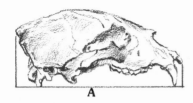

A

B

The black bear's four long, pointed canine teeth and many flat-crowned molars enable him to feed with equal ease on meat or vegetables. The Boone and Crockett method of measuring the skull is shown at left: greatest length without lower jaw (A) and greatest width (B).

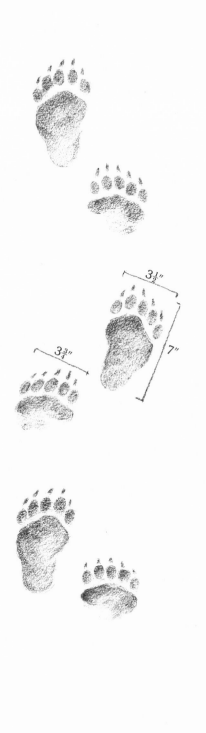

There is a marked difference between the bear's forefoot and hind-foot tracks. The hind-foot track is larger and resembles that or a human footprint. (Dimensions of all tracks are for an average-size bear.) When a bear walks at a brisk gait, he places his hind foot in front of his forefoot, which accounts for the peculiar pattern of the tracks. When moving at a slower pace, the bear often places the hind foot directly in the track of the forefoot. The claws of the black bear, which are shorter than those of the brown or grizzly, register as small marks just ahead of the toes.

Olive Fredrickson, the remarkable Canadian woman with whom I collaborated in writing the story of her life of adventure on the frontier, *The Silence of the North,* tells of watching one such fight that was a savage duel with no quarter given.

Olive and her husband John were hiking along a creek in northern British Columbia when they heard a sudden breaking of brush on a slope to their left. It didn't sound like deer, moose, or caribou, for there was the thudding noise of blows mixed with the cracking of brush. Plainly they were hearing a fight of some kind, but there was no growling or grunting, nothing to reveal the identity of the fighters.

But Olive, who had seen fights between male bears on two or three occasions, quickly guessed what was going on. The time was June, the mating season for black bears, and she decided that she and John were listening to two males brawling over a female. John was carrying a .30/06 Winchester, so they crept close enough for a ringside seat.

It turned out to be a strange fight. The two bears, both big boars, were standing on their hind legs, sparring like human boxers. First one and then the other would spread his arms, lunge in and strike a savage blow. Most of the blows landed on the head or shoulders of the other bear, and seemed to do little damage. Now and then one got walloped in the belly, however, and that brought sharp grunts of pain.

Twice one of the bears locked a forearm around a tree as if bracing himself, and delivered a haymaker with the other paw that knocked his opponent to the ground. But not once did either of them do any fighting on all fours.

Both were snarling and whining now, as the battle mounted to a climax. Finally they went into a clinch and began to use their teeth for the first time, biting at each other's neck and shoulders. Then one made a swift lunge, caught a forepaw of his opponent in his jaws and crunched down.

The victim let out a scream that was almost human, and tried frantically to free himself. But the teeth of the other were locked in his paw like spiked trap jaws. He screamed, clawed and bit in vain.

Both were snarling and whining now, as the battle mounted to a climax. Finally they went into a clinch and began to use their teeth, biting at each other's neck and shoulders.

A shift in wind direction brought the affair to a sudden and surprising end. A sow, out of sight in thick cover nearby, caught human scent and blew a loud snort of warning. The two males separated as if a lightning bolt had hit the ground between them. The one with the injured paw limped off on three feet as fast as it could go. The unhurt one ran into the brush in the direction of the sow. Minutes later the two of them came into sight in an opening, looked back briefly and vanished on a run.

"We had watched a fight of a kind that is rare for humans to witness," Mrs. Fredrickson says. "In a lifetime in bear country, only a very few times have I known anyone to see a battle between boars. Bears do most of their prowling, and also of their courting and fighting, in the black of night."

Once the sow leads her young cubs out of the winter den, if any male, including their father, threatens them she will defend them with savage determination. Most of the time she has only to threaten in order to protect them, but now and then a big and surly boar has been known to kill the cubs in spite of all the mother could do.

One such encounter that turned out to have an amusing rather than an unhappy ending was described to me by Frank Blair, former director of the Minnesota Division of Fish and Game. It involved a very spirited clash between a CCC camp cook and a prowling male black, followed quickly by another clash between the same male and a sow with cubs.

The camp was located in the Superior National Forest near Ely, Minnesota. A bunch of bears started coming in to feed on garbage and in a short time they became so tame that they were taking food from hand at the door of the cook shanty.

A female with three cubs wandered in to the garbage dump one afternoon. One of the cubs went up a tree. The old lady and the other two were pawing around in the garbage when a big male bear came along. He went straight up to the cook shanty door, found it open and walked in.

In about ten seconds those watching outside heard a terrific clatter and commotion inside the place, mixed with some loud and eloquent cussing. The next thing they knew the bear came flying out the door with the cook at his heels, swatting him over the rear with an iron fryingpan at every jump. The bear wasn't trying to defend himself. He'd been caught in the jam pot and he was a thoroughly crestfallen looking critter. If he had had a tail it would have been curled clear up between his front legs. But his troubles were only beginning.

As he sailed out the door, with the cook yelling and belaboring him, the female bear on the garbage dump swung around and pricked up her ears. The commotion must have upset her, and she decided instantly that the other bear was looking for trouble.

She took it to him! She met him a few yards outside the door of the cook shanty, just about the time the cook was turning back, and lit into him like ten furies. She was growling and bawling, and she was all over the male before he knew what had hit him. She mauled him mercilessly for a few seconds, while the three cubs looked on, two on the ground and one in the tree.

The male never did fight back. Either he was too confused or too much of a gentleman. He disentangled himself as fast as he could and took off across the clearing. The last anybody saw of him he was a black streak at the edge of the timber. The she bear returned to the garbage pile as if nothing had happened, and the cook shut the shanty door, fastened it and went back to his stove.

Bear hibernation remains something of a riddle. To begin with, it is not true hibernation. Wildlife authorities are not sure what triggers it in autumn or terminates it in early spring, but as with all hibernating animals it is clearly keyed to weather and food supply.

The duration of the winter nap varies greatly from one part of the country to another. In the southern states and in Mexico, bears, with the exception of pregnant females, often do not den at all or if they do they stay dormant for very short periods of time. In the northern states most of them are in winter quarters about the time snow comes, in late November, and they wander out little if at all before April. And in interior Alaska it is standard practice for them to spend almost half of the year denning, safe from snow and cold.

The winter sleep is light. I have seen kangaroo mice, taken from their cold-weather quarters, curled in a tight ball that could be rolled across the floor like a furry pingpong ball without showing the slightest sign of awakening. That deep torpor does not happen with the bears. Their temperature remains normal and they breathe at about the rate of a human in very heavy sleep. They are often half awake in the dead of winter, as more than one hunter has discovered by accident to his great surprise, and it is not uncommon for them to flee the den for good if disturbed. Many a rabbit hunter in the north woods has been alerted to a denning bear by the yapping of his beagles, or has broken through the top of a brushpile or windfall and landed squarely on top of a dozing black, which exploded under his feet like a hand grenade. Luckily, the bear shows little tendency to pick a quarrel under those circumstances. He clears out without an argument, and is not likely to return to that den. Cases have been recorded of sows with young cubs abandoning den and family permanently if disturbed in that fashion.

A spell of warm weather in midwinter is likely to coax the bear out of winter quarters voluntarily, to do a bit of prowling, especially if the den happens to get flooded by melting snow. Such bears normally go back to the same bed (in a cavern under a log, or stump, lined with dry leaves, grass or ferns, or in rock cave or a self-excavated hole) as soon as the weather turns severe again.

Strangely enough, the bear, which went into its semihibernation with a very heavy layer of fat under its skin, emerges in spring about as fat as when it retired. If it has lived on accumulated fat through the winter it shows little evidence. Perhaps that is the reason for the old belief that it subsists during hibernation by sucking a forepaw.

THREE

His Menu and His Weight

It is doubtful that any other game animal in this country has a food list as long and varied as that of the black bear. He relishes almost anything edible, either animal or plant.

"A bear will eat anything a hog will eat, and some things the hog won't look at," an oldtime woodsman once told me.

If any animal on this continent can be said to be totally omnivorous, this bear qualifies, although, perhaps from necessity, he is more of a vegetarian than a carnivore.

When he emerges from winter quarters food is not abundant in the spring woods, but he makes do with what he can find. On the vegetable side, he turns readily to grass and sedge and the peppery new leaves and flower horns of skunk cabbage. Carrion is also likely to be available, mainly in the form of the carcasses of deer killed by hunters the previous autumn, and the bear stoops readily to the role of scavenger. If there are sheep in the area, and if renegade dogs or coyotes are taking a toll of them, he is almost sure to feed on the leftovers. While he is quite capable of killing sheep on his own, more often he gets blamed for depredations he had nothing to do with, when he is found cleaning up a carcass.

Throughout the summer he eats insects and their grubs, wild honey and the bees that stored it (his heavy fur apparently enables him to raid bee colonies with complete impunity), ants, frogs, snakes, and small mammals. He is not generally credited with being a devoted fisherman, but he likes fish and in at least one place, Prince of Wales Island in southeastern Alaska, they make up a major share of his diet.

The members of a deer-hunting club in northern Michigan put up a birdhouse one recent spring, suspending it from a fair-sized branch on a tree not far from club headquarters.

It wasn't long before a swarm of bees moved in and took over. Toward the end of summer a bear came along, climbed the tree, inched out on the branch as far as his weight would allow, and swatted the house down. There wasn't enough left of it when he finished to be worth picking up.

As a predator on other game he has little effect, not because he chooses to leave deer, moose, and elk alone but because he is too slow to hunt them effectively. He does, however, pick up young fawns and calves now and then.

Olive and John Fredrickson once watched a distressing incident of that kind. They were hidden in brush near a woods-bordered airport, watching a sow bear with two cubs. The cubs romped and frolicked, and finally their mother sat down, leaned back against a tree, and fed them.

"There is something almost humanly tender about the sight of a she bear suffering her cubs to nurse at her breasts," Olive told me.

Once full fed, the cubs curled up and went to sleep. But suddenly the sow threw up her head, tested the wind, and raced for the airfield. A whitetail doe and her fawn had come into the open there.

The doe fled but the fawn ran headlong into the airport fence and bounced back, almost into the arms of the bear. The kill was swift and clean. There was one agonized bleat from the fawn, then the bear crunched down on its skull and it was dead.

This bear is not above cannibalism, and there are many records of one feeding on another. While most of these represent instances of cleaning up a dead carcass, a big bear does not hesitate to kill and feed on a cub if he gets the chance.

In parts of the West where they are exceptionally abundant, and especially on Washington's Olympic Peninsula where trappers once took 336 bears in foot snares in one year, the inner bark of young trees, chiefly Douglas fir, spruce, and redwood, is eaten in sufficient quantities to pose a serious forest-damage problem.

Midsummer brings berry season, and no pioneer housewife was ever a more devoted harvester of wild fruit than the black bear. Blueberries, wild raspberries, and blackberries, saskatoon berries in the north of western Canada (the same fruit that is called the shad berry in the eastern United States), wild grapes and wild cherries become his staff of life. If he finds them in abundance he may even forsake his solitary ways and tolerate other bears in the patch. Carl Johnson, Michigan's best known bear hunter, once sent his hounds into an area of wild cherries and drove out seven bears in a group.

Mast of all kinds is a highly important food item. Before chestnut blight ravaged the timberlands of the east, chestnuts figured prominently in bear diet. Beechnuts, acorns, hickory nuts, the nuts of piñon pine, and other pine seeds still do.

In late summer bears turn to mushrooms, feeding on them so heavily that the dung turns whitish. That habit raises a puzzling question. The woods are full of mushrooms that are deadly to man, as well as the edible varieties. No instance of mushroom poisoning in bears has ever been recorded. Does that mean that blackie is immune to such poisoning, or has he acquired in some mysterious fashion the instinctive ability to recognize the dangerous kinds? It is hardly likely the answer will ever be known.

No listing of bear foods would be complete without making mention of garbage dumps, of his occasional killing of domestic sheep, pigs, and cattle, his raids on bee hives and back-door garbage cans, and his endless appetite for apples. I was told by a backwoods farmer years ago that a bear in an orchard never stops feeding of his own accord. He only slows down, and because the fruit passes quickly through his digestive tract, he rids himself of it almost as fast as he takes it in.

He is not content with windfalls, either. He climbs into the trees and rakes in fruit with both forepaws, and the damage he does in broken branches is hard to believe.

Once he finds a bee yard he smashes hives to get at the honey, and in some places this problem is severe enough that beekeepers resort to an electric fence to keep bears out.

As for the bear himself, except for his bigger kinsman the grizzly (from which he flees in precipitate haste and without argument), he has no natural enemies apart from man. All of the major carnivores would certainly welcome a meal of cub meat if they could get it, but the she bear is too vigilant and too dangerous for that.

Now and then the bear attacks prey that is almost too much for him. The story of one such incident was related to me back in the 1940s by Elbert Wilkey, a lumber scaler who was working in the Nantahala National Forest in western North Carolina at the time. Wilkey and John Rogers, a woods foreman, were actual witnesses to the fracas.

Without warning, on a ridge above them, the shrill agonizing squealing of a hog ripped the stillness of the summer afternoon.

The two men knew there could be no domestic shoat or razorback in that place. This was wild boar country, and the squealer had to be a wild hog, the kind commonly called Rooshians by the local people.

"Somethin' has grabbed a Rooshian up there," Rogers exclaimed. "Bet it's a bear!" There was no other animal in those mountains likely to tangle with one of the wild boars.

They dropped their work and ran up the ridge toward the squealing. The timber along the crest was open, and when they got within fifty yards of the top they could see a bear and a boar engaged in a fight to the finish.

The boar was small, hardly more than 150 pounds, but still big enough to be a formidable antagonist. The bear was big; the men guessed him at 400. As near as they could piece the story together, he had lain in wait for the hog, hidden behind a fallen tree, and jumped his prey when it fed within reach, catching it completely by surprise.

The bear was holding the boar by the hind quarters with his forefeet, hugging it up to him and tearing at belly and back with his teeth. The hog was swinging his head from side to side, trying to use his razor-sharp tusks, but couldn't reach around far enough to bring them into play. He was being hurt badly, too, and all the while he kept up his tortured squealing, like a farmyard porker at butchering time. The bear fought in complete silence. They were both spattered with blood, but so far as Wilkey and Rogers could tell it all came from the boar.

Hog and bear went down on the ground, still locked together, and rolled into a hole left by the roots of an upturned tree. The hog was still fighting gamely, but he had no chance.

The two men moved in to within seventy-five feet, hoping to scare the bear off. It was plain that he saw them but he showed no fear of them and they did not dare to go closer.

Hog and bear went down on the ground, still locked together, and rolled into a hole left by the roots of an upturned tree. The boar was still fighting gamely, but he had no chance, and at last his agonized screams died away. Then the bear turned on the two humans who had barged in.

He came lumbering around the upturned stump, with hog blood all over his face and head, and the men could see he was mad clear through. When he climbed up on a log and reared erect, swinging his head from side to side and growling, they cleared out.

They went back the next morning to find out what had happened. The bear had carried his prey out of the hole to a level spot nearby and fed. Then he had bedded down for the night beside what was left of the carcass. From the evidence that remained, Wilkey and Rogers concluded that he had finally made his kill by biting through the boar's skull.

It's not often the black bear actually bites off more than he can chew in the matter of prey, but it does happen. There was one such case in Colorado, where a two-hundred-pound bear made an attack on a herd of about fifty range cattle, plainly hoping to single out a calf for the kill.

There was one mature bull in the lot, and he went for the bear with such rage that he sent it scrambling up a convenient cottonwood. The entire herd promptly formed a circle under the tree, bawling and bellowing. The bear climbed to a height of thirty feet and showed no inclination to risk coming down.

Willard Smith, a trout fisherman from the nearby town of Silt, was fishing the Colorado River that morning with two partners. They watched the strange encounter, and when the bear stayed treed Smith ran to his car and drove into town for his rifle. It was a Sunday morning, but he contacted a friend who ran a sporting goods store and bought a bear license. When he got back to the scene the bear was still in the cottonwood and the cattle were still making an angry fuss under the tree. Smith collected a bearskin rug with no difficulty.

The weight of an average black bear is commonly overestimated by hunters. At the same time, few outdoorsmen are aware of the huge size reached by an occasional male, in the prime of life and rolling in autumn fat. On the other hand, persons with little or no knowledge of wildlife have estimated the weight of bears in Great Smoky Mountains National Park as high as one thousand to two thousand pounds.

To begin with, bigness in bears is measured in two different ways, depending on who does the measuring. With few exceptions, hunters judge by weight alone. A 500-pound bear is automatically bigger than one that weighs 450, regardless of height, length, paw size, or the measurements of the skull.

But the prestigious Boone and Crockett Club, which keeps score on all North American trophy game and publishes new lists of the records every few years, accepts only skull measurements as the yardstick of bigness. Frequently those measurements bear little relation to weight.

In the Club's most recently published edition of North American Big Game Records, that of 1971, the No. 1 black was a bear killed in Utah in 1970. Its skull measured $13^{11}/_{16}$ inches in length and $8^{11}/_{16}$ in width, adding up to a total score of $22^6/_{16}$.

No. 2 is a bear taken in Arizona in 1968. It scored $22^4/_{16}$. No. 3, a 1964 kill in Colorado, scored 22; and No. 4, from Wisconsin, $21^{15}/_{16}$.

Of the four, I have weight records for only one, the Wisconsin bear. A male, it was killed near its winter den in the Land O' Lakes area in the fall of 1953. The dressed weight, with entrails, heart, lungs, and excess fat removed was a whopping 585 pounds. Wisconsin game men believed the bear had weighed close to 700 alive. Ed Strobel, the lucky hunter who killed it, thought he had taken the biggest black ever shot, and for a time it did stand in No. 1 place on the Boone and Crockett record list.

To me, and to almost every bear hunter I know, the weight of a bear is more impressive and dramatic than skull size. For many years I have kept track of the heaviest kill in my home state of Michigan and in neighboring Wisconsin. Some of the animals on my list are certainly among the biggest by weight ever taken anywhere, and one is probably a world record for a black bear.

In 1966 Bob Haataja, a young Naval Reservist from Ahmeek in the Michigan Copper Country, downed a bear near the tip of the Keweenaw Peninsula that dressed 570 pounds. It was the heaviest ever recorded from Michigan up to that time.

In 1971 D. S. Pope, a hunter from the Detroit suburb of Troy, killed one in the Shingleton area on the south shore of Lake Superior that weighed 650 before it was field dressed, 580 after, with heart and lungs removed. It was a big bear, but its dressed weight fell 72 pounds below that of the heaviest black on record for the country. That giant, killed near Glidden, Wisconsin, in 1963 by Otto Hedbany, dressed an incredible 652 pounds with heart and lungs out. It could hardly have weighed less than 725 alive, probably more than that.

That same fall, four days before Hedbany took his record-breaker, Linda Lunsman, a 16-year-old school girl from Danbury, Wisconsin, had shot a black bear that dressed 635 on certified scales. It stood at the top of the list until Hedbany beat it.

In 1972 two downstate hunting partners, Ed Phelps and Estille Johnson, hunting in the Grand Marais area of Michigan's Upper Peninsula, shot the heaviest black recorded for the state up to that time. It dressed 612 pounds.

Two years later the Michigan crown changed hands again, under circumstances that many hunters regarded as highly extraordinary. A bowhunter, Hawley Rhew from the town of Carp Lake just south of the Straits of Mackinac, got on the trail of a huge bear in Wilderness State Park west of Mackinaw City.

He bushwhacked it and killed it with one arrow. It dressed 613 pounds, a pound heavier than the bear taken by Phelps and Johnson. Up to that time the heaviest killed in Michigan with bow was a 555-pounder shot in 1955 by Dean Lovelace of Hamtramck. Rhew's was also the only bear among Michigan heavyweights to come from the Lower Peninsula of the state.

I have records from a few other states, but they fall short of being satisfactory, since most of them do not indicate whether the weight given is dressed or live.

Alaska says males there "may weigh as much as 500 pounds." New Mexico puts the top weight at that same figure. Virginia reports one of 635 pounds and another of 640. California lists as its heaviest a male live-trapped in Yosemite National Park in 1969. It weighed 690 pounds, and obviously that was live weight.

In 1957 New York game biologists live-trapped two bears in the Adirondacks that tipped the scales at 562 and 605 pounds respectively. Two years before that a New York hunter killed one that hog-dressed 540 and may have been heavier than either of the two captured alive.

One of the strangest things about black-bear weight is the ability of blackie to put on pounds at an incredibly fast rate when he has an abundant food supply. A wild adult has been known to gain ninety pounds in three weeks. Another gained sixty pounds in thirty-one days, and a male almost doubled its weight in five months. They can lose pounds almost as fast as they put them on, too. A winter loss of a pound a day is not unusual.

FOUR

Enigma of the Woods

Up to the early 1950s, little more than twenty years ago, wildlife researchers and hunters alike possessed less solid information on bears, the black included, than on any other big-game animals on this continent. This was a surprising situation, in view of the close association between bear and man since the time of earliest settlement, the role of the bear as a nuisance and predator, the relentless war humans have waged against him, his importance as a game animal, and the fact that many hunters regarded him as the most desirable trophy they would ever have a chance to take.

Partly because of his wariness, his secretive and furtive ways, and more because of the fact that most of his activities were carried out under the cloak of darkness, he remained for many decades a puzzling enigma of the woods. As one wildlife authority put it, "The things we are not sure of, but guess at, would fill a book. All the accurate information we have about the black bear and his way of life could be put in one short chapter."

Nobody knew with any degree of certainty how long this animal lived in the wild, the size of his home range, how extensively male and female bears traveled. There was uncertainty as to the precise time of the breeding season and the rate of reproduction. Did the female breed only every second year, as was commonly believed? If she lost her cubs the first spring, did she breed again that same summer? How old did the cubs have to be to survive the loss of their mother? Did they need to be protected under the game laws? Under what conditions did bears hibernate, and what was the nature and degree of torpor in hibernation? No one had the answers.

Most important of all, no way was known to make reliable estimates, or even good "educated guesses," of the number of bears in a state or area. The latter situation still prevails in many states, despite the fact that such figures are vital as a basis for drafting necessary regulations to govern bear hunting.

One of the pioneers in scientific bear studies was Al Erickson, a game biologist with the Michigan Conservation Department, now the Department of Natural Resources. When Erickson began his research in the Upper Peninsula of the state in 1952, dart guns that made it possible to inject an immobilizing drug into a bear from a safe distance were not yet available. But with dedicated researchers such as Erickson, where there's a will there's a way, and he improvised some clumsy but effective methods for drugging, weighing, measuring, and tagging bears.

To catch them he devised a culvert trap, using a section of corrugated steel pipe three feet in diameter and six feet long. Surprisingly, for an animal as wary and canny as a bear, blackie proved a pushover for these cumbersome devices. Probably his normal determination to push, tear or rip his way into any place where food is available overcame his normal caution.

Anyway, Erickson had little difficulty trapping bears in his culverts. The next and more difficult step was to render them safe to handle without doing them lasting damage. For that Al fell back on ether.

I was eager to photograph the whole procedure, and after two or three years of trapping, and refining his procedure, he offered to phone me right after daybreak the next time he found a bear in a trap. I was living at the downstate village of Holly, fifty miles from Detroit, at the time, and I'd have 350 miles to drive north from my home to his trapping area around the Cusino Game Research Station near Munising. It would take six or seven hours, but Al assured me the bear would wait.

His call came early one morning, and I headed north. When I reached our place of rendezvous, he was waiting with helpers and a bear that would weigh around 250 pounds.

I had expected to find a thoroughly angry black, growling and slobbering and popping his teeth, probably lunging at the bars of the trap door every time a man came near. Instead I found a resigned and crestfallen animal that acted neither annoyed nor scared. He was sitting on his rump at the back end of the trap, and the look on his face said as plainly as words, "How did I get into this mess?" What followed had become routine by that time.

Erickson had started his project while he was still a student in wildlife biology at Michigan State University, working for the Conservation Department in summer.

"As game men we needed to work out a bear management program that would keep pace with the growing importance of the black as a game animal, and insure an adequate harvest of the bear crop as well as the future of the hunting," he told me. "We just didn't know enough about bears to do that."

He began with a livetrap that weighed five hundred pounds. The back of the culvert was closed with wooden planking reinforced with steel rods. Three-inch apertures had been cut at intervals in the sides of the pipe for ventilation, and also in the hope that it might be possible to fix an ear tag in a captive bear through one of the holes. The latter failed to work.

The drop door at the front of the trap, made of steel bars, was fixed to a trigger that required a pull of at least thirty-five pounds to be tripped. That was intended to prevent skunks, porcupines, coons, stray dogs, and other lesser fry from springing the trap.

Erickson and his crew loaded their trap onto a pickup truck, drove out into the woods to a place where they had seen bear sign, and lugged the contraption a few yards to what looked like a good spot. For bait they had a quarter of a young deer that had died in a pen at the nearby Cusino Wildlife Station, from which the bear trapping was to be carried out. They dragged the slightly ripe venison back and forth across a woods road to lay a scent trail leading to the trap, fastened the bait firmly on the trigger, and went away.

They could hardly wait for morning. If they caught a bear it would be the first one, so far as they knew, ever taken anywhere in the country in a livetrap for the purposes they had in mind.

They drove out to the trap shortly after daybreak, and even before they climbed out of the pickup they saw that the door was down. Inside they found a small bear that turned out to weigh 115 pounds.

This one didn't like the proceedings. He wasn't trying to tear the trap apart. In fact he was wasting no energy at all. But everything about him made it plain that he was in a very resentful frame of mind, and if he got a chance he'd take it out on somebody.

Erickson had decided beforehand to anesthetize any bear he caught with ether. That called for converting the trap into a fairly airtight chamber. The men began by stuffing rags into the holes in the culvert, but the bear unstuffed them as fast as they were poked in. Next they tried wooden plugs driven firmly into place. They stayed. Dirt was then banked around the door, and $3\frac{1}{2}$ pounds of ether was pumped into the trap.

When the bear was completely inert they dragged him out, determined his sex, measured and weighed him, and watched a very drunk bear stagger to his feet and reel off into the woods. Capture of the first black bear ever caught for purposes of research was an accomplished fact.

A few days later a second and larger bear was trapped. He ripped the reinforced planking out of the back of the culvert and went his way. That ruined the trap and ended the work for that summer.

The following year Erickson resumed the project. A few bears were taken, including a female with two young cubs. The trapping crew found them sitting on top of the culvert, waiting for their mother to get out.

In 1955 Al was able to make his bear trapping a full-time job. It was that summer that he phoned me to come up for pictures. By that time he was using a trap of a new design, with no apertures in the culvert and with a welded steel back replacing the reinforced wooden planks. But the basic procedure remained the same.

In the meantime, somebody had suggested trying the wooden livetraps used in taking deer. They proved fine for catching bears, but no good for holding them. The captive simply ripped the drop doors to splinters or reduced most of the trap to kindling, and as Erickson put it, went out through a hole big enough to let a small elephant escape. That type of trapping was quickly abandoned.

Erickson had learned that to keep a bear anesthetized long enough for measuring, weighing, and tagging he needed a way to administer ether as he

For his study of bears in Michigan's Upper Peninsula, Al Erickson devised a culvert trap, using a section of corrugated steel pipe three feet in diameter and six feet long. Blackie proved a pushover for these cumbersome devices.

went along. He devised a metal cone to fit over the muzzle of the animal, the small end closed by a diaphragm of thick cloth onto which the ether could be sprayed. Before the summer was over, thirty-four bears were knocked out that way without the loss of one.

The black I had gone north to photograph was anesthetized by spraying ether into the trap. He was then dragged out, the cone placed over his muzzle, more ether was given him as it was needed, and he was measured, tagged and winched off the ground in a square of canvas for weighing. When the job was finished we stepped back to await his recovery.

After a while he opened his eyes, blinked drunkenly, raised his head and looked around in obvious confusion. He rolled to his feet and fell sprawling. He got up and fell down three or four times, shaking his head to clear the fog away. Finally he lumbered off, steering an uncertain course through the trees and brush.

Not all of the bears reacted that way. One smallish female came for the research crew the minute she could get to her feet and chased the men into the cab of their truck, diverted only by a dog they had along. They called the dog off and drove away, leaving the bear staring after them in obvious rage.

Before that summer was over, Erickson was taking bears in steel traps as well as livetraps. By using No. $4\frac{1}{2}$ traps, any but the biggest bears could be held without injury to a foot. That meant that any bear caught had to be roped by the legs, tied up and anesthetized, all in the open. The most ticklish part of the job was getting the ether cone in place and keeping it there. Erickson solved that problem with a neck noose that could be twisted tight enough to control the bear's head, although it left his jaws free to snap like a rat trap. With the bear's legs securely snubbed, and a member of the crew diverting his attention, Al would clap the cone in place, throw his body and arms down on it to keep it there, and hold it until the ether could take effect.

A year or so later, Erickson left Michigan and went to Alaska, where he became engaged in the same kind of research on brown and polar bears. His place was taken by another game biologist, El Harger. By that time, Erickson had tagged and released 159 bears. Between 1958 and 1970, Harger caught and handled 314 more, running the total Michigan score to 473.

Harger started with the same methods that Erickson had worked out, but by 1964 drug guns had come into use, and after that he took his bears that way, or by injecting a drug into trapped animals with a syringe on the end of a six-foot pole. He learned that by using the proper dose of two drugs, a bear could be kept asleep for three or four hours, loaded into a truck and moved to a distant release point. Because almost all of the bears handled were nuisance animals, it was necessary to learn how far they had to be moved to prevent them from coming back.

The most astonishing thing to come out of the Michigan research was the discovery of an almost unbelievable homing instinct in black bears.

One female, trapped by Harger and released with her two cubs 168 airline miles away, headed straight home with her family. In less than two months she and the cubs covered forty-two miles. One of the youngsters was then killed by a car. A week later the sow was shot while raiding a garbage can in the village of L'Anse. She had returned ninety-eight miles toward her home area in sixty-four days, in almost a straight line.

An adult male moved a hundred miles and was killed by a hunter thirty-five days later, within six miles of the place where he was caught originally. Another male returned forty-nine miles to the exact spot where trapped, in eight days. A sow, separated from her cubs and trucked sixty-four miles, was recaptured after 120 days within nineteen miles of home. She had had to follow a roundabout route around two cities and several bays of Lake Superior to get there.

The record for homing was set by a female in the summer of 1968. A local conservation officer live-trapped her in early August, in an orchard near the western end of the Upper Peninsula. She was released 142 miles to the east as the crow flies. Eleven months later, the same conservation officer caught her a second time, exactly half a mile from the site of the first capture.

With many of the homing bears, the rate of travel was surprising. Two made six miles a day, one covered nine miles, and another hurried along at an average rate of thirteen miles each twenty-four hours.

This homing instinct is all the more remarkable when it is considered that all of the bears involved were moved to the distant release sites while unconscious from drugs. There was no possible way for them to know where they had been taken. They found their way home entirely by instinct.

"We simply don't know how they do it," Harger conceded.

The homing instinct seems to be entirely lacking in cubs and yearlings, however. None of that age group made it back.

Since the Michigan bear research was begun, a number of other states with huntable populations of black bears have undertaken similar studies. New York began the trapping and tagging of bears in the Adirondacks in 1956, and by 1958 had captured and handled some five hundred. In 1970 another study was launched in that state, this time in the Catskills, where the kill of bears by hunters was dropping steadily. Seventeen blacks were caught the first year, most of them in foot snares.

The foot snare consists of a loop of aircraft cable with a trigger, a spring-activated throw arm, and a lock that prevents the loop from being loosened once it is drawn tight. When set, the loop is attached by a swivel to another length of cable securely anchored to a tree or heavy log.

It turned out that the most effective set was one New York game men called the pen-cubby type, in which the snare was placed at the entrance to a roofless, horseshoe-shaped pen of poles and brush, and bears were lured in by bait placed at the back end of the pen.

The snares seem to do little injury to the bears, and are also considered safe where humans are concerned. Nevertheless, each set was marked with a conspicuous sign which read: "Warning—Bear Foot Snare set in this area. Bears caught in snare are dangerous. Stay away."

Once caught, each bear was immobilized with a drug fired from a pistol-type syringe gun. It was then weighed, measured and tagged, its sex determined, and a small premolar tooth extracted for determination of age. The bear was finally given a drug to counteract the one that had immobilized it, and released none the worse for the experience.

The Catskill project has been plagued by a shortage of funds, but it has resulted in one interesting conclusion on the part of New York game men. They now believe that it is useless to try to protect bear cubs by law.

In 1938, a New York law went into effect that prohibited shooting any bear less than one year old. It was repealed for the Adirondacks region in 1956, but is still in effect in the Catskills. Despite the prohibition, an average of seven out of one hundred bears taken there by hunters have proven to be cubs.

Authorities believe most of them are killed not in deliberate violation of the law, but rather because hunters are unable to estimate the live weight of small bears and so cannot tell which are cubs and which are not. Many New York hunters try to follow the rule that any bear is a cub if it weighs less than one hundred pounds, but they are not able to guess the weight reliably. That rule has proven hardly more dependable than the one followed by many Michigan hunters, which holds that if a bear looks "bigger than a sack of potatoes" it is not a cub and can be shot legally.

The list of states where bear research of one kind or another has been carried out or is presently under way includes Tennessee, Pennsylvania, Georgia, North Carolina, Vermont, Alaska, Montana, Massachusetts, California, Louisiana, Washington, Virginia, West Virginia, New Hampshire, and Idaho.

In a number of these projects, radio collars have been fitted to bears, to enable the researchers to keep track of their daily movements and determine the size of their home range. Inevitably, a great deal of interesting and valuable information has come from the various studies. Perhaps the most important has been improved methods of gathering statistics on the number of bears killed annually by hunters, and more accurate ways of estimating the bear population of a state or a given area. These facts must be known if the black bear is to be managed in a way that insures his future.

40

The home range of the black bear is now fairly well known. Erickson learned that the home territory of Michigan blacks averaged about twenty miles across. He had records of some that were tagged but not moved away, that wandered only a mile or so in an entire summer. Others roamed as far as twenty-five miles.

"They are inclined to follow a regular route in traveling, much as wolves and other animals do," El told me. "But a bear's foremost interest is food, and if he finds a good supply he stays near it as long as it lasts."

Montana studies have shown that adult males there have home ranges of about twelve square miles. Females are satisfied with smaller areas, often spending most of their lives in a territory as small as two square miles.

Alaskan game men call this bear a homebody. Studies there have shown that individuals may spend the greater part of their lives within five miles of the place where they were born. Again, however, males wander more widely than females.

Male bears, live-trapped in Minnesota and released in Louisiana to boost the population there, stayed in a home territory covering twenty-five to sixty square miles, at times traveling twenty miles in one direction or another. Females ranged far less widely.

Bear age is now determined accurately by studying growth layers in a cross section of tooth, which show up much like the annual growth rings in a tree. Between 1964 and 1972, New York researchers aged close to two hundred bears that way.

Another thing that has been learned is that the black bear possesses a remarkable ability to recover from broken bones and even from the loss of a leg. A case in Georgia is typical.

A young male caught in that state in a foot snare in August of 1972 suffered a broken hind leg in fighting the snare. He was tracked by radio signals and observed several times in the next three or four weeks. During that time he sheltered himself in dense laurel thickets or in a hollow tree.

The most effective trap used by New York game men was called the pencubby. A snare was placed at the entrance to a roofless, horseshoe-shaped pen of poles and brush. Once caught, each bear was immobilized with a drug fired from a syringe gun.

He was finally retrapped, when it was found that the leg had been amputated at the point of the break. Ovbiously, the bear had done the surgery himself, probably soon after the injury. The wound had healed over, swelling was moderate, and he appeared in good physical condition. Unfortunately, radio contact with him was lost after that, so the final outcome was not learned, but there was every reason to believe that he survived the injury without serious handicap.

Far more is understood today about bear denning, the effects of a mast-crop failure, the breeding habits, rate of reproduction, and the life span of wild bears than was known twenty years ago. In short, many of blackie's secrets have been ferreted out by painstaking scientific effort, and much of the guesswork has vanished from the job of allowing him to be hunted but not overhunted. He has not yielded up answers to all of his riddles, however. Much has been learned about him, but much remains unlearned. He is still a creature of mystery, likely to do no man knows what.

The Alaska Game Department still labels him one of our least understood big-game species. A Montana authority says he is probably the most misrepresented of North American wildlife, adding that he is not "the hat-wearing Smoky, the overfed Gentle Ben or the food-begging Yogi of national park highways. He is a wary native of the forest, rarely seen outside of zoos and national parks."

Study bears as they will, men will never learn all there is to know about their behavior and way of life. One trait that hinders wildlife researchers is their refusal to follow a set pattern. Deer, elk, moose, wild sheep, even the mountain lion, all react fairly consistently to any given set of circumstances. Not so the bear.

Near the conclusion of his research project in northern Michigan, El Harger summed it up this way: "If I have learned anything in trapping, drugging, weighing, measuring, tagging, moving, and releasing more than three hundred black bears, it's that nobody knows what they are going to do next. I have a firm rule even in talking about them. I never say never.

"It doesn't matter how much dealing a hunter or trapper or researcher has had with them, let him say that they always do so and so or never do so and so, and along will come a bear to prove him a liar."

It seems safe to say that to a large degree the black bear will always be what he has always been, an unsolved riddle of the wild places of North America.

FIVE

The Trouble Hunter

Much about the black bear may be cloaked in secrecy, but he has one trait that is clear to all who know him. He goes out of his way to look for trouble, and he does it more often and with greater determination than any other animal on this continent.

I remember an experience when four of us were camped, with four Cree guides, on a willow-grown island where the Harricanaw River spills out of the Quebec bush into the southern end of James Bay.

The time was September and the blue and snow geese were pouring south from their nesting grounds along the rim of the continent and on the polar islands beyond, halting to rest and fatten in the salt marshes at the foot of the bay before pushing down the final leg of their autumn flight to wintering places along the coast of Louisiana and Texas.

We had some twenty drawn geese hanging on the meat pole. Some were ours, some would go into the winter brine barrels of the Crees.

The days were warm but the nights were frosty, and because the ground turned cooler than the air at night we were heaping the geese in a pile and covering them with tarp each evening, to prevent spoilage.

We rolled out of our sleeping bags one morning to find them missing, gone to the last bird.

The verdict of the Indians was instant and unanimous. A bear had raided us during the night, they agreed. He'd be back, and unless we killed him we'd lose geese as fast as they were shot. In addition, the bear would be almost sure to ransack our food supply, and probably the tents as well.

The situation was on the hairy side. The only guns in camp were shotguns, and the only loads No. 2 or No. 4 shot, intended for geese; poor medicine for a bear. But we didn't seem to have much choice, and so we formed a plan.

We'd take turns standing guard, perched in a fork of the only tree around, a scrubby aspen only twelve or fifteen feet high. Whoever got the chance would try to kill the bear, at very close range.

After breakfast I took a turn out in the willow thickets that surrounded the camp, hoping to find bear tracks or some other evidence of what had happened. I had completed about half my circle when I came to a low hummock with half a dozen small-animal burrows leading under it. From every one of those burrows part of a goose was sticking out.

I yelled for the Crees. They took one look and burst into laughter. "Shegak, shegak!" they cried.

Shegak. A family of skunks living beneath the hummock had stolen our geese. We went back to the tents greatly relieved.

The point of the story is that the Indians, who knew far more about bears than we did, automatically put the blame for the pilfered geese on a bear. I might add that that was about the only time when I have ever known blackie to be blamed for mischief undeservedly. Almost always he is guilty as charged.

He breaks into a closed barn to kill sheep, cattle, and hogs. He raids beehives. He climbs into apple trees and the damage he does has to be seen to be believed.

He turns into a panhandling bum in parks and campgrounds, dangerous because through the fault of people he loses all natural fear of man. He breaks into wilderness cabins despite every precaution to keep him out. I knew one bush trapper in northern Ontario who nailed discarded crosscut saw blades along the edge of his cabin roof, teeth up, to discourage prowling bears from climbing onto the roof, tearing a hole through the hand-split cedar shakes, and making an incredible shambles of everything inside. The saw blades did no good.

At campgrounds in many a state and national park, bears get to be intolerable nuisances, smashing into tents, tearing open food containers, lugging off bacon and bread and other food, even biting into tubes of toothpaste and urinating on sleeping bags.

One other thing blackie does in state after state that results in more complaints of bear damage than can be counted. He prowls around camps and summer cottages in the woods, knocks over garbage cans, eats what he wants of the contents—and after a few visits he is likely to grow bold and even quarrelsome.

A bear that robs garbage cans, whatever his disposition and intentions, is just about sure to scare the wits out of the human occupants of the place, and they complain to state wildlife authorities in a hurry, demanding that the bear be liquidated or removed.

However, I knew one case, some years ago, where the owner of the garbage can did not ask for help. The encounter had its amusing side, although it ended in disaster for an overly persistent bear. He picked the wrong person to impose on.

It happened at Howard Lowry's fishing camp on Quesnel Lake in British Columbia, west of Wells Gray Provincial Park. Howard's wife, Vi, a pretty little thing who, despite the job of cooking for the camp, managed to look like an attractive Junior Leaguer ready for an afternoon of bridge (she baked some of the best homemade bread I have ever encountered, twenty-three loaves to the batch) was working in the kitchen one summer afternoon when she heard the clatter of her garbage can being mauled just outside the back door. She stepped to the door to find a black bear that weighed around 125 pounds gobbling garbage, with his head in the can up to his shoulders. A deep dent in the side of the can indicated that he had been a trifle careless in getting the lid off. Vi said nothing. She picked up a broom, stepped out and swatted the bear across his black rump for all she was worth.

He tossed the can twenty feet in his hurry to get his head out, and ran for the timber like forked lightning.

Vi went back to her chores in the kitchen. But fifteen minutes later the garbage can clattered again, and when she went to the door the same bear was up to the same tricks.

"OK, Buster," the little camp cook said grimly. "If you want it you shall have it."

She stepped to a corner of the kitchen, picked up her rifle, and poured a shot in at six feet. The bear's raiding days were over in less time than it takes to tell the story.

A number of years back I spent some time with Ralph Richardson, a northern Wisconsin conservation warden who was an expert on bear depredation and damage. In more than twenty-five years in the north woods of that state he had had a hand in liquidating thirty-odd blacks that had to be gotten rid of because they were doing serious damage.

"No other animal in this country can hold a candle to a black bear for troublemaking," Richardson told me. The stories he related read like a catalog of bear misdeeds.

"They hunt for deviltry every chance they get, whether they need to or not," he said. "They kill stock. If there are beehives around they find 'em, and when a bear opens a hive there isn't much left that is worth salvaging. Apple orchards are their specialty, and they do terrific damage in cornfields in late summer and fall.

"They go into the corn when the ears are passing out of the milk stage, and pay nightly visits until hibernation time unless the crop is harvested before that. The havoc they wreak is beyond description. Raccoons, porcupines, squirrels, even blackbirds, can be doing substantial damage in a patch of corn, but let a bear move in and you don't need to find his tracks to know he has been there. His depredations are in a class by themselves. He smashes down stalks, breaks off ears, ruins more than he eats. One bear can make as bad a mess as a whole drove of hogs."

The first marauding bear Richardson was called on to do away with was a sheep killer. A farmer in the Crandon area, where Ralph was stationed at the time, phoned in a complaint. Richardson was new to the business of hunting down outlaw bears, and thought he might need help, so he picked up a state fire warden by the name of Gene Nelson and drove out to the place without taking time to put gun or traps in his car.

The farmer led the two men to a woodlot pasture three hundred yards from his house. The sheep had been killed there the night before, and partly devoured. Because he had no equipment along for dealing with the bear right then, Richardson stalled.

"That bear has had enough mutton to hold him for a day or two," he said. "He won't be back tonight."

Just then the farmer's thirteen-year-old boy looked off across the pasture and blurted, "The heck he won't! There he comes right now!" In the fading light, a big black bear was sauntering across the woodlot, straight for the men. The party started to sneak back to the farmhouse for a rifle, but the bear saw or heard them and was gone like a black ghost.

The next day Ralph and Gene fixed up a pen, dragged the sheep carcass inside and set a trap at the entrance. But the bear proved trap-shy and wary in the extreme. He walked all around the pen without going in, finally tore open the back end, pulled the bait out and ate his fill.

He killed a few more sheep on that same farm, then transferred his attentions to a neighbor's place and started raiding a flock there. Richardson put out baited traps at the new location, warning the farmer to keep his two dogs tied up.

"Don't worry about them, they never go off the porch," he was assured.

In the next three nights he caught both dogs and a three-hundred-pound brood sow, but not the bear.

"For quite a while after that I had a highly unusual reputation around that neighborhood as a bear trapper," he told me with a chuckle.

By that time it was plain that he was not likely to take the sheep killer in a trap. He and Nelson kept watch with rifles at sheep carcasses a few more nights, but accomplished nothing. Finally, in desperation, they decided to build a scaffold over one of the kills, high enough that the bear couldn't get their scent, and try to ambush him.

Neither of them had had any previous experience with platforms for bear shooting. If they had they would have made different plans. As it was, they lashed a plank, six feet long and about ten inches wide, between two trees, where they could look down on the dead sheep. The carcass lay in thick brush and, concerned that they wouldn't be able to see the bear if he came in after dark, Ralph rigged a fishline around the bait and ran it up to the scaffold. The bear couldn't get to his kill without walking into the line. They would sit on the plank, and when the cord jerked one of them would turn on a flashlight and the other would do the shooting.

They climbed to their perch shortly before dark and settled down on the plank. Gene had the rifle. He was sitting straddle of the plank at one end, with a tree in front of him, his left arm around it and the gun in his right hand. It turned out he couldn't shoot without making quite a bit of advance commotion.

Richardson was perched side-saddle at the other end of the plank with his feet dangling, hanging on with his right arm through a tree crotch and holding the fishline and flashlight in the other hand.

They hadn't been in place very long before they realized that the narrow plank was little better than a torture rack. Ralph's right arm and both legs went to sleep, and he figured if Gene was in the same shape he'd fall off the plank if he tried to shoot.

It was about 10:30 when they finally heard the bear coming. He was extremely cautious and walked in very slowly, but at last they heard him moving, a step at a time, right under them. About that time they smelled him, too. He had been feeding on ripe sheep for weeks, and he was a very rank bear.

There was man smell or something about the place he didn't like. They could hear him put one foot down real slow and careful, then wait and sniff, letting out long puffs of breath, and finally move another foot.

At last Richardson felt the fishline pulled through his fingers. "Now!" he hissed, and flicked on his light. There was no bear to be seen. Only brush foliage, glistening with the moisture of a wet, very dark night. The bear had cleared out so quietly that they didn't even hear him go.

In the end it was a trap, set in one of his trails, that was his undoing. Richardson found him in the trap, snarling and growling and tearing things apart. He weighed 360 pounds, and both his front feet were deformed from previous encounters with traps. No wonder he had been so careful.

There was another bear, a cattle killer, that Ralph had special reason to remember.

A local logger had bought eighty acres of swamp and cutover land, with a small house and a barn that had seen better days. He moved in, acquired a cow and calf, and housed them in the barn. They lasted less than twenty-four hours.

The very first night a bear ripped a hole in the side of the barn, walked in and killed them both. He dropped the cow with a murderous blow of a forefoot. She was unmarked save for claw wounds near her head, but the bear had smashed the vertebrae of her neck. He killed the calf by biting it through the head, ate part of it and the udder of the cow, and left.

Richardson got the complaint the next day, and he and Gene Nelson went to the place to investigate. This one looked easy. There was a small doorway leading into the barn, about three feet high and two wide, a perfect place for a trap. Sure that the bear would come back to his kills, they made their set there, nailing up with planks and heavy spikes the entrance hole he had made.

He came back that same night, but he showed only disdain for their trapping efforts. His tracks revealed that he had walked to the doorway, sized things up, turned away, gone back to the place where he had gained entrance the night before and ripped the planks off. He went in, ate his fill, picked up the calf and decided to use the doorway on the way out. What was left of the calf was in the trap the next morning, where he had dragged it across the pan, careful not to put his own feet in the wrong place.

The farmer hauled the two carcasses out to the edge of a swamp some distance from the barn, and a few days later he reported that the bear was using on them again.

Gene and Ralph sneaked in at dusk that night, and caught Mr. Bear flat-footed. Nelson made the kill with one shot from a .30/06. Blackie fell across what remained of the cow and calf.

It would have been a lot better for the hunters if he had run fifty feet or so before he went down. He was lying on top of a pile of very high beef, and because he weighed around four hundred pounds they couldn't move him. Dressing and skinning him there would be a nauseating job, but they had no choice so they went at it. They managed to finish the dressing, but the stench was sickening and they gave up on skinning him in that location. The logger enlisted the help of a neighbor with a team and wagon, and the four men loaded the bear and moved him where the air was sweeter.

Although Richardson believed that cornfield damage by bears (it accounted for a majority of the complaints he had had) was peculiar to Wisconsin, that is not the case.

Virginia game men say the chief damage done by black bears in that state is to cornfields, especially in the area adjoining Shenandoah National Park. Park bears, accustomed to feeding at dumps in summer, look for other food as visitors desert the park at the end of August and the dumps shrink. Corn is then in the milk stage and the bears take full advantage of it. Not only do they eat and destroy quantities, they actually frolic in the field, knocking down half an acre at a time. As many as forty-five bears have been trapped and moved in Virginia in a two-year period, largely as a result of corn-damage complaints.

Sheep killing is another major problem in Virginia. One county there had a bear bounty on the books as recently as 1972, possibly the only place remaining in the country where such a bounty was paid. The reason? Sheep raising is a major industry in that county.

In any state where sheep and bears share a common range, trouble is close to inevitable, although it has to be said that the bear's habit of feeding on any carcass he finds often results in him being blamed for sheep kills when he is not guilty. In one such case in northern Michigan, steel traps took a wild dog that was the real culprit. The bear had only cleaned up the leavings.

In many places, hogs fare no better than sheep at the hands of the black bear. It's a common practice with him to climb into a hogpen, grab up a shoat that may weigh one hundred pounds and clamber out, carrying the squealing porker in his forearms or with his teeth fastened in its neck.

In that connection there was an unusual and amusing incident in northern Michigan a few years ago. A sow bear climbed into a pigpen and ate the pigs' food but did not molest them. Wildlife authorities trapped and moved her three times, but she insisted on coming back, and finally the farmer lost patience and shot her.

Beekeepers have good reason to hate bears. Damage to beehives in North Carolina, for example, is widespread enough that the Wildlife Resources Commission has developed a policy of urging beekeepers to keep their hives on elevated platforms, out of reach of bears, or protect them with an electric fence. The latter calls for four strands of heavy barbwire a foot apart, the lowest ten inches above the ground, with all four electrified, and strips of old tin roofing laid all around the outside, to ground any bear that touches one of the hot wires.

One of the most serious damage problems on record cropped up on the Olympic Peninsula in the state of Washington in the 1950s. Bears were stripping away the bark of young trees to get at the sweet sapwood, which they scraped off for food. Some of the trees were girdled and killed outright, others died a few years later.

In the north of western Canada bears do major damage in oat fields, either in late summer when the grain is ripening or in early spring in fields that have been left unharvested. They sit on their rumps or lie flat on their bellies and rake in and pull down all the grain they can reach, a handful at a time, then move to another spot.

"They can harvest oats like a combine," says my old bush-trapper friend Ted Updike.

One of the most serious damage problems on record cropped up on the Olympic Peninsula in the state of Washington in the 1950s. Foresters there reported extensive damage to stands of young trees. Bears were stripping away the bark to get at the sweet sapwood, which they then scraped off for food. The damage was most severe with trees of pole size, and although Douglas fir was preferred, hemlock, spruce, redwood, cedar, and other varieties were also being attacked. Some of the trees were girdled and killed outright, others died as long as five years later.

In response to complaints from timber interests, the Washington Game Commission removed the black bear from the game list and classified him as a predator, stripped of all protection, in the five counties of the Olympic Peninsula.

The Washington Forest Protection Association, an organization of timber owners, opened an all-out war on bears in those counties, putting a number of paid trappers in the field with foot snares. In 1968 a miniature radio transmitter was developed for use with the snares. This device sends out a signal when a snare is sprung, enabling the trapper to monitor his sets by simply driving around his snare line and listening for beeps.

The total kill that has resulted from this control program will never be known, but it has run well into the thousands. One tree farm took 545 bears in five years. With few exceptions, the pelts were left in the woods to rot.

The Game Department approved the program, but Washington hound men criticized it bitterly, charging that the timber interests were out to exterminate the area's bear population.

In 1969 the black bear was reclassified as a game animal throughout the state, and steps were taken to encourage sport hunting and reduce the need for paid trappers. A spring bear season was opened in 1973, with the use of foot snares suspended for its duration to avoid snaring hounds. But the damage problem remains a grave one.

As long as tree farming is the backbone of Washington's economy, the problem will be around, says the Game Department. But the policy now is to encourage the taking of bears by sportsmen in every way possible, and so keep to a minimum the necessity for other means of bear control.

Nowhere does the black bear make a worse nuisance of himself than when he decides to break into a camp or cabin in search of food.

"Any time that happens, you can count on the place looking like a garbage dump," Ted Updike once told me.

Olive Fredrickson, the pioneer Canadian woman I mentioned in an earlier chapter, has had as much experience with this brand of mischief as anybody I know.

"Once bears have raided a place and found something they like, they won't stay away," she says. "We have had bears at our garbage dumps, bears prowling around the buildings, bears at the doors and windows at night, bears in our meat house and bears in our sheep pen. They were blacks and we weren't really afraid of them, although now and then one tried to pick an argument. But any bear that makes up his mind to break in on you is a first-class nuisance, whether you are afraid of him or not."

There was one that ripped the screen off the Fredrickson meathouse at night, climbed in, and either ate or carried off all the bacon, sausage, and pork in the place. Apparently he had no liking for fresh beef. He left a quarter untouched.

Olive and her husband John decided the best way to get rid of that bear was to cut a four-inch peephole in the door of their cook house, overlooking the scene of the raid. They would keep watch for him out of the cook house window and shoot him through the peephole.

He didn't keep them waiting. He came back after more pork right after dark the next night, walked to the window out of which they were watching, stood up with his front feet on the glass and looked in.

John could have shot him then and there, but didn't want to break the window, so he waited until the bear started for the meathouse. The shot hit him in the ribs and he bawled and ran. John ran after him, but changed his mind about chasing a wounded bear in the dark, and came back. They found him half a mile away the next morning and killed him.

Another black prowler that Olive remembers vividly started killing their lambs and calves one spring, at their ranch on the Stuart River. They kept watch of the stock in the daytime and penned it near the buildings at night, but that did not discourage the bear. Morning after morning they continued to find sheep killed and partly eaten.

With the help of their dog, they located a bear den in a big hole under a stump, not far from the ranch buildings. They were not sure it was the same bear, but John poked into the den with a pole. The bear made no response, so John took off an old shirt he was wearing, wrapped it around the end of the pole, touched a match to it and shoved it, smoking, into the hole.

There was a sneeze, a grunt, more sneezes and coughing, and then a bear poked his head out from under the stump, looking greatly displeased. John killed him at six feet. He was the right bear, too. The Fredricksons lost no more stock that spring.

Then there was another bear that broke into their henhouse and killed poultry right and left, tore the top off a rabbit pen and helped himself to the rabbits, and finally took to raiding the meat house. John killed that one at the corner of the house at ten feet.

An unusually bold case of attempted breakin occurred in June of 1975 in the northern part of Michigan's Lower Peninsula.

A farm wife named Charette, sleeping on a closed porch, was awakened at daylight one morning by something scratching on a sheet of plastic stretched across a window. She thought it was her cat and climbed out of bed to send it packing. To her astonishment she found herself face to face with a big black bear that had reared erect and was looking in at her.

She ran to call her husband, asleep inside the house. The bear promptly ripped the plastic away and reached in far enough to leave dirty paw prints on the wall two feet inside the window.

While Charette was getting his 12-gauge single-barrel shotgun, it moved to a kitchen window, stood up again and looked in there. When it dropped back on all fours and walked a few steps away, Charette thought it was leaving and yelled to hurry it off.

The bear ran back to the kitchen window and upreared again, growling and slobbering. The farmer decided things had gone far enough. He killed it with a load of No. 2 shot, fired through the window 18 inches from its head.

His wife commented afterward that she had lived more than fifty years in bear country in that same neighborhood without ever seeing a bear. She saw enough of that one to last her the rest of her life.

"If I ever get mixed up with a thieving bear again it will be because I can't avoid it," Olive Fredrickson once told me.

Small wonder.

SIX

His History and Present Range

When settlement by white Europeans began along the eastern seaboard of this continent, the black bear was an abundant animal wherever he found habitat that suited him, from the Atlantic to the Pacific, from northern Mexico to Alaska, and north across all of Canada to the limits of timber.

No one will ever come close to knowing what the total population of black bears was at that time. Ernest Thompson Seton, one of this country's foremost naturalists and wildlife writers fifty years or more ago, put together all the evidence he could gather of their primitive abundance, and then made an educated guess of the total numbers.

He told of Hearn, the early explorer, seeing eleven killed in the north of Canada in one day; of a settler in upstate New York killing ninety-six in three seasons; of a Pennsylvania hunter who took four hundred in his lifetime. Seton also cited sales by fur companies in the north in the early days of eighteen thousand bearskins a year, of eight thousand shipped from Ohio in three years.

On the basis of all the information he could get, including the old fur records, Seton put the continent's original population of black bears at not fewer than five hundred thousand. This compares with at least thirty million buffalo, an estimated ten million mule deer, and forty million whitetails roaming the American wilderness in the same period. Bears, like all flesh eaters, never attained more than a small fraction of the numbers of the feeders on grass, forbs and browse.

Whatever their numbers, however, there were too many of them to suit the pioneers and settlers. From the beginning, they proved troublesome neighbors. To begin with, humans feared them, and now and then the fear proved well founded. In the second place, they could not be tolerated in the vicinity of sheep, swine, or even cattle. They killed adult sheep, carried off shoats, preyed on calves and occasionally took a full-grown steer or cow. And because of their habit of cleaning up any carcass they came across, they were blamed for even more depredation than they committed. In consequence, every man's hand was set against them as settlement moved westward.

There were other reasons for trapping and hunting them, too. Bear pelts moved briskly in the fur trade. Thousands were exported to Europe for use in making showy bearskin shakos used by the military. At home they provided the makings of warm, durable, and highly prized coats for men.

When I was a small boy my father had such a coat, acquired from my grandfather. I can still see dad, driving his team into town for the weekly marketing on a cold and windy winter day, standing erect in the front of our two-horse sleigh, warm and snug in his bearskin coat, while mother and I huddled under lap robes with a slab of heated soapstone at our feet.

In the beginning, the bear was commonly taken in a device known as the deadfall. A log pen was built with a narrow entrance, and over that entrance a heavy log was suspended. One end rested on the ground, the other was held up by a figure-four trigger, a simple arrangement of stout sticks notched and fitted together so that any animal tugging on the crossbar of the 4 would trip the trap. Bait was fixed on the end of the bar, far enough inside the pen that a bear had to stand under the deadfall log to get at it. If the log was not heavy enough, a rock or some other weight was added. Any bear that tried to take the bait was as good as dead.

The deadfall was soon replaced by the steel bear traps. Those traps were highly effective, and also savagely cruel. I have seen them, hand-forged by a blacksmith, that weighed more than fifty pounds. They had double springs, so powerful that the trapper needed short poles to use as levers in depressing the springs and setting the trap. Short, sharp steel spikes known as teeth were welded to the jaws so that they meshed when the trap was sprung, driving the teeth into the foot or lower leg of the bear.

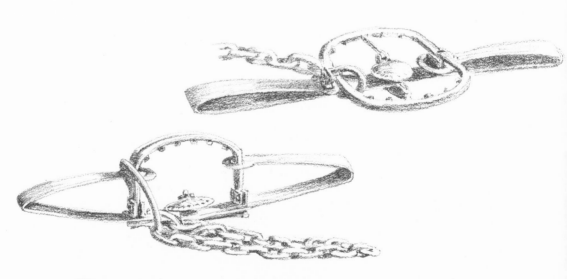

Even with this deadly contraption, the trap could not be fastened by its short heavy chain to a tree or stump. Given that kind of solid resistance, a big bear could tear the teeth out of his flesh and escape with a permanently mutilated foot. Instead the trap was chained to a clog, a short length of stout log which the bear could drag off as it fought the trap, leaving a plain trail for the trapper to follow. By the time the clog became entangled in brush or trees the bear was too exhausted to get away.

Now and then a bear caught by a hind foot would climb a tree in his struggles to escape the trap, dragging the clog up behind him. When it became lodged in the branches he jumped or fell out of the tree. Sometimes the force of his fall tore a mutilated foot out of the trap. More commonly he hung by one leg until he died.

Happily, bear trapping is today a thing of the past in this country, with the exception of a single state, Maine, and also excepting bears that have to be killed because they are doing damage.

In addition to trapping, settlers waged war on raiding bears with guns, hunters took them as often as they had the opportunity, many states paid bear bounties, and nowhere until recent years did they have any protection under the game laws. It is not to be wondered at that their numbers shrank and that they disappeared altogether from much of their original range. The wonder is that they have survived over as much of the continent as they have.

As a child, my grandmother, who was born in 1857, stood in the kitchen doorway with her mother and watched a neighboring hunter shoot a bear that had stretched up to leave claw marks on a tree that stood just beyond the family's clearing. That happened in southeastern Michigan, within fifty miles of the downtown Detroit riverfront. So far as she knew, it was the last bear killed in that neighborhood.

Blackie has been gone from southern Michigan for more than a century now, and from much of the settled areas in other states as well. But that does not mean that he is a vanishing species, by any means.

When I began work on this book, I undertook a complete survey of the remaining black-bear numbers in the fifty states of this country and in all of Canada. The results surprised me. The accompanying table tells the complete story.

Only twelve states are without at least a remnant population of bears. They are Delaware, Illinois, Indiana, Iowa (the last one was killed there about 1880), Hawaii (where they were never found), Kansas (where two strays wandered in from Arkansas in 1965), Nebraska, North Dakota, Ohio, Oklahoma, Rhode Island (gone since 1880), and South Dakota.

Of the states that have black bears, by far the highest number is found in Alaska. Wildlife authorities there estimate the population at 40,000 to 50,000. Other leading bear states are: Washington, with 27,000; Idaho, with 17,000; California, with 11,000 to 15,000; Montana, with 8,000 to 10,000; Maine, with 7,000 to 10,000; Wisconsin, with 6,000 to 8,000; Colorado, with 4,000 to 7,000; Michigan, 5,000 to 6,000; New York, with 3,800 to 4,000; Pennsylvania, with 2,000 to 2,500.

These eleven states account for a total of 130,000 to 150,000 bears, if the estimates of their game departments are reasonably accurate.

It must be admitted that the numbers cited are in many cases no more than guesswork. One state game department supplied me what it called "a ball-park figure." Another frankly labeled their figure a "guesstimate." Michigan biologists admitted they know no way to make an estimate, but from the fact that hunters in that state kill at least 500 to 600 bears annually, a guess of 5,000 to 6,000 for the total population seems reasonable.

Several states asked me to pass along to them any information my research turned up as to how to go about calculating bear numbers.

New York is one state that has made a concerted effort for the last twenty-five years to find out how many bears it has. Careful records are kept of hunter kills, and painstaking scientific studies have been carried out in the Adirondacks and Catskills to arrive at the best possible population figures and fix proper hunting regulations.

My efforts at a survey of bear numbers in Canada met with only limited success. I contacted all of the provinces of that country except Prince Edward Island, which does not have bears, plus Yukon and Northwest Territories.

Only four were able to supply any estimates of their bear populations. British Columbia reported 80,000 to 120,000; Yukon, 3,000 to 5,000; Newfoundland, 3,000; Ontario's "very rough estimate" was 90,000.

Alberta could furnish no valid estimate, but a game biologist in the Department of Lands and Forests there offered a guess of 100,000 animals, plus or minus. He added that there has been a dramatic increase in the black bear population over the last fifteen years, and that the outlook for the future is excellent. Ontario also calls this bear's future bright.

In very few cases today are the black bears distributed over an entire state or province. They are found only where there is wild country to suit them and where cover and food conditions are to their liking. In many instances a state may have two or three entirely separate populations, each limited to an isolated island of suitable habitat.

Georgia, for example, has one population in the huge Okefenokee Swamp and its vicinity, near the Florida border; another where the Southern Appalachian Mountains end in the northern part of the state. New York has three separate populations: one of about 3,500 animals in the Adirondacks; another, numbering 250 to 350, in the Catskills; a third of 50 to 100 in the Allegheny Mountains in the southwestern corner of the state.

One of the most surprising situations exists in New Jersey. It has one of the most dense human populations in the country—and it also has, in the northwest corner of the state, a small population of black bears that continues to hold its own in the face of odds. Just how many is a matter of speculation. Game officials I contacted put the number at twenty to forty, but others tell me you can get estimates of 20 to 100, depending on which wildlife manager you are talking to.

Even with that remnant population, New Jersey allowed ten hunting seasons in the 15-year period from 1958 to 1972. A total of 46 bears were taken. In some years bears can also be taken during deer season.

The hunting is permitted mainly to hold down bear numbers and reduce conflicts between bears and people. Something like nine out of ten New Jersey residents are afraid of bears. Several have been captured and moved away from centers of population, but in a number of cases local police have destroyed a prowling bear before state game men could reach the scene.

New Jersey wildlife officials believe the day may come when residents of the bear area will demand that the animals be totally done away with.

The situation reminds me of a similar one on Beaver Island, which lies in the north end of Lake Michigan about 20 miles off the Michigan mainland. The island covers 54 square miles and has a human population of around 200, almost entirely of Irish descent. Considerable restocking of game has been done. Deer and beaver have been brought back and ruffed grouse and wild turkeys introduced with highly satisfactory results. But when someone suggested, a number of years ago, that black bears be released, the residents rejoined almost to a man that if bears came they'd leave!

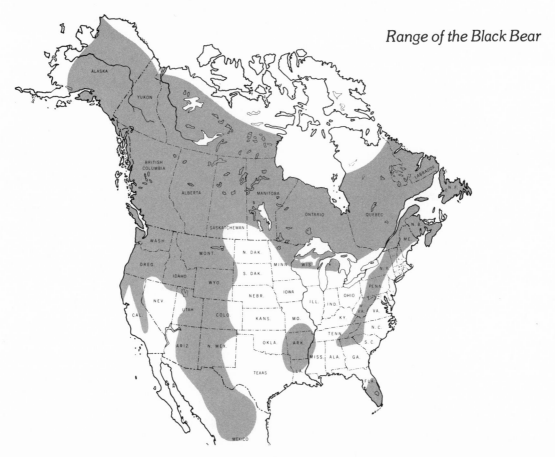

Range of the Black Bear

Kentucky is another state with an unusual bear situation. It maintains a stable population, year after year, of about twelve bears, in the eastern part of the state only. As more drift in from Virginia, West Virginia, and Tennessee, poachers take a toll sufficient to hold the number virtually unchanged.

The oddest situation in any state — it has its amusing side as well — exists in Hawaii. The black bear was not native to the Islands, but in February of 1976 Ron Walker, chief of the Wildlife Branch, told me in a letter that he believes his state may have a population of one bear.

A 20-month-old black escaped from a private zoo and took to the wilds in 1956. It was last seen in 1968, but there has been no report of its death and Walker thinks it may still be alive. If so, it is now more than twenty years old.

It's not uncommon for states or areas that have no bears of their own to be visited by strays from a neighboring population. An amusing incident of that kind occurred in Massachusetts in the fall of 1969. Two bears showed up in a residential area in the town of Florida in the Northern Berkshires. Their erratic behavior and total lack of fear of humans led to the theory that they were drunk, probably from feeding on fermented fruit.

The bear season was open at the time, but game authorities moved quickly to suspend it for two days until the two skid-row bears wandered off. The affair drew headlines all across the country and coupled with a legal kill of eight bears that year, it led animal-protection advocates to launch a campaign to "save the bears." The following spring a public hearing was held, a bear study was initiated, and changes were made in bear-hunting regulations.

There is surprising variation in the rules under which bears can be hunted in the various states and provinces.

Maine and Vermont permit the use of dogs. New York does not. All efforts by hound men to get bear dogs legalized in that state have been blocked by loud outcries from deer hunters, who charge (and honestly believe) that bear hounds would "run all the deer out of the country." Actually, a bear dog that will run deer is worse than useless and is quickly eliminated from the pack of any bear hunter.

Ontario allows dogs to be used in hunting both deer and bear. California, Massachusetts, New Mexico, South Carolina, Tennessee, Vermont, and Virginia permit dogs but prohibit baiting. In Minnesota, New York, and Wyoming the reverse is true. Montana and Pennsylvania allow neither.

A number of states allow bears to be killed at any time, and taken in traps or foot snares, if they are threatening human life, threatening or killing livestock, or doing other damage. And Washington provides for year-round killing under permits issued to the state's timber industry.

What does the future hold for the black bear? Is he destined to grace the American Wildlife scene indefinitely, or will his numbers dwindle in the next few decades until he disappears?

At the present time the odds for his survival look very good indeed.

To begin with, the population figures I have cited from Canada are high enough to preclude any possibility that this bear may become extinct. Three provinces there, British Columbia, Alberta, and Ontario, probably have something like 300,000 black bears. The population in the United States is sufficient to bring the total numbers up around 450,000, which is only 50,000 short of what Seton thought might have been the primitive numbers when settlement of the continent began. (One is compelled to wonder whether his estimate was not far too low.)

In this country, in the last ten to fifteen years, in thirty-seven of the thirty-eight states where he is still found, blackie has been elevated from the status of an unprotected predator, widely despised and often with a bounty on his head, to that of a prized game animal, given adequate protection under the wildlife code. The single exception is Maine, and even there he has a measure of protection.

No state pays a bear bounty today, and only in Maine is trapping permitted. The black bear is classed there as a furbearer, and trapping is allowed under the same regulations as hunting.

Of the states that presently have a bear population, ranging in size from rare up to Alaska's 40,000 to 50,000, only four believe the animals are decreasing in numbers. They are Pennsylvania, Texas, Virginia, and West Virginia. In only one state, Virginia, is the blame put on overhunting. Pennsylvania cites the loss of animals killed on recently opened interstate highways as a factor in the decline. Texas blames human intolerance of bears. West Virginia reports a heavy toll taken illegally, and has recently enacted a law providing compensation for bear damages, in the hope of reducing the take of "sheep-killing" bears. Virginia has shortened its hunting season, closed a number of counties to hunting outright, and protected bears under one hundred pounds, all in an effort to reverse the decline in bear numbers.

Bear stocking has been tried with great success in at least two states.

A stocking project was carried out by the Arkansas Game and Fish Commission (the population of native bears was down to no more than 50) between 1958 and 1963. Between 250 and 275 animals were obtained from Minnesota and Canada and released in the Ozark and Ouachita Mountains. The stocking proved highly successful. Today the two regions, from which bears had disappeared entirely, hold an estimated 800 to 1,000.

From 1964 through 1967, 161 bears live-trapped in Minnesota were tagged and released in Louisiana, where hunters had been allowed five bears a year in the early 1900s but where numbers had fallen so low that the hunting season was closed in 1965. In the next five years 30 of the tags were returned, from animals shot illegally, killed on the highway or by train, or by an overdose of tranquilizing drugs. The survivors spread into 37 parishes, and a few strayed into Texas, Arkansas, and Mississippi. But enough remained in Louisiana to build up a present population estimated at 400. The state opened a limited hunting season in 1974 and expanded it in 1975, and Richard K. Yancey, assistant director of the Wildlife and Fisheries Commission, tells me that Louisiana is strongly opposed to any federal effort to class the black bear as a threatened or endangered species in that state.

THE BLACK BEAR IN THE UNITED STATES

States	Population	Hunting Seasons	Are Dogs Permitted?	Is Baiting Permitted?	Hunter Kills	D—declining I—increasing S—stable
Alabama	150	None				S
Alaska	40,000 to 50,000	Aug. to June	Yes	Yes	1,000 to 1,500	I
Arizona	1,500	Fall	Yes	Yes	200	I
Arkansas	800 to 1,050	None				I
California	11,000 to 15,000	Fall	Yes	No	1,275	I
Colorado	4,000 to 7,000	Fall, Spring	Yes	Yes	500 to 600	I
Connecticut	Rare	None				No info.
Florida	Less than 500	Fall	Yes	No	25	S or D
Georgia	300 to 500	None				I
Idaho	17,000	Aug. 30 to June 30	Yes	Yes	1,750	S or I
Kentucky	12	None				S
Louisiana	400	Fall	Yes	Yes	2 or 3	I
Maine	7,000 to 10,000	May to Nov.	Yes	Yes	750 to 1,000	Not known
Maryland	Rare	None				S or D
Massachusetts	75 to 100	Fall	Yes	No	3 in 5 years	No answer
Michigan	5,000 to 6,000	Fall	Yes	Yes	460 to 990	S or I
Minnesota	No estimate	Fall	No	Yes	650	S
Mississippi	Rare	None				Sighted only occasionally
Missouri	Rare	None				S or I
Montana	8,000 to 10,000	April to Nov.	No	No	1,500	S
Nevada	Less than 25	None				S
New Hampshire	No estimate	Fall	Yes	Yes	No figures	S
New Jersey	20 to 40	None				S
New Mexico	3,000	Fall, Spring	Yes	No	470	S
New York	3,800 to 4,000	Fall	No	Yes	435 to 725	S
North Carolina	1,000	Fall	Yes	Yes	100 to 200	S
Oregon	15,000	July to Dec.	Yes	Yes	1,700	I
Pennsylvania	2,000 to 2,500	Fall	No	No	225 to 370	D
South Carolina	150	Fall	Yes	No	8 to 10	S
Tennessee	400	Fall	Yes	No	20	S
Texas	Less than 50	Fall	Yes	Yes	No figures	D
Utah	No estimate	May to Oct.	Yes	Yes	125	S

State	Population	*How Classed	Hunting Seasons	Are Dogs Permitted?	Is Baiting Permitted?	Is Trapping Legal	Hunter Kills	D–declining I–increasing S–stable	Future Outlook
Vermont	1,200 to 1,500		Fall		Yes	No	300	I	
Virginia	1,000 to 1,300		Fall		Yes	No	300	D	
Washington	27,000		Spring, Summer, Fall		Yes	Yes	3,400 to 4,100	S	
West Virginia	600 to 650		Fall		Yes	Yes	50	D	
Wisconsin	6,000 to 8,000		Fall		Yes	Yes	400	S	
Wyoming	No estimate		Spring, Fall		No	Yes	200	S	

THE BLACK BEAR IN CANADA

Province	Population	*How Classed	Hunting Seasons	Are Dogs Permitted?	Is Baiting Permitted?	Is Trapping Legal	Hunter Kills	D–declining I–increasing S–stable	Future Outlook
Alberta	100,000 +/–	GA	Spring, Fall	No	No	No	5,000 +/–	I (dramatic increase)	Excellent
British Columbia	80,000 to 120,000	GA	Spring, Fall	Yes	No	No	2,400 to 3,750	I	Very good
Manitoba	No estimate	GA, FB, P	Spring, Fall	No	Yes	Yes	No figures	S	Good
New Brunswick	No estimate	GA	Spring, Fall	No	Yes	No	600	I	Good
Newfoundland	3,000	GA	Fall	No	No	No	200	S	Good
Nova Scotia	No estimate	GA & FB	Fall	No	Yes	Yes	150 to 225	I	Good
Ontario	90,000	GA	Spring, Fall	Yes	Yes	No	6,000 to 9,000	S	Bright
Quebec	No estimate	GA & FB	Summer, Fall	No	Yes	Yes	430 to 490	No answer	No answer
Saskatchewan	30,000 to 40,000	GA	May, Sept.	No	Yes	Yes	750 to 900	I	Stable
Northwest Territory	No estimate	GA	Summer, Fall	No	No	No	200	S	Good
Yukon Territory	3,000 to 5,000	GA	Spring, Fall	No	No	Yes	110	S	Stable

How Classed   GA – Game animals   FB – Fur bearer   P – Predator

Other states have considered stocking as a way to establish new populations of bears.

Warren Jackson, director of the South Dakota Division of Game and Fish, told me in a letter in the autumn of 1975 that he believes habitat in the Black Hills of his state would support bears if livestock interests would tolerate them. A population could probably be established easily by stocking.

Texas also has given some thought to importing and releasing bears, but has held back because of a belief that the public is unwilling to accept the animals as a resident wildlife species. Bears were exterminated in all but a few counties of that state by 1900. The few that remain, probably less than fifty all told, are decreasing in numbers because of incompatibility with humans.

"While most people say they would like to see the remaining bears protected, they admit that if one is seen they are all too ready to kill or capture it," says a Texas wildlife official. "In this state the black bear has simply not been able to cope with contact with man."

Happily that is not true over most of this country and Canada. Bears and men have coexisted for a very long time, and in general the bear has made out quite well.

As long as there is wild country left in America, this animal will have a place to live. And so long as he is legally hunted, those who hunt him will see to it that he has the protection necessary for survival.

SEVEN

Never Trust a Bear

Maurice Day and Lloyd Hillbourn were running a survey line in the Warroad district of northern Minnesota, for the state Forest Service, when they saw in the brush ahead what they first took to be a black wolf. Then they got a better look, and realized it was a cub bear instead.

The cub disappeared and before they had gone thirty feet farther an adult bear that they later estimated to weigh five hundred pounds stood up from a bed two hundred feet away and made a determined rush for them.

They were in a stand of small trees, only three or four inches in diameter. They scrambled up the nearest two, but Hillbourn didn't make it high enough. The bear stood on her hind legs, grabbed him by a heel and yanked him down.

She bit him around the legs, arms, and shoulders. Both men yelled, and she dropped Lloyd and climbed after Maurice. The tree bent with her weight and he jumped and ran. But she overtook him and closed her jaws on his neck. Only a miracle of chance saved him. Her teeth went into the back of the neck and out under the side of the jaw.

Then Hillbourn started to get back on his feet, and she let go of Day and went back to her first victim. For the ten or fifteen minutes the attack lasted she mauled first one man, then the other, turning time after time on the one that was trying to get up.

Hillbourn finally fought back with his jackknife, stabbing her around the neck and shoulders, and Day fought her off with a four-foot club broken from a dead tree. At the end she broke off the attack, stood and looked at the two men, then ran into the brush.

Day's throat was torn and he was bitten about the head, shoulders, back, and hips. Hillbourn had more than two hundred tooth and claw wounds. Other members of their mapping crew took the two men to a hospital at Warroad, where Hillbourn spent two months. Both will carry the scars of the encounter to their graves.

It had been their misfortune to be involved in a sudden surprise encounter with a female bear that had cubs along. There is hardly a more explosively dangerous situation in the outdoors of this continent.

Just about everybody I have ever known who has lived long in bear country has blundered into a meeting of that kind at one time or another. Often the confrontation ends with the bears in full flight. About equally often it ends with both parties in that same condition.

Sometimes the sow warns the human off with growls and puffing, and popping of her teeth. She may make short and angry, but abortive, rushes at the intruder, breaking them off if he clears out. But now and then she flies into a rage and decides to eliminate once and for all the threat to her young.

When that happens, the consequences are an attack that the victim, if he

survives, never forgets. An angry female bear is not only a terrible adversary, she is also unbelievably persistent.

Often the human who is attacked does not see a cub and has no warning there is one in the vicinity. The case of Art Le Gault was typical.

Le Gault was a woodcutter living near the village of Engadine, not far from Newberry in Michigan's Upper Peninsula. He was seventy-one at the time.

Hiking on an old brush-grown logging road one June afternoon, he saw something move in a big willow swamp eighty yards away. He looked again and made out a full-grown bear sneaking toward him through the brush. If there were cubs with her, he saw no sign of them, and at the time that possibility did not occur to him.

But sure that he was being stalked, and unable to run because of a bad heart,

The bear mauled first one man, then the other, turning time after time on the one that was trying to get up. Hillbourn finally fought back with his jackknife, stabbing her neck and shoulders.

he turned and walked away as fast as he could. When he looked over his shoulder the bear had broken out of the brush and was coming at a gallop.

She overtook him, grabbed him by a thigh and tried to wrench him to the ground. He twisted around, screamed at her and drove a fist into her face. She reared up, tore one sleeve away with a swipe of her forepaw and raked his arm so that blood streamed down. Le Gault punched her again, she stayed erect on her hind feet, and for the next twenty minutes they clawed and pummeled and pushed each other like two rough-and-tumble fighters in a ring.

At the end Art Le Gault was clawed on the face, arms, legs, hips, and back. His shirt was hanging in rags, his pants torn half off; he was dripping blood and on the verge of blacking out from exhaustion.

It was then he thought for the first time of the old pocket knife he was carrying. It had a blunt, worn blade no more than two inches long but it was better than no weapon at all. The old woodsman reached for it, got it open and jabbed the bear around the nose. She dropped back on all fours, staring up at him, and he lunged for one of her eyes with the knife. He felt the blade sink in, and he believes he blinded her on that side. In any event, she flinched, spun away from him, and then was gone. He staggered out to the truck he had parked on the road, almost a mile away, but he had lost the key and had to walk another half mile to his home.

He lived and recovered completely, which was more than anyone expected.

Michigan conservation officers and two experienced bear hunters, who went to the scene late that same afternoon in a vain attempt to run the bear with dogs and dispose of it, found a big area trampled and torn up where man and bear had fought. They considered it a miracle that Le Gault had not been killed on the spot.

They also found what appeared to be plain evidence of the reason for the attack. Not far from the place where the bear had first grabbed the man, they came on a big birch tree with claw marks in the bark, of a size that only a cub bear could make. Apparently the bear had driven one or two youngsters into the tree, and had then stalked and attacked Le Gault when he walked close enough that she decided he was threatening the cubs. Blood sign showed that when the battle ended she had gone back to the tree, called the youngsters down and led them off into the swamp. It was too wet there for dogs to follow her.

When I was at Woody Wheaton's fishing camp on Grand Lake, at Forest City, Maine, a few years ago, bears were feeding at the town garbage dump nearby and a number of people were making daily visits at sundown to watch them.

Included in the lot was one fairly small sow that for several years had showed up regularly with three or four cubs in tow. That family was a stellar attraction.

In the summer of 1973 one of the visitors, a man named Graham, was watching them when one of that female's cubs started to climb a small tree. The she bear was nowhere in sight just then, so Graham walked in close to get a picture.

She descended on him like a thunderbolt, grabbing him in the thigh from the back. He suffered injuries that put him in a hospital for weeks, and more than a year later the leg was still troubling him.

A Florida man, Frederick Chapman of Indialantic, related the story to me in a letter, and added the whimsical comment, "Satchel Paige said: 'Never look back. Something may be gaining on you.' In the wilderness I have always found it advisable to look back now and then, just to be sure nothing is gaining on me."

Anytime you find yourself in close proximity to a cub bear, it pays to look back — and ahead and on both sides as well. Most of all, it pays to clear out if the she bear will give you time.

That does not mean that such females unfailingly attack, by any means. El Harger, the Michigan wildlife biologist who headed up that state's field research on black bears for a number of years, puts it this way:

"Almost every outdoorsman believes that a female bear with cubs adds up to a risky combination. There is good reason for that belief, yet only four times in trapping and handling more than three hundred bears have I encountered sows that actually ran us off while we were trying to remove cubs from a live-trap."

Far more often, Harger told me, if the cub squalls at any point in the proceedings, you hear the mother out in the brush, circling around and puffing but not showing herself. Only two or three times had such a she bear come close enough to him to enable him to use a dart gun on her.

One of the angriest sows El ever encountered was the mother of a cub he was trying to release from a coyote trap, where it had been caught unintentionally. The cub squalled and the mother came for the trapping crew in a headlong rush, hair standing the wrong way, ears laid back, moaning and popping her teeth.

"I know nothing in the woods more certain to make a man take to his heels," Harger admitted.

The crew ran, but when the bear reached the cub she stopped. They rushed her, yelling and waving their arms, and she backed off. But when they attempted once more to free the cub, it squalled again and the enraged sow repeated her charge.

That happened half a dozen times. Finally the men set a coyote trap in the trail she was using. She put a forepaw in it, and it held her long enough for Harger to jab her with a pole syringe loaded with an immobilizing drug.

"Don't get the idea that I think a bear with cubs is ever to be taken lightly," El warns. "My advice to any unarmed human who encounters one is to give her as wide a berth as possible and leave the neighborhood without delay if the bear will permit it. Only now and then one is likely to attack, under those circumstances, but there is no way to guess beforehand which one it will be."

Incidentally, Harger carries only two scars to show for all his bear research. They are small and faint, on his right forearm, and he got both of them at one time, from a five-pound cub. It had climbed a tree, he climbed after it, and when he got close enough it turned on him like a tiny spitfire.

Attacks on man by bears fall into two categories, provoked and unprovoked, but there is widespread disagreement among outdoorsmen as to what constitutes provocation.

It must be conceded in the beginning, of course, that any attack by a female with cubs has to be rated provoked. The mother obviously believed her young are in danger.

There agreement ends. Wildlife protection extremists argue that there is no such thing as an unprovoked attack. They contend that the mere fact that a human is in the neighborhood is provocation enough and justifies any action the bear may take. I even know one Alaskan guide who feels the same way.

"The charge may seem unprovoked to you, but in the mind of the animal your presence is all the reason he needs for running you off or attacking you if you fail to run," this man says.

I disagree. If the bear is not wounded, threatened, or crowded, and if cubs are not involved, I class the attack as unprovoked.

It often happens that there are no witnesses, and the circumstances of the attack are never known.

Before Ike Cooper, the bear hunter I talked about in the introduction to this book, left Cheboygan he was involved in a very unusual case of that kind. An Indian woman walked into Cooper's drugstore one hot day in blueberry season.

"Man dead," she announced. "In woods. I find."

From her description of the place, Cooper was sure he knew the identity of the dead man.

Frank Devereaux, a veteran of the Civil War, was living a hermit's life in a cabin on the small, pine-bordered lake that still bears his name, a few miles south of Cheboygan. He made it a practice to carry an old muzzle-loading musket whenever he went into the woods, but Cooper said the gun was rarely loaded with a conventional ball. Instead, Devereaux usually used small pebbles, broken nails or whatever was handy, on top of a charge of powder. From what the Indian woman said, Cooper smelled bear trouble.

We got together a burial party and the men drove out to Devereaux's place in a buckboard. Not far away, where the woman had indicated, they found Devereaux.

He was sitting upright on a log, leaning back against a tree with his chin in his hand. He had been severely bitten through one leg, and the bear had killed him with a blow on the side of the head that broke his skull from temple to ear.

Next the men found the bear, also dead, half hidden under the branches of a small evergreen. Except for one unanswered question, how it had all begun, it was easy to piece the story together.

Between man and bear there was a trampled space of ferns and brush, indicating a long and savage battle. The roof of the bear's mouth was cut to ribbons where Devereaux had used the muzzle of his musket as a blunt bayonet, jabbing to fend off the attack. But the bear had not died from that. A gunshot wound in the flank had killed it.

How did it start and how did it end? No one will ever know. Almost certainly man and bear had blundered into one another, both intent on berrying. Did the bear attack on sight or did the man wound it first and arouse it to battle rage? At the end it probably knocked him down with a blow of a forepaw, and then bit and mauled him as he lay on the ground. But who broke off the fight? Did the bear crawl away under the evergreen to die, leaving Devereaux to drag himself to the log where he was found? Or did he retreat first? There was no way to tell.

The men buried Devereaux on the shore of the lake, near his cabin. For years only a rough pen of poles marked the lonely grave, but in the 1930s a wooden marker was put up, bearing a curious inscription, relating the story in Latin. It read: "Here lies F. Devereaux, killed by the ferocity of a famous bear, in whose memory this monument has been erected out of generosity of his grandson." Years later a marble headstone was added.

Frank Devereaux was the first human in the history of Michigan to be killed by a bear, but he was not the last. The next time the circumstances would be tragic in the extreme. That story will be told in a later chapter.

The bear that made a night attack on the Wesley Heyer party, at a campground in Montana's Sun River country in 1967, certainly had no provocation.

In August of that year, less than two weeks after grizzly bears had made history of the most unbelievable and terrible kind in Glacier National Park in Montana, by killing two college-age girls in a single night in two separate and unrelated incidents, Heyer took his family and a neighbor boy to Gibson Reservoir for a few days of camping and fishing.

Heyer was from the small town of Fort Shaw, about fifty miles east of the reservoir. The party consisted of him, his wife Irene, their little girl Debbie; two sons, Allen, fifteen, and Steven, thirteen; the neighbor boy was Jerry Brown, twelve years old and a friend of Steve's.

They reached the campground on the reservoir after dark, and stored their food under a picnic table near their tent. The mother and father and Debbie went to bed in the tent. Steve and Jerry decided to bunk in a double sleeping bag on another picnic table nearby, and Allen bedded down on the ground under a tree beside them. There was no food under the table where the two boys elected to sleep.

About two o'clock in the morning Steve was awakened by something. He opened his eyes and saw a three-hundred-pound black bear up on the table, standing over him and Jerry. Before he could cry out it bit him savagely in the shoulder. He yelled, jerked free and slid down inside his bag for protection.

The bear turned on the Brown boy, biting and clawing at his head and arms. Jerry screamed at the top of his voice, and Wesley Heyer woke up.

There was a Winchester .300 Magnum in his gear. He grabbed it and rummaged for shells, but he was too late. Fifteen-year-old Allen, aroused by the outcries, jumped up and clouted the bear over the head with his pillow, the only thing he could lay hands on. It jumped off the table and ran, and was out of sight by the time the father got out of the tent with the loaded rifle.

The family left at once for Choteau, thirty miles away over a dirt road, stopping on the way to phone ahead for a doctor. The doctor was waiting when they arrived.

The bear turned on the Brown boy, biting and clawing at his head and arms. Jerry screamed at the top of his voice, and Wesley woke up.

Steve was treated for the shoulder bite. Jerry was patched up and put to bed in a hospital. He had suffered severe lacerations but no major injuries.

The following day Heyer went back to get the family's gear and boat. The bear had returned, eaten most of the food, ripped the tent open, torn the sleeping bags, and smashed everything in sight, scattering the wreckage in blind rage.

Heyer told me he had no theory as to what accounted for the attack. So far as he knew, the bear was not a campground panhandler, accustomed to people and lacking normal fear of them.

Another bear attack that has to be rated totally unprovoked occurred in Colorado in the summer of 1971.

John Richardson, a thirty-one-year-old Denver man, and Linda Moore, the girl he planned to marry in a few more days, were asleep in two bags on the ground at a campsite on the Never Summer Ranch, just west of Rocky Mountain National Park on the western slope of the Colorado Rockies. In a bus-type camper a few yards away, Richardson's sister and brother-in-law, Gus Wedell, were sleeping with their children.

John and Linda were looking forward to an outdoor wedding at a nearby site they had chosen for its scenic beauty. Nothing could have been farther from John's mind than the fact that before daybreak he would become the first man in the history of Colorado to be killed by a bear.

As frequently happens with bear attacks, the trouble struck without warning. Sometime after midnight, when the moon had set, the peace and stillness that lay over the campground were suddenly shattered. Linda was awakened by John screaming at her.

"Run!" he cried. "Run for the camper!"

She scrambled out of her bag, saw dimly a big shaggy bear standing over John, and did as she was told, yelling "There's a bear out there!"

The bear came for her the instant she moved. It overtook her in a couple of jumps, clawing her on the back and hips as she ran. Then it turned back to Richardson, biting and clawing him savagely. Doctors concluded afterward that he had died almost instantly.

Linda went on screaming, pounding on the door of the camper, and Wedell came running out, armed with a heavy iron skillet, the first weapon he had been able to lay hands on. He turned on the lights of the camper and saw the bear. It was a black of the cinnamon color phase.

By that time it was fifty yards away, dragging or carrying the body of its victim. It had dragged him under a barbwire fence and was making off with him.

Wedell went after it, clouting it around the head with the skillet. When it refused to drop Richardson he whacked it on the nose with all his strength. He pummeled it severely enough that when it was killed and pelted, a couple of days later, the bruises showed plainly under the skin. Finally it let go of the man, turned and ran.

The following night it broke into a garbage can nearby. Ray Lyons, a bear-hound man and professional guide from the town of Collbran, was called in by Colorado game authorities. His dogs picked up the track near the garbage can, ran it a couple of miles, and Lyons shot the bear. It proved to be a three-hundred-pounder.

An autopsy performed at the Colorado State University lab at Fort Collins showed beyond question that the right bear had been killed. In the stomach were chunks of plastic, dish cloths, chicken bones, and other table scraps, the result of the garbage can raid.

Had it attacked Richardson out of hunger? The answer to that will never be known, but it seems a logical guess.

One other thing the autopsy proved. The bear did not have rabies, as wild-life authorities and even Ray Lyons had suspected might be the case.

That disease had been offered many times, by game men, hunters, and writers, to excuse so-called abnormal behavior on the part of a bear that has attacked humans. I have never known a case where such a bear proved rabid, and it is my opinion that the alibi of rabies fails completely to hold up. A bear attacks a man for the same reasons it attacks anything else, because of anger, in what it considers self-defense or to protect cubs, or in extreme cases because it is hungry and the man represents a meal.

The most extraordinary story of black bear attack I have ever heard was related to me by three young married couples from Green Bay, Wisconsin.

In the early summer of 1964 they went on a fishing-camping vacation in the Blind River district of Ontario, east of Sault Ste. Marie. They engaged an out-fitter to fly them to a remote campsite on a lake deep in the bush for six days of wilderness fishing. Flown in on a Saturday, they were to be picked up and brought out the following Friday. For those six days they would be on their own. It was an adventure they were looking forward to.

They put in Saturday afternoon cleaning up the campsite and doing a little fishing. Sunday they fished and hiked.

Still tired from a sleepless all-night drive to Blind River, they were sleeping soundly two hours after sunrise on Monday morning when a bear walked into camp, slashed the back of the tent open with a forepaw and tore a deep gash in the hand of one of the men.

The victim screamed and the six people rushed out. The bear was standing at the edge of the brush, ten paces away, watching insolently. When the three men ran at it, brandishing an ax, it walked unhurriedly off. Plainly it was not afraid of people.

The six campers, deeply concerned and frightened, attended to the torn hand, ate breakfast, mended the tent as best they could, and went out on the lake to fish. When they came back in midafternoon their camp had been ransacked.

The tent had been torn apart, food cartons stored under a pole table outside had been smashed, and most of the supplies eaten. There was still enough food to see them through, but they'd be on short rations the rest of the week. At the moment, however, it was not food they were worried about. They were thoroughly scared of the bear that had done the damage.

They concluded they might as well go fishing again. They returned to camp shortly before dark and as they neared shore, to their dismay they saw a medium-sized bear walk out of the torn tent and another that looked twice as big walking around it. Both of them padded boldly down almost to the water's edge to meet the boats, but finally turned and walked into the brush.

Sick with dread at what darkness might bring, the six collected enough firewood to last through the night and got a fire going. They agreed to take turns standing watch. Their only weapons were an ax and a hunting knife, but at least they would not let the bears take them by surprise.

They were still gathering wood when they heard noise in the brush. The light started to fail, and then the two bears walked into the small clearing, growling as they came.

When neither shouting nor the fire did any good, the camping party loaded mattresses, sleeping bags, warm clothing and food into their two boats and took to the safety of the lake.

It was a wretched night. The boats leaked and the bags were soon watersoaked. Toward morning a storm came up. When it ended six shivering people elected to go ashore and build up their fire again, bears or no bears. A cheerless dawn broke while they were starting the fire, and in the gray light they saw the two bears watching them only a few yards away.

The same pattern was repeated for three more nights. Each evening the bears came padding out of the brush, growling and popping their teeth. They paid no attention to fires or gasoline flares, and each night six people were driven to their boats.

In desperation, they considered dousing the more quarrelsome of the bears with gasoline (it would have been easy to do) and setting him afire by means of an oil-soaked rag on the end of a pole. But in the end, they dared not risk the retaliation they feared might result.

The bears grew more and more surly, finally smashing dishes, pots and pans and even the camp table in blind fury.

The outfitter's plane came to the rescue on Friday. One of the women later described that Cessna slanting down to the lake as the most beautiful sight she had ever seen. The six campers have scars they will carry the rest of their lives, not from the bears but from the terrible onslaught of blackflies and mosquitoes while they huddled unprotected in the open boats for four sleepless nights.

Another party of fishermen who camped at that same site a year later had rifles and bear-hunting licenses. The camp raiders tried to repeat their performance of the previous summer, and both were quickly gunned down.

So runs the almost unbelievable record of black bear attacks.

Many people, completely unschooled in the ways of wild animals and lulled by the gentle behavior of trained bears on TV shows—or by feeding half-tame but always dangerous blacks at campgrounds and in parks, often while standing beside a sign that warns "Don't Feed the Bears"—regard this bear as no more dangerous than a big friendly dog. To them, a bear is never anything to be afraid of. They couldn't be more wrong.

As an old bear hunter told me once, "Nobody knows one minute what a bear is going to do the next. Most of the time the bear himself doesn't know. There is no more dangerous mistake in the woods than to take his good nature for granted."

There are even experienced hunters who argue that a human has no cause to fear a black bear under any circumstances. They are likewise in grave error. Any time a man finds himself in the presence of a wild bear he is potentially in danger. None of them is ever to be trusted, the black included.

A few years back I exchanged letters with K. B. Mitchell, superintendent of Jasper National Park in western Canada, regarding the killing of an eight-year-old girl in the Calgary district of Alberta by a black bear.

The bear involved was four or five years old, in good condition, not short of food. It had spent most of its life in the area, had frequent contact with people, and was considered good natured and harmless. But it was also a genuine "highway bum," Mitchell said, accustomed to panhandling.

The child was playing at a campground when the bear walked out of the brush near her. Startled, she grabbed up a small tablecloth with cookies on it and ran to her cabin steps. At the steps the bear, presumably after the cookies, grabbed her.

Two teenage girls who worked at the camp heard the commotion, ran after the bear and whipped it about the head with switches until it dropped the child. She died of her injuries shortly after.

The bear did not threaten the older girls or make any attempt to fight them off. Mitchell summed things up very well when he wrote: "It was an unfortunate and dreadful thing that this small child had to lose her life to prove that there is no such thing as a tame, quiet, or gentle bear. They should all be treated as dangerous animals."

EIGHT

Pull the Trigger Hard

Before the late 1940s, virtually all the black bears killed by hunters in my home state of Michigan—and in many other states in the eastern half of the country as well—were taken in connection with deer hunting. With few exceptions, the hunter encountered the bear by accident and luck, and a bearskin rug was considered a highly prized bonus from a deer hunt.

The Michigan kill was running one thousand to fifteen hundred a year, which was surprisingly high in view of the fact that most of the state's bear population had denned up for winter by the time deer season opened in mid-November. In the meantime, much was being heard in outdoor circles about the registered hunts with packs of bear dogs that were being staged by the Tennessee Conservation Department in the eastern mountains of that state.

I was then outdoors editor of a chain of metropolitan daily papers published in eight major Michigan cities outside of Detroit. I had believed for several years that hunting the black bear with hounds was a far more exciting way of taking him than shooting him as a result of a chance encounter in the deer woods. And I had also come to believe that bear dogs could be used as successfully in Michigan as in the southern mountains.

In the autumn of 1945, with World War II at an end, in my capacity as an outdoor writer I made a trip to Tennessee to get a first-hand look at the hunts and size up their Michigan possibilities.

Randy Shields, a game man with the Tennessee Conservation Department, made the arrangements. We spent three or four days hunting in the Cherokee National Forest, behind a pack of bear hounds owned and trained by Bert Woody, the guide regularly hired by Randy's department for the registered hunts.

I didn't kill a bear, but I wasn't disappointed, for I had hardly expected to. But I did get in on one very lively chase, when the dogs drove a black out of a mountain cove, so close that we heard the brush break as he crashed past. I had never listened to such hound music.

That one crossed the state line into North Carolina and got away. Two of the dogs came home at dusk that evening, weary and footsore. Twenty-four hours later the remaining five of the pack had not yet showed up, but eventually all of them made it home.

Two days later one of the hunters in the party killed a bear after a long, hard chase and a no-quarter fight between bear and hounds.

I returned home convinced of two things. Bear hunting with dogs was like no other hunting I had tried, a sport as exciting as an outdoorsman could hope to find. And it was every bit as feasible in the tangled cedar swamps of northern Michigan as in the laurel hills of the Great Smokies.

I passed my ideas along to the leadership of Michigan United Conservation Clubs, a statewide sportsmen's federation with 120,000 members, and proposed that they sponsor a test hunt the following year. The proposal met with an enthusiastic welcome, the Michigan Conservation Department offered complete cooperation, and the plans were laid.

In October of 1946, at the invitation of MUCC, Hack Smithdeal of Johnson City, Tennessee, came north to Michigan with his pack of bear dogs and a group of handlers and hunting partners, for the first bear hunt with hounds in the history of the state.

Any doubt as to the reaction of Michigan sportsmen had been settled ahead of time. The Dead Stream Swamp area in Missaukee County had been opened to dog hunting by the Conservation Department, and three hundred permits made available. Applicants for those permits totaled more than a thousand. The lucky three hundred were chosen on a first come, first served basis.

Only two bears were killed in the four-day hunt, but there were a number of exciting chases. The dog handlers reported running eight bears in one day. Only the dense cover of an almost roadless swamp, coupled with inexperience on the part of the hunters, prevented a higher kill. At the end it was clear that this method of hunting was destined to take deep root among Michigan sportsmen.

Among the hunters who took part in the pilot hunt was Carl Johnson, an insurance man from the upstate city of Cadillac. An enthusiastic hound man and coon hunter, and chairman of MUCC's big-game committee, Johnson would become the father of the sport in Michigan.

He purchased a bear hound from Smithdeal at once, and began the building of a top-grade pack. Within a year he had organized the Michigan Bear Hunters Association. He served as its president for many years, while it developed into one of the most active conservation groups in the state. And Johnson's own career as a conservationist paralleled that of the association. In 1963 Governor George Romney named him to the Michigan Conservation Commission, a non-salaried post carrying a great deal of prestige. The commission is now the Natural Resources Commission, Johnson is still serving with distinction, and has been chosen chairman three times.

In the meantime he has continued to promote the use of bear dogs, encourage high standards of sportsmanship in bear hunting, stage organized hunts, and encourage the sport in every way possible. This method of hunting now accounts for more than a third of the bears killed annually in Michigan, a kill that has run above six hundred in recent years.

In 1963 Johnson did for Wisconsin what the Tennessee hunters had done earlier for Michigan, taking his dogs there for three demonstration hunts. The total kill was only six bears, but one chase lasted for seventeen hours, and that method of bear hunting caught on as quickly as it had in Michigan.

I have no way of knowing how many hound men in other states were encouraged to acquire and use bear dogs as a result of the publicity given Michigan hunts by *Outdoor Life* magazine over the years, but I do know of several instances where that happened. Today bear hunting with hounds is a widely followed sport, and its followers are firmly of the opinion that it is by far the most exciting way to take blackie.

As Carl Johnson once told me, "For the houndman who wants his hunting big and tough, no other sport compares with running bears with dogs. There is more excitement in one black bear taken that way than in a dozen shot by any other method. Until you have listened to a pack of good hounds on a reeking hot bear track, you have not heard the most blood-pounding music in the hunting world."

El Harger, Michigan's top bear research specialist who has hunted blacks longer than he has studied them, agrees. Harger tells of a hunt when he and his companions put five dogs down on a cold track where a bear had left an apple orchard, at the border of a big swamp in Michigan's Upper Peninsula. The pack cold trailed the bear into the swamp, jumped it in five minutes and overtook it in five more. It made no effort to outrun them, preferring to fight.

Because Harger was no longer greatly interested in killing a bear, he had started out that morning without a gun. This black went only a short distance before making a stand. By the time El reached the scene, it had grabbed one of the hounds and killed the dog with a bite through the spine. It then moved on at a walk.

Twice more in the next half hour, Harger was close enough to see it dodge out of sight behind a stump or blowdown and ambush a dog deliberately. Both hounds were bitten in the back and disabled. Once the bear dived for Harger instead, but the remaining dogs went for it and gave him time to clear out.

The bear made its final stand at a drained beaver pond. By that time another member of the party had caught up, carrying a bow and four arrows.

He put one arrow through the bear too far back, buried a second near its spine, missed the third and drove the fourth into the lungs. The bear charged from fifteen feet, the bowhunter tumbled backward off the beaver dam, retrieved the arrow that had missed, and wound things up with a neck shot.

"It's that kind of bear that makes a hunter's dreams come true," El told me when he finished the story.

The hunter who uses dogs has one major advantage over those who do not. He does not need to find a bear. He needs only to find a track fresh enough for his hounds to handle.

One of the best ways of doing that, where conditions permit, is by dragging woods roads and trails at dusk, with a farm implement or a treetop pulled behind a vehicle. Any bear track made in the freshly dragged road during the night shows up plainly the next morning, and is certain to be fresh enough to run. Most bear hunters will tell you that if a hound cannot follow a track at least twelve hours old, under ordinary conditions, he does not belong in the pack.

Bears like thick cover, the bigger and wilder the tract the better. In the northern states, east of the Mississippi, and in many places in the South, they

frequent big swamps. In the southern mountains they are found in tangles of laurel and rhododendron. In the mountains of the West, they show a preference for canyons and rough country grown thick with brush and evergreens.

There is one other rule that the hunter must keep in mind. The black bear is where his food is. He is a gluttonous eater, and if he locates a supply of berries, beech, or oak mast, or a convenient apple orchard, he is not likely to leave the neighborhood as long as the groceries hold out. On the other hand, he does not hesitate to move miles as his food conditions change. Fresh bear sign found in late summer is often meaningless by the time hunting season rolls around.

The bear hunter going into an area he is not familiar with does well to seek tips from conservation officers, big-game biologists, farmers or sheep growers, beekeepers, and others who have reason to know where the local bear population is feeding. In most cases such people are more than willing to pass the information along.

There is one other productive way of finding fresh bear tracks. The black is a lazy traveler. Once an individual finds the easiest way through a dense cedar swamp or in and out of an abandoned orchard, every other bear that comes along will follow precisely the same path. The result is a worn trail, with bear footprints deeply imprinted in earth or moss, that an experienced bear hunter learns to recognize on sight. Unless a seasonal shortage of food has forced the bears to move out of the neighborhood, the tracks in those trails are almost sure to be fresh.

Some bear hunters have strong preferences in hound breeds. Others believe that a bear dog is where you find him, whether he is of Plott blood, Walker, bluetick, redbone, black and tan, or a mixture of breeds. Performance is far more important than pedigree. Many packs have airedales or airedale-and-hound crosses to do the hard, close fighting needed to hold a bear that refuses to tree and comes to bay on the ground instead.

Whatever his blood line, the bear dog must have certain basic qualifications. First of all, he must live to run bears. He must also be rugged enough for it, although size is not a prime consideration. More than one bear hunter has told me that he has had forty-pound dogs that turned in as fine a performance as any seventy-pounder. It's stamina and eagerness that count most.

The best packs I have hunted behind included one or two old and seasoned strike dogs with superb noses, that could be counted on to fool with nothing but a bear track and that had the ability and patience to unravel it no matter how old. A pack must also include a dog or two with a good voice, to enable the hunter to follow the chase. Every dog must be tireless at the tree, and most of the pack has to possess the guts for a finish fight. The hound that holds back when a bear is brought to bay is of no help to the others.

Carl Johnson, who has owned some of the best bear dogs in the country, has a basic formula for building a pack: "Select and cull," he advises, "whether you are buying or breeding. Keep only the dogs that prove themselves. If one has a poor nose, performs badly at the tree, doesn't have his heart in what he is doing, or hangs back in a fight, get rid of him."

It's hardly to be wondered at that a really good bear hound fetches a price of $1,500 or more, if he can be bought at all.

One other qualification is essential in such a dog. Because the black bear and deer share common range in most places where the bear is found, the bear hound must be completely deer-proof. If he will take a deer track, no matter the temptation, he is worthless and worse, likely to get himself shot on sight by any deer hunter who intercepts him. No bear hunter wants him.

Deer-proofing a young dog is not easy, but if he comes from a line of top-notch bear hunters the battle is half won.

Experienced hunters start their beginners with old deer-proof hounds, preferably in an area where there are not many deer. The dog must learn, first of all, what he is there to do. Before you can teach him not to do the wrong things, you must show him what the right things are.

A second rule is never to turn a young hound loose on a cold bear track. Leave the cold-trailing to old dogs that are completely trustworthy. Follow as closely as you can with your young hounds on leash until the bear is up and running and the chase is at white-hot pitch. Then let them go only one at a time, the second not until the first is in full cry after the bear, and so on. A deer crashing out under the nose of an inexperienced dog presents an almost irresistible temptation, unless the dog has his hands full of more important business.

The best bear hunters I know follow the hot-track-only and one-at-a-time rule with every dog under three years old. A hound is not likely to be at his best at this kind of hunting before he reaches the age of five.

If a promising young dog can't resist the temptation to fool around with deer, he can usually be cured by the use of an electric shocking collar. Drive around with him until you spot a deer feeding in an open field or at the edge of cover, if possible. If not, make sure you have a smoking hot deer track. Put the dog down and let him take it full throttle. With no word of reprimand or discouragement, give him the shock treatment. Don't scold him. Call him back and take him to the car. You want him to think it was the deer scent, not you, that hurt him.

Two or three treatments of this kind are usually enough to break the most stubborn deer chaser. He comes to the conclusion that all deer tracks are charged, and he wants nothing to do with them. Coming across one, he is likely to sail over it in one long jump, as he would clear a water-filled ditch.

The shock treatment may sound like harsh medicine, but the dog is not injured by it, only stung painfully enough to leave a lasting impression in his mind.

Bear hunting with hounds has one other essential requirement. Both the hunter and his dogs must be in good condition. They are going up against one of the toughest and most long-winded animals in North America. He is almost sure to take the pack out of hearing. If necessary, he can travel an entire day, fighting the hounds off as he goes. He is ready to kill any dog that gets reckless. He keeps to the thickest, most impenetrable cover he can find. In the country where I have hunted him he likes nothing better than a thick evergreen swamp with water underfoot, laced with beaver ponds.

Hunting him calls for endurance and grit, on the part of the hunters as well as the dogs. I know hound men who harden their dogs by running them on the road for ten to fifteen miles a day, for two or three weeks before a hunt. They also take as great pains to put themselves in condition, hiking, hill climbing, running upstairs.

I have not followed bear dogs in the West, but I am told that most of the time in that part of the country the black bear trees ahead of hounds. That is not true in the places I am familiar with. Where I or friends of mine have hunted, except for cubs and youngsters something like three bears out of four refuse to climb unless they are crowded by fast, hard-fighting dogs.

It isn't until the pack overtakes the bear that their mettle is really tested. Whether he keeps traveling and fights them off or chooses to make a stand, a full-grown black bear is a highly dangerous adversary for dogs. If he comes to bay in a dense thicket or windfall, as he usually does, he stands a fair chance of whipping the entire pack, no matter their courage and fighting ability.

He also stands a good chance of killing one or more of them. The bear hunter is rare indeed who has not lost dogs to bears that refused to tree. Carl Johnson's losses total at least a dozen, and Carl told me once that he had never owned a really top-notch hound that did not get badly hurt sooner or later.

In general, it's the dog whose courage outweighs his judgment that is bear-mauled. Now and then a thoroughly enraged bear makes up his mind to break through the ring of dogs around him, and he is very likely to kill one in doing it. The heaviest bear can move with the quickness of a cat, and once he gets his eye on a dog and makes a determined rush for it, the chances are slim it will escape unhurt.

The pack that runs a track together and overtakes the bear all at the same time has the best chance of avoiding injury. A lone hound that reaches the bear first is likely to get hurt or killed, and the one that arrives late is likely not to count for much. Holding a bear at bay calls for teamwork and furious infighting. A cautious pack can't do the job. On the other hand, if they are reckless the hunter loses dogs needlessly.

More than once in recent years, the charge has been made by those who oppose all hunting that running bears with hounds is totally devoid of sportsmanship. Touching word pictures have been painted of the poor doomed bear, driven into a tree by slavering dogs, waiting resignedly for some bloody-handed hunter to come and kill him.

Bear hunting with hounds isn't quite like that. I know no one who has summed up the real story better than Bill Mason, a houndman from upstate New York who must hunt elsewhere because his own state does not allow the use of dogs in bear hunting.

"The black bear is the greatest animal that can be run with hounds on this continent," Bill once told me. "He's a natural for it, tough and long-winded, more than ready to fight back. Nothing else in the outdoors can match for excitement the sound of dogs on a bear track."

No one knows better than Carl Johnson what the climax of a bear chase can be like. He will remember as long as he lives the black his dogs cornered in a swamp in northern Michigan back in the 1950s.

The bear had been doing damage and causing concern around the little town of Brimley, near the eastern end of the Upper Peninsula. Sheep pens and orchards had been raided and beehives knocked over, and as time went on the troublemaker grew more and more bold.

There had been a tragic case of child killing by a black bear in that area a few years before, and the community was understandably jittery about bears. When this one took to walking around cabins and houses in broad daylight, and watching children from the roadside as they walked home from school, the local people clamored to have the animal done away with. Finally Johnson was asked to bring his dogs north and take care of it.

He picked seven of his dogs for the job, five hounds and two airedales to help with the close-quarter fighting. He also took along two hunting partners, Howard McDaniel and Danny Porter. Porter lived not far from Carl's home at Cadillac, and kenneled and helped train Johnson's bear pack.

At Brimley a local woodsman and hunter, Alex Van Luven, led the party out to an area frequented by the bear. At the border of a small clearing where a logging camp had once stood, they found fresh sign where a bear had cuffed a crumbling log apart to get at a colony of ants. The tracks were those of the bear they were after, and Johnson let Banjo and John, his two strike dogs, go.

The time was early May, and the bear was spring-lean. It was five hours after the dogs took his track before he finally came to bay in a swamp on the shore of Lake Superior. By that time he had been goaded into rage in a long-running fight.

Years before, a storm had cut a wide swath through the swamp, piling big trees like jackstraws. Young cedar and alder had grown up among them, forming a tangle so thick it shut out the sun. That was the place where the bear elected to make his stand.

Johnson and Porter were within hearing when the fight began. They did their best to reach the scene, clambering over blowdowns and creeping through underbrush on their hands and knees, spurred by the racket of the most savage bear-and-dog battle they had ever listened to.

The dogs were screaming their hatred of what they had caught, and the bear was snarling, making pig-like grunting noises, and popping his teeth loud enough to be heard fifty yards away. At the end Johnson could even smell the rank scent of bear, mixed with the stink of churned mud and stagnant swamp water. He clawed his way within five yards of the fight, but he could see neither bear nor dogs. The battle was raging under a windfall, hidden by a thick screen of young cedars.

The dogs were screaming their hatred of what they had caught, and the bear was snarling, making pig-like grunting noises and popping his teeth. Then one of the dogs came sailing out, flying end over end through the air.

Suddenly there was the sound of scuffling and flailing. One of the dogs had grabbed and was hanging on. Then one of the dogs came sailing out, flying end over end through the air. But however badly she was hurt, she whirled and went back into the fight before Carl could get his hands on her.

Next the bear came lunging out and the hunter saw him for the first time, only three or four steps away.

He didn't care much for what he saw. The bear was a four-hundred pounder, muddy, bedraggled, and hard looking. The hair on his neck was pointing the wrong way, his ears were laid back, teeth bared, boarlike eyes blazing. Johnson tried to jerk his rifle up, but the barrel tangled in brush and before he could free it Duke, the second airedale, flashed in front of him, blocking a shot. Right then Carl wasn't sorry to have the dog between him and the bear, either.

The bear dodged back into the cedars, and the fracas ended as if a switch had been thrown. The uproar died away and the swamp got as still as a grave — and not much more inviting. Carl waited for the dogs to open again, but when the silence hung on he wormed into the windfall.

His pack, which he had thought a match for any bear, had quit cold. Five of them lay sprawled in the trampled mud where they had fought, whining and licking their cuts. Banjo and Rocky were missing, and Johnson concluded they had crawled away to die.

Porter came panting up and heard the story. The two men were debating what to do next when, off in the swamp, Banjo's rolling bawl suddenly broke the silence. The old hound was still in action after all. His throaty warcry rang out again, and on the heels of it came the thud of a rifle shot. Crossing an old brush-grown logging road with Banjo and Rocky snapping at his heels, the bear had had the bad luck to run headlong into Howard McDaniel. The hunt was over.

Carl found Banjo stretched out on the ground beside the dead bear, battered and exhausted. Rocky lay on a coat nearby, whining from the pain of a broken jaw.

Johnson knew now what Shook Vance, an old bear hunter from the Tennessee mountains, had meant when he said, "Any man that shoots a b'ar when he's fightin' the dogs has to pull the trigger powerful hard!"

NINE

Hunting Without Dogs

The hunter who sets out to take the makings of a black-bear rug is after one of the most coveted trophies in North America.

Just about every big-game addict I have known harbored a deep hankering to shoot a bear. But because there are not enough bears to go around, and also because they are difficult animals to hunt, hardly more than a handful succeed. In my home state of Michigan, for example, the annual deer kill ranges from 60,000 to 100,000, but only 500 to 700 bears are taken each year. Vermont estimates that in a fall when it has a deer herd of around 150,000, its black-bear population may number 1,200. And so it goes.

The hunter who tries for a bear deliberately is also going up against one of this continent's most superbly equipped game animals. If he hunts without dogs he will need determination, patience, stealth, hunting craft, and some luck.

This bear's natural defenses are surprising in view of the fact that he has no enemies apart from man, and, occasionally, bears bigger than himself. His ears and nose are fully as good as a deer's. He can smell a man half a mile away if the wind is right, and the sound of a small twig breaking under a hunter's feet is enough to warn him that the neighborhood has suddenly become unhealthy. If either man scent or an unnatural noise alerts him at close range, he is likely to let go a grunting woof that is sufficient to lift a nearby human out of his boots, and go crashing off through the brush like a runaway truck. But if he picks up danger signals at a distance, he will probably melt away with hardly more commotion than a shadow. For an animal of his size, he can move through thick cover with astonishingly little noise—an ability he shares with deer, moose, and various other game animals.

Many authorities believe, and many writers who talk about the black bear say, that his eyes are poor, especially that he is nearsighted. I am not prepared to argue that theory, but I have never seen evidence of it. The bears I have encountered seemed able to make me out as readily as any other animal could, and as far away.

The black is also extremely wary and crafty, an expert at keeping out of sight unless he wants to show himself. In my lifetime I have spent about as much time in places where he is found as in deer country, yet I have seen at least a hundred whitetails for every bear I have laid eyes on.

Outside of parks and campgrounds and the vicinity of garbage dumps, where the black bear loses all fear of man through frequent association and frequently turns into a brazen panhandler, it is probably safe to assume that anybody who has camped, hunted, or fished for any length of time in bear country has been watched by one or more bears. But of a thousand such persons, it would be hard to find one who has seen the bear that watched him.

This elusiveness, coupled with his keen sense of smell and hearing, makes the black bear a difficult animal to hunt unless dogs are used. But there is one chink in his armor and, aside from the bears that are killed literally by accident when they blunder within range of a deer hunter, that chink accounts for most of the blacks taken today by hunters without dogs.

The first thing the hunter must keep in mind is that his chances will be far better if he lets the bear come to him than if he tries to go to it. Under most circumstances, stillhunting for a black bear pays very few dividends.

The life of this bear is centered around food, and the surest way to outwit him is by the use of bait. Shooting a bear over bait is not new. A few hunters, familiar with blackie's habits, have been doing it for a long time. Basically, it was the method resorted to more than seventy-five years ago by Ike Cooper, the oldtime bear hunter whom I talked about earlier. But it has remained for bowhunters to recognize its effectiveness and bring it into common use in the last fifteen or twenty years.

The bowhunter needs to get close to his target, and bait enables him to get close indeed. Most of the black bears killed with a bow are shot at ranges under forty yards, many of them at less than half that. I know one outstanding hunter in northern Wisconsin, who has accounted for more than thirty black bears with bow, who tries to arrange things around the bait station so that he can be no farther than fifteen or twenty feet from the bear when he releases his arrow.

A bear comes to a bait station cautiously. He is likely to stop in thick cover nearby, test the wind, take time to decide whether there is danger in the neighborhood. If nothing threatening happens, he starts to feed.

The first step in baiting is to locate a place where bears are feeding on natural food or traveling regularly. Trails, tracks, dung, broken branches of fruit trees are often the clue. So is hair rubbed off on the underside of fallen tree trunks, where a bear has crawled underneath.

The range of baits is wide. Beef scraps, bacon, table leavings, apples, syrup, honey all appeal to the black's appetite. New York game men who carried out bear research in the Adirondacks concluded that smoked or burned pork jowls, bacon fat, and honey were especially attractive baits.

Some states, Wisconsin among them, permit the use of only liquid bait, partly to appease anti-baiters, partly in the interests of keeping the environment clean. And it is common practice today for bear hunters to be required to clean up all scraps and refuse at a bait station when the hunt ends.

Success in baiting depends in large degree on careful planning ahead of time, and putting the bait in the right place. Some of the best black bear guides in Canada, in provinces where spring hunting is legal, make it a practice to locate promising areas in the fall, before the bears go into hibernation, and then put the baits out in early spring before the animals leave their dens. The food is there waiting, and the emerging black is likely to start using it at once. The bait should be in the kind of dense cover bears like, but it must also be placed to allow the hunter a clean shot.

The bear comes to a bait station cautiously, particularly the first few times. He is likely to stop in thick cover nearby, test the wind, take time to decide whether there is danger in the neighborhood. If the bait is in a box or container and is wired in the low fork of a tree, a method some hunters use to circumvent coons, skunks, wandering dogs, and ravens, the bear will pull it down, but if it falls with a thump he is likely to beat a fast retreat. He does not run far, however. When nothing threatening happens, he stops, sniffs, pads cautiously back and starts to feed.

The blind from which the bait user intends to do his shooting, whether with gun or bow, does not need to be elaborate but it must blend into the surroundings sufficiently well to escape the bear's attention. A small evergreen tree, dropped and lying on the ground, serves about as well as anything. The bear is not likely to notice a motionless hunter if he is screened enough to break his outline. It's essential that he stay motionless until he raises up for the shot, and if possible he should do that when the bear's head is turned away. Camouflage clothing is a help, and some bowhunters tape their bows to prevent any chance of sun flash.

The blind must be downwind from the bait, whether it is fifteen feet or forty yards away, and it should not be placed in the thickest cover in the vicinity. That is very likely the route the bear will take in approaching. More than one novice hunter has made that mistake, heard some small noise behind him, and looked over his shoulder at a bear only a few feet away.

I know one who hid behind a log in a very thick growth of low brush and ferns. Just after sundown he heard a rustle in the thicket behind him, no louder than a red squirrel would make. He raised up for a look, and at that same instant the bear did the same thing, just two short steps away.

"I'll never make that mistake again," the man told me.

Bait watching calls for unlimited patience. The hunter should be in his blind by midafternoon, but usually the bear will not come in much before dusk. Another requirement is complete silence on the part of the hunter. The black bear relies on his ears about as much as on his nose, and the faintest whisper of sound that does not belong in the woods is all the warning he needs.

Many states and provinces prohibit baiting, and there are questions raised even among hunters as to its sportsmanship. It is inevitable that such doubts should arise, especially in these days when those who bitterly oppose all hunting are flooding the country with emotional propaganda.

But because of the nocturnal habits, craft, and cunning of the black bear, it is almost the only sure way of taking him, and those who do it defend it as no more unsportsmanlike than hunting geese in a cornfield.

For the hunter who does not want to rely on it, or who hunts where it is not legal, the best bet is to locate a place where bears are feeding on natural food, wait in late afternoon for one to show up, and hope to ambush him.

My friend, Ken Peterson, outdoor writer on the Flint, Michigan, *Journal,* tells an amusing anecdote about that technique. Ken asked a bear-hunting farmer in the Escanaba district of Michigan's Upper Peninsula about his methods.

"I know you don't use dogs," Ken said. "What do you do, bait?"

"Bait, hell!" the farmer retorted. "Bears come into my cornfield and knock down half the crop. When I want one I just go out and sit in that field."

I have known instances where bears were killed raiding oat fields in that same fashion, and many times a hunter takes one in an apple or peach orchard they are using.

Thickets of wild cherry or wild grape, places where beech mast or acorns are plentiful, wild apple trees or old trees on abandoned farms back in the woods, all are likely places to find bear sign and waylay a feeding black. Beech trees often show evidence of an unusual kind. The bark is scarred with the claw marks of climbing bears, and a crotch may hold a tangle of brush and leaves that somewhat resembles an outsized squirrel nest, where a bear has sat, raking in and breaking branches to strip off the nuts.

Whatever the food may be, the hunter who locates a place where bears are feeding while the hunting season is open has a good chance of success. On the other hand, simply to walk through woods and swamps in hope of catching a bear unawares is a waste of time.

Many hunters collect a bearskin while on a stand in deer season. There are enough humans abroad at that time to rout bears out and keep them on the move, and frequently they blunder into a lucky stander entirely by accident.

For the hunter that can be as exciting an experience as anything that can happen to him. The symptoms of bear fever are identical with those of buck fever, and the sight of a bear stepping into the open within easy gun range, black and big and burly, is fairly likely to bring on a severe case.

I remember a young hunter in a deer camp in northern Michigan who was watching a deer runway that crossed an old brush-bordered logging road in a tangled evergreen swamp. He had picked a stand at a place where the logging road forked, and he had a clear view down both branches. Without warning, a big bear walked into view, following the deer runway. The hunter was carrying a .348 Winchester, an entirely adequate dose of bear medicine, but he froze, unable to bring the rifle to his shoulder, and sat shaking and paralyzed while the bear ambled across the road and disappeared in the evergreens. A couple of minutes later it repeated the performance at the other fork, and the hunter like-wise repeated his. He was still close to incoherent when he got back to camp.

When it comes to guns for the black bear, any hunter who has a rifle adequate for deer, and one that handles well in thick cover, can consider himself the owner of a bear gun. But if he is buying one specifically for bear, my advice is to pick a caliber that speaks with a bit more authority than the lower range of deer rifles.

There can be no question that more black bears have been done in with the .30/30 than any other firearm, in part because oldtime bear hunters commonly regarded it as totally satisfactory, more because it was for many decades the favorite deer rifle in this country and most of the black bears shot each autumn fell to deer hunters as a matter of luck — bad luck for the bear, good for the hunter. The .32 Special probably rates close second to the .30/30 as a bear caliber, for the same reasons.

But the black bear is a much bigger animal than either the whitetail or mule deer, and far tougher to kill, in part because of his pelt, thick layer of body fat, and heavy bone and muscle structure, in part because he is by nature more tenacious of life and likely to carry off lead that would be almost certain to drop a deer in its tracks.

All of these factors make a rifle in the elk or moose class more suitable for bear hunting than the lighter deer calibers. There is no need for a high-velocity, flat-shooting rifle. The places where the black bear is found rule out long shots almost completely. My guess is that very few of these bears are killed at ranges exceeding fifty yards.

This applies only to hunting in the United States east of the Mississippi and in the thickly timbered country of Canada north of the farmlands, however. In the mountain West, black-bear hunting is another ball game, and the same is true in Alaska, where game men tell me the black shows a decided preference for open rather than dense forests.

I have not hunted this bear in Alaska or in the western states, and so cannot speak from firsthand knowledge. But every western hunter and guide I know agrees that it is a common experience to spot a black in the open, especially in mountain berry patches, and get within range by stalking. Under those circumstances a rifle that can reach out a couple of hundred yards with very little drop in bullet trajectory gives the hunter a marked advantage, of course.

My own favorite big-game rifle, for the places where I have done most of my hunting, is a featherweight model Savage in .300 caliber. My preference is based on the fact that I like the feel and balance of the gun, the way it handles, and the action. There are many others with similar ballistics that are every bit as good.

I carry that rifle in all of my deer hunting, and I have relied on it many times when I was after black bear. If the shot is placed where it should be (and that is vital with any gun), the .300 is entirely adequate for the job.

Other black-bear calibers in favor with today's hunters are the .270, .30/06 (in general the heavier bullets in these calibers are better for use in the cover where the bear is hunted), .300 magnum (more rifle than you need), .308, and the old .348 if you happen to have one. In factory loads, all of these push good brush-bucking bullets out with a muzzle energy varying from 2,700 to 3,600 foot-pounds, and that is enough for the biggest and toughest black bear any hunter will ever encounter.

One other factor needs to be kept in mind in choosing a rifle for this bear if the hunter intends to follow dogs. The gun will get hard use. It should be rugged enough to stand up to water, dirt, mud, and sand. And there is no need for a scope in eastern black-bear hunting. The ranges are short, and a scoped rifle can be an abomination in dense brush. But again, a scope can be a big help in the open country of the West.

I know bear hunters who use dogs who have rejected a rifle outright, as too heavy and awkward to carry. They rely on one of the Magnum handguns, in either .357 or .44 caliber.

The handgun has advantages. It leaves both hands free for crawling through thickets and keeping balance when walking a log over a stream. It doesn't hang up in the brush. And at the short ranges commonly involved, if the hunter can place his shots the Magnum sidearms will kill a bear about as well as a rifle. But I also know hunters who have gone back to a rifle after one hair-raising face-to-face meeting with a dog-harassed bear.

Speaking of placing shots, which ones are best? The neck shot is likely to drop a bear in its tracks, but if a fight with hounds is going on it is usually impossible. The same is true of a head shot, and if the bear is of trophy size a bullet in the skull is likely to cause damage, make accurate measurements impossible and cost the hunter his rightful place in the record list of big game.

All things considered, the shoulder shot is probably as good as any, especially if it is placed to damage the lungs or heart as well as to break the animal down. Above all, no hunter should ever risk a shot back of the chest cavity. A wounded bear usually bleeds very little externally, because of layers of fat both inside and outside the body. Consequently, trailing one is likely to be difficult and often proves impossible, the more so since most bear hunting is done on bare ground. A gut-shot black will travel a long distance, and nine times out of ten will get away and not be found.

For the same reasons, no hunter should try a shot at a bear that is spooked and running away from him. No matter the caliber of the rifle, a shot in the rump is far more likely to wound than to kill, and a bear wounded in that part of his anatomy is a bear lost.

As for bow weights, in the early days of bowhunting it was common practice for the few hunters who went after a black bear to carry a bow with a draw of not less than sixty or seventy pounds. With a straight bow, such power was necessary to insure adequate penetration.

The advent of the recurved bow, coupled with improved hunting arrows that penetrate deeper and result in more extensive hemorrhage, altered the situation. Most bowhunters today rate a fifty- to sixty-pound bow entirely adequate for black-bear hunting. One factor that has contributed substantially to the use of less powerful bows has been the introduction, in the last five years, of the compound bow. The power of these is augmented by an ingenious arrangement of pulleys.

The largest archery outlet in this country, and probably in the world, is Anderson's, at the village of Grand Ledge, Michigan. I talked with Gene Schroeder, a top authority there, about bows for black bear.

His recommendation is a compound bow of fifty-five- to sixty-pound draw, fifty pounds or less for women hunters. Such a bow has marked advantages. At full draw, a fifty-five pound top-grade, four-pulley compound is reduced to a pull of forty-five pounds, making it far easier for the hunter to hold it at full draw while he waits briefly for the right shot. (Compounds achieve twenty to fifty percent reduction in pull at full draw, depending on their design.) But at the same time, such a bow drives an arrow with the speed and penetrating capability of a sixty-five-pound recurved. The compound bow has one disadvantage. In general, it tends to be less quiet than a recurved bow.

One highly important consideration is that the bow "fit" the hunter, with a pull no greater than he can handle comfortably and with no loss of accuracy.

For example, Hawley Rhew, the Michigan bowhunter who in the autumn of 1975 took the heaviest bear ever killed in that state (it dressed a whopping 613 pounds), was using a fifty-three-pound bow. Thirty-eight years old, of muscular build, and a man who takes pride in keeping himself in good physical condition, Rhew had tried bows of greater power but found he could not shoot as accurately as with the fifty-three-pounder.

"I'll stick with a bow that fits me," he says, "but I'm a nut about sharp arrows. You can't get your hunting heads too sharp."

Other bowhunters agree. Razor-sharp arrows are fully as important as the right bow weight. The arrow must penetrate thick fur and slice through inches of fat and tough muscle to reach vital organs. More than one bear, killed by a rifleman, has been found carrying a hunting-arrow head buried just under the skin or in the flesh of neck, chest or legs. Now and then a shot of that kind can be the result of accident, but such finds give bowhunting a bad name it does not deserve. It's not likely to happen with a hunter who carries the right equipment and is expert at using it.

The most deadly shot for the bowhunter is from the side, with the bear facing away from him at a 45 degree angle, placing the arrow just behind the shoulder where it will not encounter heavy bone and can knife its way into the lungs or heart. On a five-hundred-pound bear the target area for a clean kill is no bigger than a football. But bears hit there often drop in their tracks, and few of them run more than fifty yards before they go down for keeps.

One final question arises. Is there any element of danger in hunting this least aggressive of American bears?

The answer has to be yes. Most of the time the hunter who goes after a black bear is in no more danger than one who hunts cottontail rabbits. But now and then a wounded black turns on his human tormentor, and he can then be as dangerous and formidable an antagonist as the grizzly or brown.

It does not happen as frequently as might be expected. Black bears are mortally hurt by either bullets or arrows, and something like 999 times out of 1,000 their one thought is to escape.

The Wisconsin bowhunter I mentioned earlier, who has killed more than thirty blacks over bait, often drives an arrow home from the shelter of a frail blind at fifteen feet. He has never been seriously threatened with attack. The bear screams with pain when the razorhead slices in, and runs, apparently in blind panic.

At the opposite extreme was an attack that took place on the Yukon River in the interior of Alaska in 1950. It resulted in the most terrible mauling I have ever known a man to suffer from the teeth and claws of a black bear.

The victim was a sixty-five-year-old Indian by the name of Pitka. Hunting by canoe along a slough ten miles from his fishing camp on the Yukon, he spotted a bear on an alder flat half a mile away. He took it for a grizzly.

Pitka had killed ten or a dozen black bears but had never shot a grizzly. Like many Alaskan Indians, he was disposed to leave the latter alone. But he needed camp meat, and also, after seeing the bear in the same place for several mornings in a row, he came to the conclusion that it knew he was there and meant to make trouble for him if it got the chance. He decided to make the first move.

He stalked it, and when he got close enough for a shot with the .30/30 he was carrying he discovered that it was a big black bear instead. He dropped it with one shot, watched for a minute to make sure it was dead, and walked in. For reasons he himself did not understand, he leaned his rifle against a bush and went the last few steps with no weapon but a belt knife. He was three yards away when the bear rolled to its feet and leaped on him.

It knocked him unconscious with one blow, which proved a merciful happenstance. When he came to he was lying on the ground, the bear was standing over him, he could feel its fur against his arms and smell its foul breath. The bear's face was only a foot from his, but the luckless Indian no longer had a face.

As he floated up out of unconsciousness he remembered his knife. He freed it and drove the four-inch blade into the bear's belly as hard as he could. The bear gave no sign that it felt the knife thrust. It was probably dying on its feet from the bullet wound.

Pitka stabbed the animal repeatedly. He could feel blood spurting down on him. Finally, as he put it, he went to sleep again, and when he awoke the bear was no longer standing over him. He could hear it thrashing and bawling in the brush a few yards away. When the noise died out the Indian knew the bear was dead.

He had taken incredible punishment. The entire right side of his face from the eye across to the nose and down to the chin had been torn away. The right eye was ripped out of the socket, and he could barely distinguish light with the left. His nose was torn off, with cartilage sticking out of raw flesh. The right cheek and part of the left were gone, and his mouth was so mangled that he could not manage a drink of water. Three teeth were left in the jaw; the rest were dangling loose. All the torn flesh and skin of his face were hanging down beneath his chin like a grisly, bloody bib, and the pain in his head was beyond description.

His only hope of survival lay in getting back the half mile to the canoe that he had left on the bank of the slough, where members of his family or other searchers could find him. Back in the brush where he had shot the bear, he knew he would never be found.

Part of the way to the canoe led through thick alders, part across a grassy flat. Almost blinded and unable to stand, Pitka began his terrible journey. Part of the time he crept on his hands and knees. When he was too weak for that he crawled on his belly.

He left the dead bear in the evening. The month was June, and there is no real darkness in the Yukon country at that time of year, but when the air got cold and mosquitoes swarmed out to torment him, he knew it was night.

He reached the slough the next morning, too exhausted to search along the bank for his canoe. He lay in the grass all that day and another night, finally made out the blurred shape of the canoe and crawled to it. There, more than fifty hours after the attack, his wife and a neighbor found him, more dead than alive.

He spent a total of ten months in the hospital, while doctors tried first to save his life and then to rebuild his mutilated face. As the Indian said later, what remained wasn't a very good face but it was better than none. The bear had left him permanently crippled and close to blind.

Any hunter who believes that a wounded black bear is ever something to be taken lightly would do well to remember that dreadful mauling.

The rule of safety is simple. A wounded bear, of whatever kind, is a dangerous bear, and the hunter who approaches him should be prepared for trouble so long as a spark of life remains in the animal.

TEN

Bear on the Table

Is bear meat good to eat?

That depends almost entirely on the age and condition of the bear, what it has been feeding on, and whether the carcass is dressed carefully and cooked properly.

Nobody has stated the case better than Alaska game officials. Along the coast of that state the flesh of black bears is seldom palatable because the bears eat dead fish and carrion, the authorities warn. But they add that in the interior, unless the black is feeding on carrion, bear meat is very good.

A few years back, in early September, I drove north to the Upper Peninsula of Michigan to spend two or three days with El Harger, a Michigan game biologist then stationed at the Cusino Wildlife Research Station east of Munising. Harger, mentioned earlier, is Michigan's foremost authority on bears and their habits.

I stayed overnight in Munising, and when I walked into El's office the next morning there was a row of beautiful shaggy-mane mushrooms lying neatly along one side of his desk.

I exclaimed with pleasure, and asked where he had gotten them.

"I could pick a bushel," he replied. "You like shaggy-manes?"

My answer was an enthusiastic yes, and El followed with another question.

"Like bear meat?"

Again I said I did.

"I shot a medium-sized bear the other day," he explained. "I try to take one each fall for the table. This one was fat and in good condition. Just got the meat back from the butcher. How would you like to come to dinner tonight?"

That bear roast, as El's wife prepared it, served with mushrooms and fresh vegetables from the Harger garden, was more tasty than some prime rib of beef I have been served in expensive restaurants.

For many years the Michigan Bear Hunters Association, a sportsmen's group organized by my friend Carl Johnson when bear hunting with hounds started to gain popularity in the state, has staged an annual banquet at which bear meat is always featured.

Usually something else is offered as well, beaver or chinook salmon, for the sake of those who spleen at the idea of eating bear, but the latter is the foremost item.

It goes without saying that an old bear will be tougher and stronger in flavor than a young animal. Those responsible for the MBHA dinner are careful to pick a young bear, usually killed by one of the members. It is skinned and butchered very carefully, and the meat is frozen until banquet time, in late winter. I have never eaten any that was other than excellent.

At the end of one of the banquets, Carl came to me, said there was plenty of bear left over, and offered my wife and myself a supply to bring home. We accepted eagerly.

It had been cut into serving-size chunks and roasted. We invited friends in for bear dinner, heated it in the oven with slices of bacon laid over the pieces to keep them from drying out, and the verdict of our guests was unanimous. They had never sampled anything better.

Somewhat surprisingly (or maybe it is not surprising in view of the black bear's frequent descent into the role of scavenger), the meat shares with pork the dubious distinction of being a carrier of trichinae, the small parasitic worms that cause trichinosis, a rare but dread disease in humans.

Instances of infected bears, or of human infection from eating bear meat, have been reported from states as far apart as Alaska and Vermont. In 1964 a number of persons in Vermont became ill from eating bear meat. But again as with pork, thorough cooking eliminates all risk.

Recipes for cooking bear can be found in a great many cookbooks. The Michigan Bear Hunters Association has one for broiled bear steak that I have not tried, but I suspect it would produce a highly appetizing dish.

The steaks are marinated for twenty-four hours in a marinade made of 1 cup of cider, 2 tablespoons of orange juice, 1 tablespoon of lemon juice, 1 finely chopped onion, 1 diced carrot, 2 stalks of diced celery, 1 teaspoon of paprika, 1 clove of garlic mashed, 1 bay leaf, dash of nutmeg and $\frac{1}{2}$ teaspoon of mustard. Boil the marinade for five minutes, let it cool and cover the steaks.

At the end of twenty-four hours remove the meat from the marinade, dry thoroughly, sear on both sides under high heat, and broil until well done, basting frequently with the marinade.

The recipe I can vouch for is the one used in cooking bear roasts for the MBHA banquet. It was given me through the kindness of two friends at Lake City, Michigan, where the annual dinner is held. They are Russ Reeder, a former president of MBHA, and John Stih, who for several years cooked the bear. It is complicated, but here you have it just as Russ and John sent it to me.

Prepare a marinade of 10 pounds of uniodized salt, 3 bunches of celery cut up, 5 pounds of carrots sliced, 10 pounds of onions sliced with the peelings on, and 2 quarts of vinegar.

Cut 100 pounds of choice bear meat into rolled roasts. Place the roasts in several large containers, add the marinade ingredients except the vinegar, cover with water, add the vinegar and stir well to dissolve the salt.

Let the meat stand 12 hours, then bring the roasts from the bottom to the top and from the top to the bottom. Let stand another 30 hours. Remove from the brine, rinse under running cold water, put in containers and let stand in cold water overnight. Remove and dry, and rub each roast with salt, pepper, and garlic powder as you would a beef roast.

Put in roasting pans, add $\frac{1}{4}$ inch of water in the bottom of the pans, and roast uncovered for one hour at 325 degrees. Turn the pieces, if dry add more water, and roast for another hour.

Meanwhile, grind 4 pounds of carrots, 5 pounds of onions and 1 bunch of celery, cook in 3 gallons of water until well done. Pour into the roasting pans with the bear meat on top, add $\frac{1}{2}$ pound of butter on top of the meat in each pan, and continue roasting at 325 degrees. Next dry sherry wine and dry gingerale are poured over the meat. The recipe calls for 2 quarts of wine and 4 of gingerale. At the end of an hour turn the meat and add more wine and gingerale. Cook until well done. Cooking time depends on the quality of the meat and the size of the roasts.

Thicken the broth and vegetable mixture from the pans with flour, strain through a sieve, add 6 large cans of mushrooms, and pour the hot gravy over the meat after it is sliced.

I hardly need to add that if you are cooking less than 100 pounds of bear (which seems highly probable) you cut all ingredients down accordingly.

The worst bear meat I ever tried to eat was from a polar bear I killed at the south end of Hudson Bay in 1937. Our party of seventeen was meat hungry, for we had been traveling three or four weeks aboard a small trading schooner that had no refrigeration facilities, and our initial supply of beef had lasted only two or three days. After that we depended on speckled trout, available in unlimited abundance in every river we came to along the coast. Choice fare, but I learned you can tire of a fish diet rather quickly.

So we welcomed the prospect of a meal of fresh bear. We cut off a fine looking roast, dressed it with onions and apples, and put it in the oven in the schooner's tiny galley. As soon as it started to heat, the stench was enough to drive everybody out.

We had some excellent cooks aboard, and they resorted to every trick they could think of to tame that bear meat, but without avail.

When it was cooked the braver of us tried a bite. It was too rank to swallow. Finally our Eskimo engineer sliced off a chunk. He sampled it, picked up the roasting pan, walked wordlessly to the rail and dumped the roast into the sea.

Eskimos are known for being tolerant and even fond of high meat. In fact, they eat meat of almost any kind or age. Alagkok's firm verdict tells more about that bear roast than I can put into words.

A few days later, other members of our party killed three more polar bears on another offshore island fifty miles to the south. One was a youngster that weighed maybe 125 pounds.

Again we tried a roast, and I have eaten little beef that was more flavorful and tender.

We could never be sure of the explanation for the dreadful taste of my bear, but we suspected he had been feeding on carrion for some time, perhaps on a bearded seal or beluga whale washed up on the beach of the island, although he was not foul smelling until we undertook cooking the meat.

It goes without saying that any bear that has fed on carrion is not likely to be fit to eat. I have never heard of a hunter or guide with a stomach strong enough to sample grizzly or brown bear, possibly for the reason that both of them are inveterate scavengers and often smell to high heaven when they are shot. The Indians and early mountain men are said to have been fond of grizzly meat, however, and there is no reason why a young one on a clean diet should not be as good to eat as the black bear.

Polar bears rely chiefly on a diet of freshly killed seal, and so for the most part are free of taint. Explorers in the arctic have leaned heavily on the white bear for a food supply many times in the past.

When S. Andre, the Swedish balloonist, was forced down on the pack ice in his attempt to drift to the North Pole in July of 1897, he and his two companions had almost no other food supply than the flesh of the bears they shot on their long and fruitless march back toward land.

When in October they finally went ashore on White Island, northeast of Spitzbergen, where they died and where their last camp was discovered thirty-three years later, they had stocked enough bears to last them through the long winter night. At their last camp on the ice, however, the floe cracked open beneath their tent, and the meat was lost.

One word of caution is needed in connection with eating polar bear. The liver is so high in content of a certain vitamin that it is poisonous to dogs and men. The Eskimos have always avoided it and Arctic explorers learned early to leave it alone. At the Explorers Club in New York many years ago, I asked Capt. Peter Freuchen, the renowned Danish explorer, about this. He had had only one experience. A sledding party of which he was a member had killed a white bear while Freuchen and a companion were away from camp hunting. They alone ate none of the liver, and they alone escaped severe illness.

That is the story of bear on the platter. Properly selected and prepared, it can be close to unbeatable. Of the wild meat I have eaten, I rate only beaver ahead of it. That stands at the top of my list.

But if bear meat is bad it is very bad indeed. So if you plan on serving it, be sure you start with the right kind of bear and then do your homework very carefully.

ELEVEN

The "Timid" Bear as Man-eater

Does the black bear ever resort to deliberate man-eating?

If that question were put to a thousand outdoorsmen, it is doubtful that one would reply in the affirmative. No one familiar with bear behavior is much surprised to learn that grizzly, Alaska brown, and polar bears sometimes kill a human because they are hungry, and feed on what they have killed. It is as easy for them as killing a sheep or a seal, and is in keeping with their fierce nature as big, hot-tempered, flesh-eating animals.

But the black is a different bear. Many hunters deride the idea that he is ever dangerous. Reputable writers describe him as timid, more eager to shun men than they are to avoid him.

Seton, one of the most respected naturalists of his day, called the black shy and inoffensive, adding that a dangerous individual was encountered far less frequently than a dangerous dog or bull. "I am tempted to lay it down for law that no black bear ever willingly faced or harmed a man," he said.

It is hardly surprising that the average hunter, told that this bear turns now and then into a man-eater as determined and fearless as any grizzly, brown, or polar bear, reacts with astonishment and disbelief. But the record leaves no room for doubt.

I have in my files accounts of seven such instances, all verified or vouched for by reliable writers. The stories are completely true and the circumstances of the kill leave no room for question as to the bear's motives. I am sure there have been more such incidents, too, that have not come to my attention, and I am equally sure there will be still more in the future.

One of the most tragic cases ever recorded involved the killing of a three-year-old girl in the Brimley area, near the eastern end of Michigan's Upper Peninsula, in July of 1948.

Little Carol Ann Pomerankey was the daughter of a forest ranger on the Marquette National Forest, and the family was living in an isolated firetower cabin in deep woods. The father was on duty at the forest headquarters fifteen miles away that hot July day, the mother was busy in the kitchen, and the child was playing in the yard.

Her mother heard a sudden scream and looked out a window to see the little girl scrambling up the back steps of the cabin, with a smallish black bear snarling at her heels. The frightened youngster was reaching for the latch of the screen door when the bear grabbed her by the neck.

The horrified mother ran screaming from the house, grabbed up a broom and gave chase, but the bear refused to be scared off. It lumbered across the brush-bordered clearing and disappeared in the woods, carrying the child.

The mother made a frantic phone call to her husband, the alarm went out by radio, and a posse of more than a hundred men armed with rifles and shotguns quickly gathered and began a search. They were headed by Alex Van Luven, a woodsman from Brimley. Van Luven was not a bear hunter, but he had hunted coyotes for years and kept good dogs. He brought the best one with him.

Less than a quarter mile from the cabin one of the searchers found a small blood-stained shoe. The dog picked up the trail at that point and followed it, on leash, into a dense thicket, where the body of the child lay. The bear, having killed its victim with a single bite through the back of the neck, had carried her only a short distance before stopping to feed. The searchers had interrupted and driven it off.

Van Luven sent one of the two men with him back with the news. The other, a commercial fisherman from Lake Superior named Wayne Weston, he left on guard. He then turned his dog loose on the bear track and took out after it.

It fell to Weston to take revenge, and he had a very short wait. Within five minutes after the dog's bawling had faded in the woods, and while Van Luven was still within hearing of a rifle shot, the bear showed up, coming insolently back to finish its meal. Weston did not see it and had no warning until it stood up on its hind feet and stared him in the face, over the top of the brush, at twenty feet!

"I was so scared for a second I hardly knew whether to shoot or not," he confessed afterward. But he didn't take long to make up his mind. He smashed a shot into the bear's mouth and knocked it down, and as it attempted to drag itself away, thrashing and growling, he finished it with four more shots.

The carcass of the bear was flown to a veterinary lab at Michigan State College, in downstate East Lansing, for painstaking examination. Had the animal been injured, was it suffering from some disease, had it once been a pet and so lost its normal fear of man? Human flesh in the stomach proved beyond all question that Weston had killed the right bear, but other than that the experts learned little. There was no collar mark, no injury, no disease, no clue at all save that the killer was lean and hungry. The blueberry season, when all bears feast, was still a couple of weeks away. There apparently lay the answer.

The tragedy was a shocking one, and had predictable consequences. For the next two or three years people in northern Michigan were decidedly jittery where black bears were concerned. A bear track found around farm buildings was enough to throw a scare into a whole neighborhood. Any bear seen near dwellings or at garbage pits at the edge of a town—and plenty were seen, of course—touched off something close to hysteria. There was an open bear season the year around, and widespread clamor for a bounty. Any suggestion that bears were game animals and ought to have some protection met with angry opposition.

There had been two recorded cases of man-eating blacks before that one, both in Canada.

The first occurred at a lumber camp on the Red Deer River in southern Alberta in May of 1906. Two men, named Heffern and McIntosh, were chopping wood near the cook shanty when they saw a bear come out of the brush on the far bank of the river. The only other man around the place at the time was Wilson, the cook. They called him out to watch the bear and he came, never suspecting that he was walking to his death.

The bear marched into the river, swam across, shook himself as a dog does on leaving water, and charged the three men headlong and without warning. McIntosh and Heffern made it into the cook shanty, only thirty feet away. The unlucky Wilson overran the door and went racing around the building with the bear gaining on him at every jump. He was almost back to the safety of the door when the bear felled him with a blow across the neck, probably killing him instantly.

The two men in the shanty bombarded the bear with everything they had at hand. They landed a canthook and a can of lard solidly at short range, but the bear paid little attention. He picked up Wilson's body, dragged it off a few yards and stood over it, guarding his kill. Heffern and McIntosh then made a run for the bunkhouse where they had a revolver. They came back as close as they dared and fired several shots without scoring a hit. In the face of that barrage the bear backed off but took his time about it. He picked up the dead man once more and carried him a hundred yards out into the bush, determined to feed. When somebody showed up with a rifle a few minutes later, however, he cleared out.

In the fall of 1924 a black bear killed a Finnish trapper named Waino, in the Port Arthur district of Ontario. The face and neck of that bear were bristling with porcupine quills. Newspaper accounts at the time reported that Waino's rifle had been fired once and had jammed when he attempted to lever in another shell. Whether his shot provoked the bear's attack, however, or whether he shot in self-defense as it was coming at him was never made clear and probably was not known. In any case the bear, an unusually big black, came back to its kill and was shot while feeding on the body of the trapper. Whatever the reason, that bear has to be put down as a true man-eater.

In the early autumn of 1961 an Ohio man was found partially devoured by bears in a thicket near his cabin, on a remote lake in the Sudbury district of Ontario. His glasses and a smashed camera lay not far away. Inside the cabin the cold stove held a half-cooked breakfast.

How the encounter began will never be known, but the victim had told friends a few days earlier that two or three black bears were hanging around the cabin, that they showed little fear of him, and that he intended to make some exciting film of them.

Officials who investigated believed he had left the partly cooked breakfast, gone into the yard with the camera, and been attacked. The bear or bears had dragged him a short distance and fed.

The blueberry crop had been a failure that year, and local woodsmen speculated that the attacker had been an extremely hungry animal.

The next killing came in northern Minnesota in the summer of 1965. A forty-nine-year-old man named Sauvola, living by himself at the hamlet of Automba, thirty miles southwest of Duluth, was jumped by two or more bears while fishing on a small isolated stream a few miles from his home.

His pickup truck was found parked on a nearby road five days later, and members of a search party then discovered the man's mangled body, together with his fish pole and tacklebox.

Tracks showed that at least two bears had taken part in the attack. They had dragged their victim seventy-five feet to a grassy opening, fed, and later returned and moved the body to another spot before working on it again.

Two years after that another tragic case occurred, at Okanagan Lake in southern British Columbia. That time a ten-year-old child was the victim.

Two families from the Vancouver area had gone to the lake on holiday, staying in cabins at a public campground. In midmorning two of the children, girls of nine and ten, took sandwiches and pop and walked up into the hills to play. When they heard a noise in a thicket and saw a bear watching them, they ran, screaming.

The nine-year-old heard a cry from her playmate, but when she looked back she could see neither the girl nor the bear.

The child's father and mother hurried to the scene, but could find no trace of the missing youngster, and returned to the campground where a search party was hurriedly organized.

An unarmed member of the party found the body along a game trail, and almost at once saw the bear approaching. He and a second searcher tried to drive it off with rocks. It backed away, but refused to give up its victim, came back repeatedly and dragged the body farther into the brush.

Somebody then arrived with a rifle. Two shots drove the bear off and a third shot killed it. It was a male weighing about two hundred pounds, with sound teeth, fat and in excellent condition. But the berry crop had failed in that area that summer, and it was probably hungry.

In the fall of 1968 an unarmed Indian guide, fifty-three-year-old Jack Ottertail, was killed and partly devoured by a three-hundred-pound male black bear near the Neguageon Lake Reserve thirty-five miles southwest of Atikokan in western Ontario.

Searchers found the guide's bloodstained coat, and a quarter mile away came on the bear standing near its victim. It stood its ground, and was shot by a member of the search party. Ottertail's body had been partly covered with moss, leaves, and sticks.

Because the man was carrying neither gun nor knife, Ontario Provincial Police who investigated believe the attack was entirely unprovoked. It occurred in an area where an unusual number of bears had been seen during the summer, and the victim's hands were lacerated, as if he had tried desperately to fight off his attacker.

In August of 1963 I investigated a report of a kill by a man-eating black bear in southeastern Manitoba that proved not to be an authentic case, despite strong circumstantial evidence.

Mike Barkus, an elderly prospector living by himself in a cabin on Lac du Bonnet, disappeared in July of that year. Neighbors could find no trace of him, so they reported to the Mounties that the old man was missing.

A four-day search followed and a trained dog finally led officers to what was left of the body, in the bush some distance from the cabin. Bears had fed on the remains and the story gained wide circulation that a bear had killed the man for food.

But when I checked with the Royal Canadian Police at Winnipeg, G. H. Prime, the officer in charge there, told me that investigation had revealed that Barkus had died of natural causes.

"He was dismembered by black bears after death," Prime said. "Parts of the remains were scattered through the bush, and fresh bear tracks were found in a drainage ditch near by."

One of the strangest incidents that has ever come to my attention took place in the Ely district of Minnesota in 1962. A black bear invaded a family campsite on a small lake along the Echo Trail, picked up a seven-month-old child, started to carry it off, then changed its mind.

James Cremins and his family, his wife and their six boys and two girls, were camped on the lake on a fishing vacation, with their tent pitched near the shore and a picnic table set up. When they decided to go fishing after lunch, one of the boys, nine-year-old David, offered to stay in camp and take care of the baby, seven-month-old Charles.

David and the baby took a nap in the tent, and when they awakened David put Charles on a blanket outside and gave him toys to play with. A little later, looking out over the lake, the nine-year-old sensed something behind him and turned to see a bear walking toward him, only thirty feet away.

The boy panicked. He dived for the tent, not even closing the zipper front behind him, and crouched in a corner, clutching a medal and praying. Not until then did he remember the baby on the blanket outside.

When he peered out, the bear was going through food supplies. It knocked aside a log that weighted down the cover of a styrofoam cooler and ripped the lid away. There were two half-gallon cartons of milk inside, both opened, and it proceeded to lift them out and drink the milk.

Twice David started to step outside the tent to get the baby, but each time he heard or saw the bear walking around only a few yards away and his courage failed. When he looked out the third time the bear was standing over the baby, licking its face. That was more than David could endure. Forgetting his own fright, he started to scream, and grabbed up a stone and threw it. In that same instant he heard a motor, approaching across the lake. Part of the family was returning from fishing.

The bear scooped little Charles up in its right forepaw, much as a person might have done, and ran for the woods, hobbling on three legs and carrying the baby. At that point Charles started to cry for the first time. The bear covered fifteen or twenty feet, with David yelling frantically, dropped the child and went out of sight in the brush.

Two older boys, Patrick and Stephen, came ashore in the family canoe. David ran to meet them, shouting "Don't come up here, there's a bear!"

The bear was gone, the baby was lying near the edge of the brush where it had been dropped. Stephen grabbed Charles and he and David took refuge in the station wagon parked near the tent. Patrick shoved the canoe off and raced for his parents, who were still on the lake.

The terror-stricken mother jumped from the boat as it slowed in shallow water, and ran for the camp. She found David and Stephen and the baby huddled safely in the station wagon. Little Charles had been rolled in the dirt and looked it. His mother told me that his face wore what resembled a coat of fresh varnish with pine needles stuck in it. But the bear had left no marks on him and no evidence of injury.

A thoroughly shaken Jim Cremins and his wife were looking over their scattered camp gear when one of the youngsters cried "There he is!" The bear was padding out of the woods once more.

The parents rushed the children into the station wagon. They stayed outside, shouting and waving their arms to drive it off. It retreated a few yards and lay down, sniffing and eying the two people with no show of fear. Then it got up and started for them, and they too retreated inside the station wagon.

The bear scooped little Charles up in its right forepaw and ran for the woods, hobbling on three legs and carrying the baby. Forgetting his own fright, David started to scream, and grabbed up a stone and threw it.

The bear prowled the camp area for an hour, pacing back and forth but molesting nothing. Finally it disappeared in the woods. The family saw no more of it, but they broke camp and left the next morning.

There was no campground nearby and no garbage dump. The bear was a genuinely wild animal, apparently hungry and looking for a meal. The Cremins family had escaped tragedy by a very narrow margin.

What accounts for the unnatural behavior of man-eating animals? Present-day man is not the natural prey of any land predator. His primitive ancestors probably furnished food for every clawed and fanged beast that could overcome them, but the invention of gunpowder changed that. Today, man-eating has to be considered an aberration. From the human viewpoint, it is an extremely abhorrent aberration, too.

The most famous man-eaters have been the great cats, lions in Africa, tigers and leopards in India. The human victims of some of them have numbered in the hundreds, and once an individual animal of these species entered on a career of man-eating he persisted until he was killed. A bear by contrast is likely to take one victim and never repeat the offense.

Various theories have been advanced to explain what has to be considered a perverted appetite in any carnivore.

John Kingsley-Heath, the Nairobi white hunter who killed the last man-eating lion I have heard about, in the Darajani district of East Africa in 1965, found a number of the dreadful quills of the African porcupine in the chest and shoulder of the animal. One was driven nine inches up its right nostril, with the end still protruding two or three inches.

That lion had taken seven or eight human victims in the preceding three years, growing more and more bold as time went on. Kingsley-Heath suspected he had turned to man-eating in the beginning when he found his natural food supply driven out and his watering places preempted as a result of human encroachment. He probably killed his first human out of starvation. Having discovered how easy it was, when the encounter with the porcupine partly disabled him for normal hunting he kept it up.

Jim Corbett, the British army officer who liquidated a number of notorious man-eating tigers in the Kumaon Hills of northern India in the 1920s and 30s (one of the tigers he shot had accounted for the staggering total of 434 human victims), believed that any man-eater turned to what he called "a diet alien to it" because of wounds (porcupine quills included) or old age, that prevented it from killing its natural prey.

Others have suggested that the man-eating tigers of India acquired an unnatural taste for human flesh by feeding on incompletely cremated bodies from the burning ghats.

As for man-eating bears, black or any other kind, the key to such behavior seems to be hunger pure and simple. The animal is short of food, a human is at hand and not hard to kill. The quick-tempered bear needs no better reason.

PART TWO

THE GRIZZLY
AND BROWN

TWELVE

Lord of the Mountains

"If you see a black bear some ways off, you may wonder whether he's a black or a grizzly," Howard Copenhaven once commented to me. "But if you see a grizzly you won't have to wonder. You'll know him for what he is."

Howard was a Montana guide and outfitter, living at Ovando at the time. A few years before he had had an encounter with a grizzly that he would remember the rest of his life.

Bill Schneider, editor of *Montana Outdoors*, official publication of the Fish and Game Department of that state, tells me that Montana guides not uncommonly say that same thing to a client who wants to know how he can tell the two bears apart.

Nothing could reflect more accurately the awesome personality of the grizzly, the impact he has on humans encountering him for the first time – or the fiftieth. He is the bear of western legend, and also of western fact.

He has no enemy save man, and for man he displays contempt or anger more frequently than fear. He is lord of the mountains, walking his windswept domain with haughty arrogance, his gait an unhurried swagger. If he retreats before a human he does it grudgingly, and he is not likely to yield the trail to anything that walks the earth.

There have been a few reports of fights between a black bear and a mountain lion, over a kill, but I know of no recorded instance where a lion has had the courage to tangle with a grizzly. The bear has been known to walk in on a feeding lion, which reacted angrily, snarling and spitting. But in the end it fled without giving battle and the grizzly took over the kill.

There are many differences between this bear and his lesser kinsman, the black. To begin with, the grizzly averages considerably larger, although a young one or a female may be much smaller than a really big black. The average weight of adult grizzlies ranges from two hundred pounds up to about seven hundred. Now and then an individual tops one thousand, but grizzlies of that size (excluding their next of kin, the Alaska brown) are rare in the extreme. Art Young, the pioneer bowhunter, killed one in Yellowstone Park in May of 1920 that tipped the scales at 916 pounds. That bear was spring-lean and drained of blood when weighed piece by piece. Young's hunting partner, Saxton Pope, thought it would have weighed above fourteen hundred when larded with a heavy layer of autumn fat. If that was an accurate estimate, it may have been the heaviest grizzly ever taken by a hunter.

Female grizzlies average much smaller than males, and in general even the big ones weigh far less than hunters think. Many a hunter has killed what he believed to be a thousand-pounder, only to learn later that it weighed hardly more than half that. It was not uncommon for old hunters a century ago to tell of killing grizzlies that weighed one thousand to twelve hundred pounds, but wildlife authorities today doubt that such bears were put on a scale. As a zoo director once remarked, few grizzlies of record weight come from a part of the country where accurate scales are found.

With grizzlies as with blacks, most hunters measure the size of a bear by weight and pelt. But the Boone and Crockett Club, which compiles and keeps records of all North American trophy game, uses an entirely different yardstick. On the Boone and Crockett record list, skull size alone is the governing factor.

The grizzly that stands in No. 1 place in the 1971 edition of the club's book of records, the most recent published, had a skull $17^6/_{16}$ inches long and $9^{12}/_{16}$ wide, adding up to a total score of $27^2/_{16}$. That skull was picked up in the Bella Coola Valley of British Columbia in 1970.

No. 2 on the list was killed that same year at Alexis Creek, also in British Columbia, by a hunter named Edmon. The skull measured $17^1/_{16}$ by 10 inches, for a score of $27^1/_{16}$.

The No. 3 grizzly was a bear I happened to know something about. It was shot in 1965 by Jack Turner of Lonesome Lake, British Columbia, and with a score of $26^{10}/_{16}$ it stood for a time in top place.

About a year after Turner shot it, I visited him at his isolated home in the mountains and heard his story of the kill.

Jack, his wife Trudy and their daughter Susan, eight at the time, were living in the most remote location I have ever seen, a homestead on the Atnarko River two miles above Lonesome Lake, twenty-five miles by foot trail from the nearest road, seventy-five from Bella Coola, with only one other family within twenty miles of their place. They were earning most of their living by packing in grain in late summer and winter-feeding a flock of trumpeter swans at the head of the lake, a job they did under contract with the Canadian Wildlife Service.

They raised their own beef, kept hens, grew a garden, and relied largely on moose, deer, and trout for meat. Their food costs ran only $100 a year. Jack killed a cougar as often as he got the chance, mostly because they liked the meat, which they told me tasted like pork. Once a month he hiked out to the road for mail. That was almost their only contact with the outside world. It was an extremely lonely life, but they had a pleasant and comfortable log house and a good log barn and outbuildings. Jack and Trudy loved the wilderness, and the whole family seemed entirely happy.

They also had a heavy log fence around their clearing, to exclude moose and deer, and in the somewhat vain hope of keeping out grizzlies as well. The mountains along the Atnarko were prime grizzly country, and when the salmon runs began in the autumn the bears came down to the valley for the fishing. Jack had once counted ten adult grizzlies and five cubs along the river in a single day, and he said there were at least ten or a dozen of the bears hanging around within a few miles of the Turner house from September into December.

They had raided the garden, prevented the Turners from getting into the house and challenged the family on the trail. Jack had had to shoot two or three that wanted to pick a serious fight, and he had made it a rule never to go beyond his home clearing without hanging a battered old .30/30 Winchester over his shoulder on a length of nylon cord. The rule proved a wise one on the May morning in 1965 when he killed the record grizzly.

He started up the Atnarko that morning to repair a log fence, carrying an ax, and with the rifle hung over a shoulder. About two miles from the house the riverside trail he was following led through a small opening in the timber. Jack stepped into the clearing, and standing in the middle of it was the biggest grizzly he had ever laid eyes on.

He had seen more than two hundred of these bears in various parts of British Columbia, but never one that came close to matching the huge animal staring at him just forty feet away.

It came for him in a headlong rush the instant he saw it. He whipped the .30/30 off his shoulder, levered a shell into the chamber and drove his shot home, all in one swift motion.

The 170-grain softpoint hit the grizzly between the eyes and blew its brains out through a hole in the back of the head. The bear hit the ground stone dead, its muzzle just two paces from where Turner had stood when he fired the shot.

Despite some difficulties in measuring the skull accurately because of bullet damage, that bear went on the Boone and Crockett list as a new world record, a place it held for five years. Jack Turner had shot the biggest grizzly ever taken up to that time, when it was three feet from the muzzle of his gun and coming in a kill-or-be-killed charge.

Whatever he weighs, the grizzly is a low-slung, thickset and very muscular animal. His legs are short and stout, strong almost beyond belief. His heavy head is supported by a burly neck thicker than the width of his skull, and the whole impression he creates is one of great power.

He lives up to his appearance, too, and his strength is hard to believe. The early records tell of grizzlies dragging off the carcass of a full-grown buffalo bull. He handles a domestic steer, a dead moose or bull elk with no difficulty. I know of one case where a bear took a four-hundred-pound elk up and around a steep mountain for a quarter mile and finally dragged it through a series of rough washes before stopping to feed. Four or five men could hardly have duplicated that feat of strength.

In the early days in California, when fights were staged between captured grizzlies and bulls, the bear commonly waited as the bull came for him and smashed its skull or broke its neck with one blow of a forepaw. One account reported a grizzly that killed six bulls in a single afternoon, one after another.

For all his bulk, this bear can move with catlike quickness, and over a short distance it takes a fast horse to stay ahead of him, especially on the rough ground where he is most commonly encountered. In the old days in the West, Indian ponies weakened by the hardships of winter were a regular prey of grizzlies.

In addition to his greater size, the grizzly differs from the black bear in a number of ways that make him easy to identify. He has a longer head, which shows some resemblance to that of an overgrown dog. His forehead is high, his face concave, giving him a dished profile. He has a pronounced hump over the back between the shoulders, and the claws on his front feet are long and prominent, only slightly curved, perfect tools for digging out ground squirrels, something he is surprisingly fond of doing. A five-hundred-pound bear will spend half an hour moving rocks and digging for a squirrel that could be sent through the mail for a few cents. It seems doubtful that he even tastes it as he crunches and swallows it, but I suppose the same question could be raised about a human who gulps down a raw oyster.

Like the black, the grizzly varies widely in color, ranging from yellowish blond through dark brown to almost black. But on most of these bears, light or dark, the outer fur is frosted with silver, accounting for the name of silvertip by which the grizzly is often known.

Between the grizzly and black, incidentally, there exists an implacable but somewhat one-sided feud. One-sided in the sense that the black never pushes

hostilities to a showdown. If a grizzly shows up in his immediate neighborhood, he simply clears out.

In Yellowstone and Glacier National Parks, until a few years ago it was official practice to entice bears in to garbage dumps close to lodges and camp-grounds, as a tourist attraction. The nightly feeding-the-bears performance was a very popular show. The practice was abandoned after a number of cases of tragic attack on humans by garbage-dump grizzlies convinced park officials of the great danger involved in encouraging grizzly-human contact. But while the feeding was done, it was common for black bears to come to the garbage earlier in the evening than grizzlies.

As long as they had things to themselves, the blacks fed contentedly. But when the first grizzly came swaggering down a bear trail every black made himself scarce. They put up no argument, showed no evidence of the resentment they probably felt. The grizzly was boss, and they had no desire to incur his wrath by questioning his authority. If necessary, the black climbs a tree to get safely beyond reach of his enemy.

Despite their marked differences in appearance, it happens now and then under field conditions that a hunter is unable to tell whether a bear is a black or a grizzly until the last minute.

Alexie Pitka, the Alaskan Indian whose mauling by a black bear I described in an earlier chapter, believed he was going after a grizzly, something Indians are not much inclined to do. Not until he was within gun range did he discover that he was stalking a big black instead.

It was a similar case of mistaken identity in reverse that put my friend Fred Bear, head of the Bear Archery Company at Grayling, Michigan, in a very tough spot.

Fred, who rates as one of the foremost bowhunters of his generation, was on a hunting trip in the Yukon with a partner and two guides. At a lunch stop beside a small glacial creek, on a rainy day, one of the guides spotted a bear on the side of a mountain half a mile away. He picked up his glasses, took a quick look and pronounced it a black.

Neither Fred nor his partner, Judd Grindell, had any plans to hunt black bear, but this one was big enough to be a good trophy. When the party rode within a quarter mile of the place where they had seen the bear, after they left the creek, he decided to go after it.

He and Grindell climbed off their horses, shed their rain gear and chaps and started up the ridge with their bows. The two guides stayed in the saddle, grin-ning. This was a stalk on which even bowhunting clients did not need to be backed with a rifle. For the same reason, Fred left his .44 Magnum Smith and Wesson, the hand-gun he had along for emergencies, hanging on his saddle horn.

The next thing he saw of the bear, he rounded a low knoll and it was digging for a marmot on a treeless slope a hundred yards ahead. Its front legs were down in the hole it was excavating and its rump was toward Fred. He crouched low and crept up behind a small boulder just twenty-five yards from it. When he raised up on one knee behind the boulder he had a razorhead arrow on the string of his sixty-five-pound bow, ready for the shot.

But before he could draw, the bear jerked its head around his way, watching for the marmot, and Fred was looking into the grizzled, dished face of a grizzly at seventy-five feet!

He had dreamed for years of killing a grizzly with an arrow. He wanted a bear of that kind more than anything else on this Yukon hunt. If he took one he'd be the first to do it that way, so far as he knew, since the pioneer archers, Art Young and Saxton Pope, accomplished it in Yellowstone in the early 1920s, hunting down a big troublemaking grizzly under permit.

But Fred had never intended to tackle a grizzly with a bow without a rifleman behind him. He had plenty of confidence in the killing power of a properly placed arrow, but he also knew that no arrow was going to kill a grizzly in its tracks. He had made careful plans with his guide to back him with a .30/06 any time he got close to a bear—but now the guide was sitting on his horse, out of sight on the other side of the creek, and Fred's .44 Magnum was back there with him.

Fred was facing a lot more than he had bargained for, but he was also confronting an opportunity that, more than anything else, had lured him on this hunt. He took only three or four seconds to make up his mind. If he wounded the bear and it came for him, he'd count on dodging it long enough to get in a second arrow.

The shot was an easy one. The bear's head jerked around at the noise of the bowstring, and in that same instant the razorhead knifed into his rib section. It went all the way through, sliced off a rib, cut through lungs, liver, and intestines, and came out of the far side.

The bear bit at his side, then swiveled around and came for the man, growling and bawling. Charging or badly hurt and running blind? Fred never knew. In either case he was covering ground a lot faster than Fred had thought possible. But when he still had a dozen yards to come he swerved and went out of sight over the ridge. Judd Grindell saw him come down on the other side. In all, he ran eighty yards, spun around two or three times and fell dead.

Fred had his grizzly. But he had taken it under circumstances that he admitted afterward he would not recommend to any hunter.

Stranger than the occasional failure of a hunter to tell which bear he is stalking is the fact that even after he kills it he sometimes mistakes a black for a grizzly.

Present hunting regulations in Alaska require that all grizzly pelts must be presented to an officer of the Department of Fish and Game for sealing. Not infrequently a hunter, even one handled by a professional guide, brings in a black bear pelt of smallish or medium size in the belief that he has taken a grizzly. One Alaska game biologist has investigated two dozen such cases.

Are these instances of honest misidentification on the part of both hunter and guide, or of an unscrupulous guide convincing a client that he has taken a better trophy than is the case? No one can say.

THIRTEEN

The Winter Den, the Birthing, and His Food

The winter den of the grizzly may be in a convenient cavern, beneath the arching roots of a big tree, or under an upturned stump. Probably more often than he finds a natural hole of the kind that suits him, however, this bear digs his own, with a tunnel or entrance opening into a roomy chamber. His long front claws equip him to dig like a power shovel in fur, and the excavation of a den that meets his winter needs is no problem. Usually he finishes the job by carrying in branches, dry grass, or leaves to make a bed.

The length of time he spends in winter quarters depends on weather conditions, food supply, and the individual bear. Alaska game men say that in the interior of that state and in the mountains of northern Canada, where the winters are long and severe, grizzlies are in the torpor of ursine hibernation about six months of the year, denning in October and coming out in April or early May.

This bear appears prone to den later in the autumn than black bears in the same country, and also to emerge earlier in spring. Often he tunnels through snow to leave his den.

His winter sleep is not always continuous, either. A spell of warm weather in midwinter, especially if it causes melting snow to flood the den, is likely to rout the bear out for a short time. And there is some reason to believe that an occasional male may not den at all.

It was a maverick of that sort, prowling in January, when there was almost a foot of snow on the ground and temperatures were below zero, that accounted for a shocking case of man killing in the Dawson Creek area of British Columbia in 1970.

Beaver Indians on the Doig River Reserve north of Fort St. John found the bear's tracks while running their trapline, and Harvey Cardinal, a Beaver from another reserve nearby, undertook to hunt the animal down for the sake of its pelt, which he thought would be worth around $150.

119

He took the track and followed it into thick cover. The details of what happened were never known, but apparently the bear had lain in ambush near its track, let the man walk past, and then rushed and killed him in a surprise attack from behind. He had not had time to free his hands of the mittens he was wearing or release the safety on his rifle. The bear had shattered his skull with a murderous blow of a forepaw. Officers who investigated suspected the man had not seen the animal or felt the blow that killed him.

The victim's clothing was torn to shreds, the snow around packed down and bloodstained, and much of the man's upper body had been devoured. In all likelihood this winter-roaming grizzly had killed out of extreme hunger.

The bear left the area after officers recovered the body. Trailed eight miles by helicopter, he took shelter in a dense stand of timber but was flushed out and destroyed from the air.

The breeding season of the grizzly runs from late May into July, and once a male finds a receptive female he may stay with her for three or four weeks. Sometimes two males court her simultaneously. That is the only time when mature grizzlies display much inclination to live in close association with others of their own kind. They are mostly solitary animals, but a honeymooning pair is often surprisingly affectionate, feeding together, hugging one another, wrestling and rolling like overgrown cubs.

In marked contrast, there is very little affection between the sexes except in breeding season. Females with cubs either clear out if a male comes along or warn him away with angry growling. And in turn, the male displays scant liking for female company.

Researchers in Alaska, carrying out a study of North Slope grizzlies in 1973, recorded an extraordinary instance of a male making a deliberate and unprovoked attack on a small female and killing her in a savage fight. The male weighed an estimated 600 pounds, his victim around 225. The encounter took place in September, when the ground was snow covered, and the tracks told the story.

The boar, walking along the crest of a ridge, had changed direction when he was seventy-five feet from the sow, approached her obliquely to within fifteen feet and then rushed her. They had fought for thirty yards down the slope of the ridge before he killed her by inflicting deep wounds in her back and breaking her neck. He had then dragged her downhill another forty yards, but had not fed on her.

The male was immobilized from the air with a dart gun the next day, and examined. He had suffered no wounds in the fight.

Young grizzlies, commonly two or three in number, sometimes only one, very rarely four, are born in January or February while the mother is in winter quarters, in the semi-torpor of bear hibernation.

As is the case with all bears, the little grizzly comes into the world astonishingly small in comparison with the size of the mother. Cubs born to a female weighing three hundred to five hundred pounds will be smaller than a half-grown cottontail, with a weight of less than a pound.

Without food or water for herself, the mother suckles the cubs until she is ready to lead them out of the den, when the warm days of spring have melted the snow on the south slopes of the high country and uncovered a supply of grass, sedge, roots, and other springtime food.

Born almost hairless and with their eyes closed, the little bears grow fast. By the time they leave the den they have reached a weight of ten to fifteen pounds, and in midsummer they weigh double that. As one Alaskan authority comments, the birth and early life of a bear is one of nature's most remarkable phenomena.

Like all young bears, the cubs stay with the mother until their second or even third summer. That is a way of life that has developed over the long evolutionary history of the animals, to avoid dangerous and even fatal family complications. The cubs are barely self-sufficient at the end of their first summer, so the sow takes them with her into her winter den. If she had bred in June (something she does only every two or three years), the new family would arrive in the presence of the year-old young, and almost certainly there would be trouble.

When it comes to a food list, the grizzly's is at least as long as that of the black bear, although there are some items of the black's diet, such as grain and apples and other cultivated fruit, that are not found in the wilder country where the grizzly roams. In turn, he compensates by feeding frequently on fish, something that blacks do not show a great deal of interest in. The silvertip bear is not as dedicated and persistent a fisherman as his next of kin, the Alaska brown, but he relies heavily on fish wherever and whenever he can get them, especially along the salmon streams of western Canada and Alaska.

Although he is considered basically a carnivore (a trait that has brought him into endless conflict with man), the grizzly eats vegetable food at least as often as meat, in some cases more often.

When other groceries are scarce, he digs roots or grazes on grass, sedges, and forbs. He digs for ground squirrels and marmots, and even for badgers. He tears logs apart for ants and grubs, feasts on wild bee colonies and their honey as often as he has the chance, and does not hesitate to raid the nest of the dreaded yellowjacket hornet. He devours any small animal he can catch. Now and then he makes the mistake that is made occasionally by just about every wild carnivore on this continent and attacks a porcupine. Almost unfailingly, the result shows in a bear face and forearms stuck full of quills.

The grizzly eats frogs, turtles, lizards and snakes whenever he comes across them. One thing I'd like to know but have not been able to learn. Does he also eat toads?

The skin of a toad gives off an acid secretion that few animals are willing to tolerate. Snakes swallow them with no hesitation, especially the hognose snake, to which they are the staff of life. But I have seen half-starved Indian sled dogs in the North, hungry enough to eat a boot or piece of harness if it was left within their reach, prowl a river bank where the grass was alive with toads, paying the warty amphibians not the slightest attention. They knew better. Does the omnivorous grizzly share that distaste? I doubt that anyone knows.

When wild plums, wild cherries, blueberries, crowberries, and other wild fruit ripens in summer, he turns in large measure to a fruit diet. He has been known to leave a salmon stream for the berry patches. He is not fastidious about gathering his berries, either. He rakes off and swallows fruit, leaves, and twigs with equal relish.

Another of his favorite foods is carrion. He eats it as often as he finds it, and if he kills an animal too big to be consumed in a day or two he is almost sure to stay nearby, guard it and return to it to feed as long as it lasts, no matter how ripe it may become. While he feeds he lies on it and soaks the stench into his fur and skin, too. Men mauled by a grizzly often remember more vividly than anything else about the ordeal the terrible carrion smell of the bear and its breath.

Given his arrogance toward man, the innate propensity for devilment common to all bears, and an insatiable appetite for anything edible (and for some things that aren't, such as soap, tooth paste, and the down stuffing of sleeping bags), it is inevitable that the grizzly should break into isolated cabins if the opportunity presents itself.

Leon Copenhaver, a Montana guide, described the consequences to me many years ago, as eloquently as I have ever heard them cited. Not long before, he and his brother Wendell had ridden to an unoccupied forest ranger cabin on the North Fork of the Blackfoot River, intending to camp there overnight. Bears had been ahead of them.

"That cabin was the worst sight I ever laid eyes on," Leon said. "The rangers had left wooden shutters nailed over the windows, but that hadn't delayed things long. One of the shutters had been ripped from its hinges and the window smashed out, and every other window in the cabin was broken.

"The floor looked as if it was covered with snow, but it wasn't snow. It was flour, scattered from one end of the room to the other. The stove had been overturned and the cupboards torn down. Cans were strewn all over the place, dented and punctured by bear teeth, most of the contents either sucked out or drained out and lapped up. There was even a DDT bomb opened that same way.

"Unless you have seen a cabin that has been worked over by bears, it's hard to imagine the wreckage they leave behind. That one was a combination of damaged cans and broken glass, flour and syrup, beans and prunes, all scrambled together as if a tornado had gone through. I'm still sorry we weren't there to hear what the rangers said when they rode in and got a look at the mess."

Grizzly vandalism of a slightly different brand, but fully as hard to put up with, overtook an outfitting team, Louis Brown and his wife Dolores, in the Yukon some years ago.

At the end of their fall hunting season they had packed their camp gear and nonperishable grub in steel drums and left everything cached in a grassy basin beside a big wilderness lake. They were guilty of one oversight. The guide who finished the job failed to wire the lids down and chain the drums together. Probably it wouldn't have made much difference.

When the Browns rode into the basin for their first hunt of the year the following August, they found the place strewn with ripped canvas, chewed cooking pots, demolished cupboards, broken dishes, and shredded cartons. Nothing remained of the supplies. Three grizzlies had come along and done a 100 percent job of wrecking the cache and everything in it.

Louis and Dolores swung down from their horses to survey the ruins. He picked up a rolled cook tent, torn completely in two. She shoved a fist through a hole in the bottom of her favorite roasting pan. The stove top had been torn into strips. The cupboards were fit only for firewood, and the metal cannisters that had held sugar, salt or butter had been chewed until they looked like oversized wads of gum.

"I hope the bear that ate the dehydrated potatoes drank so much water he burst!" Dolores growled with deep feeling.

Because of the bear's own revolting food habits, I doubt that one present-day hunter in a thousand could be persuaded to try grizzly meat. But the old-timers relished it, especially that of a young bear, and even ascribed to it certain special, almost magic, properties.

John Muir told of an old hunter who contended that it was the best meat in the mountains, adding the claim that grizzly grease was better than butter.

"Biscuit shortened with it go as far as beans," that authority said. "A man can walk all day on a couple of them biscuit."

Any suggestion of making a meal of grizzly meat reminds me of the time I asked a hunter in the southern mountains whether he liked possum.

"I don't rightly cotton to it," he replied. "In the winter there's nothing a possum likes better than to find a dead horse or cow left out in the field, crawl inside the carcass and stay till spring. I've kicked half a dozen of 'em out of one dead horse. Ever since I found out about that I don't have no appetite for possum meat."

There is another sound reason for avoiding grizzly meat. In Alaska, scientific studies indicate that something like half of these bears are infected with trichinae, the parasite that causes trichinosis in humans. The bears themselves do not seem to be much harmed by the parasites, but there have been several recorded instances of humans contracting trichinosis from eating grizzly flesh. Thorough cooking removes the danger, of course, but all things considered, it's one wild meat that I prefer to pass up.

The grizzly is not rated a major predator on other big-game animals, not because he wouldn't like to be but because he is not too often successful in catching them. He is too large for stealthy stalking, and lacks the skill and shadow-like furtiveness of the mountain lion. Now and then he does kill a full-grown deer, elk, or moose, either when he encounters one that is old and weakened, or by creeping close enough for a short, fast rush or lying in ambush.

A Colorado rancher told me years ago of seeing a grizzly hide behind a rock where cattle passed on the way to water, wait for an hour until an unsuspecting cow came along, and then leap out and kill her almost before she knew what was happening. It has to be assumed that the same thing sometimes happens with wild prey.

Now and then this bear develops a marked liking for elk or moose, and sets out to make a career of gratifying his appetite.

Hunting in the north of Yukon Territory with his son and two Cree guides in the fall of 1973, Bob Pagel, a sportsman from suburban Milwaukee, camped in an area that had been closed to nonresidents until three years before. Moose were plentiful and extraordinarily tame. Many stood and watched with no show of fear when Pagel rode close to take pictures. Those that moved out left at an unhurried trot, and the hunters and guides concluded that they had never seen men on horseback before.

Then the hunting party rode into a valley where the reverse was true. All the cow moose they encountered were spooky in the extreme, and one even threatened the men with half-hearted charges. In a lifetime of big-game hunting, Pagel had seen no behavior like it, and the Crees were completely at a loss for an explanation.

Then, riding a gravel bar, the hunters saw a yearling cow moose crash out of thick brush just ahead and race across the river with water flying. Thinking wolves were after her, Pagel jumped off his horse, yanked his rifle out of the saddle boot and dropped prone, ready for a shot.

To the amazement of everybody, a dark grizzly came tearing out of the brush on the heels of the moose. He was running hard, with his head down, so intent on the chase that he did not appear even to see the hunters and horses. Bob killed him with one shot.

The two guides were in complete agreement now as to the reason for the strange behavior of cow moose in that particular valley. They believed this bear had taken to preying on moose calves, hunting them with such deadly determination that every cow with young had grown afraid of anything that moved, bears, men or horses.

Before the days of settlement in the West, buffalo were a major prey of the grizzly. When cattle and sheep replaced the vast bison herds, it was a short and logical step for the bear to turn to them. Many individual bears became persistent stock killers and did enough damage to bring down the wrath of ranchers on the whole grizzly tribe.

In the summer of 1923, for example, on the Okanogan Forest Reserve in Washington, a grizzly gained considerable local fame by killing 35 cattle and 150 sheep in a few weeks. Livestock owners finally called in a hunter with trained dogs, and the bear was killed. Reportedly it weighed more than 1,100 pounds.

As an inevitable result of their depredations on livestock, grizzlies were classed as predators, hunted the year around, taken in bear traps that weighed up to seventy-five pounds, poisoned, and in many cases bounties were paid on them. Today, wherever he is found, the grizzly has been given protection as a game animal, but there are still times and places where he takes a heavy toll of sheep and cattle, and stockmen and predator-control officers still kill him on occasion.

One thing that the black bear does quite frequently the grizzly does very rarely. That is to kill domestic hogs, the reason probably being that the humpback bear is not much given to prowling close to farm buildings, where swine are kept.

Occasionally a horse falls victim to this bear, usually a young colt. Adult horses, for the most part, are too hard for the grizzly to catch.

Although he is a tireless traveler, spending much of his life apart from the months of winter sleep in an endless search for food, the grizzly does have a fixed home range and for the most part he keeps to it. It varies in size with the terrain, food supply and local conditions, but on the average is rarely more than twenty-five miles across.

A study in Alaska in the summer of 1973 showed that males roam far more widely than females. Of twenty-nine North Slope grizzlies, nineteen males and ten females, kept under aerial observation, it was a male that traveled the longest distance, forty-eight airline miles. How far he wandered on the way will never be known.

By comparison, the females were stay-at-homes. None of the ten got farther than seventeen miles from the point of first capture.

Much of the wandering was seasonal, depending on where food was available. There was also considerable travel in connection with winter denning. One male walked forty-two miles to find a den site that suited him, another thirty-six miles.

The most amusing record to come out of the study was that of a nineteen-year-old boar that was observed six times between May 10 and 26, in an area no more than twelve miles from the place where he had been captured and marked—but was next sighted on June 17, thirty-nine miles away, going steady with a four-year-old female who, incidentally, in the course of the summer was never seen farther than nine miles from the point of her original capture.

But just by way of proving that amorous male grizzlies are not alone in wandering afield in search of romance, a female in that same study, captured and marked at the end of April, was sighted at the end of June, seventeen miles away (the study record for feminine bear travel), keeping company with two adult males.

Even among bears, love exerts a strong influence.

The hunters saw a yearling cow moose crash out of thick brush just ahead and race across the river with water flying . . . and then a dark grizzly came tearing out of the brush on the heels of the moose.

FOURTEEN

His Numbers and His Future

So far as I know, no one has ever undertaken to make any estimate of the number of grizzlies that roamed the western wilderness of this continent when the first trappers and fur traders pushed up the Missouri into grizzly country early in the 1800s.

The range of the humpback bear at that time extended into central Mexico in the south, north to the arctic tundra beyond the Brooks Mountains of Alaska. On the west it reached the Pacific coast of what is now California and British Columbia, eastward it reached out to the Black Hills, and beyond the mountains across the buffalo plains of Nebraska, the Dakotas, and Saskatchewan. In the far north of Canada it extended from the Yukon east almost to Hudson Bay.

Over that vast tract of wild country, did grizzly numbers average one bear for every ten square miles? For every twenty? For every hundred? No man can say. But the records of the early explorers and mountain men clearly indicate a big and thriving population of the silvertip bear.

When Lewis and Clark made their epic journey up the Missouri in the summer of 1804 they found grizzlies so numerous in the vicinity of what is now Great Falls, Montana (probably lured there by the abundance of dead buffalo drowned or killed in falling over the cut banks), and so quarrelsome, that the leaders of the expedition did not think it prudent to send one of their men alone on an errand of any kind.

The old journals tell of seeing ten or a dozen grizzlies a day, day after day, as the mountain men traveled through grizzly country. One report has it that in the early years in California it was not unusual to sight as many as thirty to forty in a day. In what is now Yosemite National Park, in the 1860s a hunter killed forty-nine of these bears in less than a decade. Seton quotes two old hunters, one of whom told of grizzlies in the Black Hills "in bands like buffalo," the other saying that up to about 1880 they were one of the animals most frequently seen in the mountains of the West. As recently as the early 1900s it was not unheard of to sight as many as fifteen to twenty a day in the Yukon. Added together, the evidence of grizzly abundance is clear. But whatever his primitive numbers, the ranks of the humpback bear shrank rapidly once white settlement started to encroach on the wilderness where he was found.

From the beginning every man's hand was against him. For one reason, he posed a genuine threat to any human who encountered him. For another, as the buffalo and other wild game animals that were his natural prey were reduced in numbers, he turned more and more often to cattle and sheep. Over all of his early range south of Canada he incurred the undying hatred of stockmen. All-out war was waged on him with guns, traps, and even poison. He was also a trophy much sought after by hunters. And he was one animal that never signed a peace treaty with his human enemies. Often, if they did not carry the war to him he took it to them.

He did grow somewhat more wary in the face of modern firearms than he had been when the Indians hunted him with arrows and lances (in part for the makings of the highly coveted grizzly-claw necklace), but he never really mastered the lessons of fear and caution. All in all, his decline to extinction or the threshold of it, in many places where he was once abundant, was inevitable. On top of the deliberate reduction of his numbers by trappers and hunters, the settlement of the West left him in large part without the wild-country habitat he required. It is logical to believe that there would be few grizzlies left today in the southern half of their original range if no bear traps had ever been set or no shot ever fired at one.

South of the Canadian border now, this bear exists only as a remnant species, found chiefly in Yellowstone and Glacier National Parks. The U. S. Fish and Wildlife Service has classified the grizzly as a "threatened" species. He is no longer hunted save for a very limited open season in Montana. Even that is under fire by those who do not believe that the remaining grizzly population can tolerate any hunting at all.

Any attempt to estimate, or even make a rough guess of, the present grizzly population is bound to end in almost total frustration.

When I began work on this book, I contacted the game departments of the four states and four Canadian provinces that still have grizzlies. They are Montana, Wyoming, Idaho, and Alaska (the latter holds a major share of the continent's remaining population); Alberta, British Columbia, Yukon, and Northwest Territories. In each case I asked for an estimate of the bear's numbers, records of the annual kill by hunters, and an appraisal of what the future holds for the grizzly.

I also went to the U. S. National Park Service and the Canadian Wildlife Service in an effort to learn how many of the bears are presently found in the western national parks of both countries. Finally I asked the Washington-based National Wildlife Federation and Wildlife Management Institute, two of the leading conservation organizations in the United States, for any estimates on grizzly numbers they could supply. Very little solid information resulted, for the reason that nobody knows how many grizzlies are left or how to take anything like a reliable count of them.

Nobody described the over-all situation better than Tom Kimball, executive director of the National Wildlife Federation.

"Accurate population determinations are extremely difficult if not impossible to obtain," Kimball told me. "Grizzly estimates are often inaccurate, and have recently been the center of much controversy."

He went on to quote a 1975 report of the Fish and Wildlife Service which stated, "There are several hundred grizzlies in the United States south of Canada, but their range has been reduced to the point where virtually all occur in three relatively small ecosystems: The Selway-Bitterroot in Idaho and Montana; the Yellowstone; and the Bob Marshall in Montana. These ecosystems are composed mostly of federal lands."

Kimball next quoted from a 1974 report of the Montana Forest and Conservation Experiment Station which said, "There is considerable evidence that grizzly bears may no longer exist in the Selway-Bitterroot Wilderness Area." The contradiction here is typical.

The Bob Marshall Wilderness Area probably contains the largest of the three grizzly populations, Kimball believes, but he added, "I will not estimate its size."

He pointed out that one scientific report, published in 1974, indicated that Glacier National Park supported no grizzlies at all, but this is certainly not true.

The Wildlife Management Institute, citing recent reports from the U.S. Forest Service, National Park Service, Fish and Wildlife Service, and the state of Montana, estimated the grizzly population south of Canada at a minimum of 764, a maximum of 1,075.

A writer for the National Audubon Society in 1975 fixed even broader limits, saying that at most there are only about 1,300 of the bears left in the Lower 48 states, perhaps as few as 500, adding that most of those were in Glacier or Yellowstone Parks.

The National Park Service, commenting that grizzlies are difficult to count, says park naturalists believe there are some 275 now living in Yellowstone, 250 in Glacier. Outside the parks, Wyoming's game department told me that there is a wintering population of 80 grizzlies roaming seasonally over 1,900 square miles in the northwestern part of the state. They go unhunted now, although as recently as 1974 hunters killed seven in a year.

Bill Schneider of the Montana Department of Fish and Game, one of that state's leading authorities on grizzlies, in a letter in April of 1976, summed things up this way: "I understand your confusion over the number of grizzlies left south of Canada. Unfortunately, I can't give you any kind of accurate estimate. Dozens of authorities in the field hedge on this question."

"There are as many estimates as estimators," one authority told me. "About the only figure that nearly everyone will accept is fewer than 1,000 south of Canada."

Of that number probably more than half are found in Yellowstone and

Glacier, and Bill Schneider among others makes a sharp distinction between park and wild grizzlies.

"Yellowstone and Glacier boast of their grizzly numbers," he says, "but in both parks the bear dwells in an unnatural environment of roads, campgrounds, concessions, and dumps. By contrast, in the truly wild places of Montana's Shining Mountains—the Missions, the Cabinets, the Bob Marshall, and the Lincoln Scapegoat—this bear goes about its business of life in a free and untamed fashion, with a self-confidence matched by no other beast and few men."

Some have called the grizzly a pensioner in the unnatural environment of the national parks. On the other hand, many believe that is the only place where an attempt should be made to maintain him.

Range of the Grizzly Bear

"I'd like to have grizzlies around, but not around me," one Westerner said, voicing what is a fairly common feeling.

Moving north into the grizzly country of western Canada and Alaska, where the humpback bear still reigns as a king among the trophy game animals of North America, things are about as cloudy.

The Alberta Department of Lands and Forests, admitting that it has no reliable data, estimates its grizzly population at one thousand plus or minus. Hunters there kill only ten to twenty a year.

Biologists of the Fish and Wildlife Branch of British Columbia put the population of adult grizzlies in that province at approximately 6,500, but say frankly that that figure is only an estimate. A leaflet put out by the Fish and Wildlife Branch claims that "British Columbia and Yukon Territory hold practically all of North America's grizzly population," but that certainly is not true. In all likelihood, Alaska has more grizzlies than the two Canadian provinces together.

British Columbia game authorities told me that the number of the bears there is stable or decreasing slightly. In the ten years between 1965 and 1975, hunters took between 280 and 563 annually.

The superintendent of game in Northwest Territories, citing an annual kill of only about 45 bears, declined to make an estimate of their total numbers beyond "probably in the thousands."

The Game Department of Yukon Territory said simply, "We do not know how many grizzlies are found in the Yukon, but their number is at least 5,000 and may be as high as 10,000."

The nearest I came to concrete estimates for Canada were figures supplied by Dr. A. M. Pearson, research scientist of the Canadian Wildlife Service stationed at Edmonton, Alberta.

He told me: "The most recent information on grizzly populations in Canada outside the national parks is as follows:

Alberta—1,500 plus
British Columbia—6,000 to 8,000
Yukon Territory—10,000 to 15,000
Northwest Territories—3,000 to 5,000
"These are estimates," he added.

Alaska calls itself "the last great stronghold of this noble beast." Except in limited areas, the state believes its grizzlies are almost as abundant today as before settlement began, and says it may have a greater number than the rest of North America put together. But it makes no claim to knowing just how many.

Several attempts have been made in that state to find ways to count the grizzly and brown bear population. Methods tried have included track counts, aerial beach counts in spring, counts of spring bear trails in the snow of alpine areas, actual counts on foot in Mt. McKinley National Park, census taking with aircraft on Kodiak Island and the Alaska Peninsula.

In every case the project failed to yield reliable data, and today the Alaska Game Department is still unable to furnish any accurate figures on the number of grizzlies and browns found in the state.

However, Donald McKnight, research chief of the department's Division of Game, did come up with a rough estimate in reply to my question.

"Alaska makes no distinction between grizzly and brown bears, since they are of the same species," he told me. "In all likelihood, total statewide numbers of the two together exceed 15,000." That is as close as anyone comes to knowing the answer.

Between 1966 and 1975 the annual kill of grizzlies and browns by sport hunters in Alaska ranged from a low of 512 in 1969 to a high of 923 in 1973.

What of the future? If wildlife authorities are unable to make more than reasonable guesses as to grizzly populations, can they offer any firm opinions as to whether the bears are decreasing, holding their own, or increasing?

Here the situation is less foggy. Frequency of bear sightings, annual kill by hunters, and information turned up in various research programs all provide clues to the abundance or scarcity of bears in a given area from year to year.

Says Dr. A. M. Pearson of the Canadian Wildlife Service, "I am optimistic regarding the future of the grizzly in Canada. Enough is known regarding the ecology of these bears that the proper management programs can be carried out. It's simply a matter now of getting agencies which plan resource development to consult with the wildlife management agencies, so that we avoid conflicts between development and grizzly populations."

Any forecast about the future of the grizzly has to be made with one key factor in mind. It is an inescapable fact that he is not compatible with man. Where human populations and activities increase in wilderness country his numbers are sure to shrink, either through deliberate programs of attrition or because the bear himself cannot and will not tolerate human neighbors on a friendly footing.

In general, the game departments that still have sizable grizzly populations to protect and manage are guardedly optimistic. But in the same breath they admit that there are clouds on the horizon bigger than a man's hand, and without exception they agree on the basic threats that lie ahead.

For example, Alaska, which has more grizzlies than any other state or province; Yukon Territory, which has enough to supply excellent hunting; and Montana, which probably has fewer than 150 outside Glacier National Park (hunters took only thirteen there in 1975), all share essentially the same concerns where the future of this bear is concerned.

"The future of brown and grizzly bears is tied directly to one thing, maintenance of bear habitat," Don McKnight of the Alaska Department of Fish and Game told me.

"For this species, habitat is not only food, cover, and water—it also includes space in which the bears can avoid interaction with humans. While black bears seem to thrive in the presence of man, their bigger cousins for a variety of reasons don't fare well when they and man must get along on a regular basis.

"Brownies and grizzlies are aggressive defenders of their young and their food stockpiles, and apparently their fear of man is overcome by these behavioral responses. Because of this aggressiveness man is more prone to shoot first and ask questions afterward in any encounter. At the other extreme, he tends to regard the black bear as a clown.

"As long as we have substantial acreages that aren't crawling with loggers, bird watchers, petroleum engineers, and hikers, our big bears will make out all right. They seem able to convert most plant and animal matter to bear quite readily, and they are capable competitors with all other species but man. The number killed by hunters we can regulate. But we can't stop people from shooting 'charging' bears or depredating bears which are after their sheep, reindeer, or food."

"Since the hunting of bears can be curtailed whenever necessary, the future of the grizzly in the Yukon should look promising," says Dr. Manfred Hoefs, assistant director of the Yukon Territory Game Department. "There are, however, a number of other factors which may adversely affect grizzlies, over which we have no control nor can we predict them. These include the expansion of human population into wilderness areas, pipeline and road construction, and increased oil and mineral exploration activity with accompanying air travel in the back country."

In British Columbia the Fish and Wildlife Branch is moving away from autumn seasons to protect pregnant sows, and quotas for nonresident hunters loom in the future. Baiting is prohibited for both grizzly and black bears, and hunting regulations are fixed to maintain the present grizzly population. For the most part problem bears are captured and moved. Only notorious troublemakers are destroyed, when it becomes necessary to protect human life or livestock.

British Columbia authorities say they can easily control the grizzly kill, but the population has fallen in some areas in recent years because of rapid human expansion.

"Habitat deterioration presents more danger for these bears in the long run than a regulated harvest," Frank Tompa, problem wildlife coordinator for the province, told me.

Says the Montana Fish and Game Department, "The salvation of the grizzly lies in the protection of the wild lands that are the bear's habitat, not in silencing the hunter's gun."

Legal hunting is not endangering the grizzly in Montana. If there was the slightest indication that that were true, the department would be the first to propose closing the season. Habitat destruction and human encroachment are the most serious threats to this bear. Remote wild lands are the silvertip's last hope. Montana has such lands in its primitive areas, and for that reason it has grizzlies. If it can keep the primitive areas in their present condition, the bears will be around for a long time.

FIFTEEN

A Man Is Never Safe

On an August night in 1967, in Glacier National Park in northern Montana, two grizzlies wrote one of the most dreadful chapters in the annals of American wildlife, when they attacked and killed two college girls, in separate and unrelated incidents at park campgrounds ten miles apart. That the two attacks should have occurred the same night, in locations so close together, was a coincidence so remarkable that it was almost impossible to believe.

One of the girls was from Minnesota, a nineteen-year-old university sophomore working a summer job at Glacier Park Lodge. For that August weekend she made plans for an overnight hike to Granite Park Chalet, a remote lodge not reached by road. She would go with another college student, a boy from Ohio who was a busboy at the same place where she worked and whom she had dated a few times.

The two young people reached the chalet in the early evening. At dark they unrolled their sleeping bags, on the ground and in the open, at a campground a hundred yards from the lodge, and turned in.

The bear came in after midnight. Later events indicated that it was a 250-pound female. The girl awoke first, tugged her companion awake and whispered "Pretend you're dead." They had been warned earlier by park rangers to do that if a bear attacked them.

The boy opened his eyes, startled and half dazed, to see a burly shape standing over him, no more than a black shadow in the darkness. Then he smelled a horrible stench, half animal and half carrion, and something struck him a hard blow, rolling him clear of his bag.

The bear ripped his clothing and bit into his shoulder, arm, back and hips. Then it dropped him and turned on the girl. She cried out once, "It hurts!" and then began to scream as the bear dragged her into the brush.

Other campers signaled the chalet with flashlights, and a rescue party came down to the campground, carrying a washtub filled with burning wood for protection. There was no gun at the place.

The boy was carried up to the lodge and flown out to a hospital before daylight. The girl was found when her moans led the rescuers to her. She died of chest injuries about 4 o'clock in the morning.

In the meantime, the other chapter of the double tragedy was being played out at another remote campground, on Trout Lake ten miles away.

Five young people working in the park for the summer had gone there on a weekend hike. One of them was a girl attending college in California.

Before dark that night, they were threatened by an ill-tempered grizzly that had been making trouble for campers and fishermen for weeks, eating scraps, stealing fish, driving people off or treeing them if they tried to interfere.

Afraid to risk hiking back to the highway, five miles away, after darkness fell, the camping party built up a big fire, intending to keep it burning throughout the night. It proved no protection.

The grizzly prowled into the camping area after midnight and padded around the fire for two hours, making up its mind. The fire, burning brightly, had little effect on it. It grabbed one of the boys, tore his sweatshirt, dropped him and went for the California girl, held captive in her bag by a stuck zipper.

The other four members of the party scrambled to safety in trees. As the bear dragged the girl into the brush, they heard her scream, "Oh, my God, I'm dead!" Park rangers found her mutilated body a hundred yards from the campground the next morning.

The bear suspected of the mauling was shot two days later, and there was proof that it was the killer. At Granite Park three grizzlies were disposed of and park rangers believed they had liquidated the guilty bear, although they had no proof.

The double killings were the first in the history of Glacier, although by no means the first instances of attack. They made front-page headlines in metropolitan papers all across the United States and Canada.

As a staff editor on *Outdoor Life,* I worked for a month, with the cooperation of one of the survivors, putting together the detailed story of that terrible night.

Park officials were completely uncooperative, probably because they faced the almost certain likelihood of costly damage suits brought by the families of the victims. Park personnel clammed up, and in a telephone interview the superintendent of Glacier offered me the astonishing excuse that lightning, which had started several fires in the park that evening, had enraged the bears and caused them to attack. I was told later that his superiors in Washington complimented him for the originality of that ridiculous alibi. Actually both bears were park bums, used to feeding on garbage or scraps and lacking all normal fear of humans.

In the end, in deference to the wishes of the parents of the two girls, the story was never published. I have omitted here the names of the victims for that same reason. The story was one that both I and my editor, Bill Rae, were sorry to lose, too, in part because it carried a clear and sorely needed warning of the danger that lurks wherever grizzlies are found.

Nine years later, in September of 1976, there was another fatal grizzly attack in Glacier National Park, again totally unprovoked.

Once more the victim was a college girl, twenty-two-year-old Mary Pat Mahoney from the Chicago suburb of Highwood, a student at the University of Montana at Missoula.

Camping with four girl companions at the park's Many Glacier Campground, she was asleep in her tent when the bear struck, shortly after daylight. It ripped the tent open, seized the girl in her sleeping bag and dragged her outside.

The screams of the other girls in the tent aroused another camper nearby and he ran to the trailer occupied by park ranger Fred Reese to get help. Reese dressed and hurried to the scene. There he was joined by Stu Macy, a state park ranger from California who was camped nearby, and the two men began a search for Mary Mahoney's body.

Her bloodstained sleeping bag was found torn open about twenty-five feet from the collapsed tent. A bloody T-shirt lay not far away.

Reese and Macy followed a blood-marked trail into the woods for three hundred yards, and there they found the mutilated body. The bear had dragged its victim into a thicket and started to feed.

Reese gave Macy his handgun, a .357 Magnum, and left the California man to stand guard over the body. The grizzly showed up almost at once. The handgun failed to fire, and the bear's aggressive behavior sent Macy up a tree. His shouts brought two park rangers carrying 12-gauge shotguns loaded with slugs.

A shot knocked the bear down, but it escaped into the underbrush. Minutes later one of the rangers saw a grizzly head again and fired a second shot. Two young grizzlies, two-and-a-half years old, were found dead in the brush. There was human blood on their claws, and little question that one of them, at least, was the killer.

This was the third grizzly killing on the continent for the year. Earlier a man had been fatally attacked in Glacier Bay National Monument in Alaska, and a woman naturalist had died under a bear's claws in British Columbia's Glacier National Park.

U.S. Park Service officials called the Mahoney killing a baffling mystery. It was the first case on record of a bear attacking a human in a tent, one declared, something that was far from true.

A board of inquiry was convened to determine whether park authorities had been guilty of any violation of the park's bear management policy (established after the 1967 double killings) and whether the young women themselves had broken any rules. The board found the answer to be no in both cases.

The young women had taken every recommended precaution. They had been warned that perfume might trigger a grizzly attack, so they were using none. And to avoid the smell of meat around their tent they had even eaten a vegetarian meal the evening before the mauling.

"They did everything right," a member of the board of inquiry said. "I don't think anybody can explain the attack."

Actually there was very little mystery about it. The bear that mauled Mary Mahoney to death did exactly what any grizzly is likely to do, any place, any time and under any circumstances, especially if he is hungry.

Wild-animal apologists, the Park Service included, simply will not admit the truth, that the humpback bear is as dangerous as a hand grenade, and that every now and then one resorts deliberately to man-eating. After this attack one official even speculated about the possibility of training wilderness grizzlies to avoid humans, something that almost two hundred years of conflict with men armed with rifles has not accomplished.

I have never heard things summed up better than by Bruce Neal, a retired Montana game warden who had lived with these bears for all his seventy years and had dealt with them as a hunter, wrangler, packer, and government predator trapper. In his lifetime he had liquidated more than a score.

"A man is never safe for a minute in grizzly country," he told me flatly. "A lot of people think if they don't bother the bear it won't bother them. That's a rule that doesn't hold."

I met and talked with Neal when I went to Montana in 1962, to get from Dick Mosher, a rancher living near the sun-baked hamlet of Augusta on the eastern slope of the Rockies west of Great Falls, the story of the grizzly that had killed his sheep herder, Josif Chincisian, on a September night in 1947.

Camped in his herder's wagon on a bluff above Cunniff Creek, Chincisian, who had herded for Dick and his father for twenty-four years, heard a disturbance among his sheep. It came as no surprise. The two thousand animals in his charge had been moved out of the foothills twice in recent weeks, seeking a safer location after a grizzly started raiding them.

Chincisian did not live to tell precisely what happened, but as Mosher was able to piece the story together from the tracks and available evidence, the sixty-five-year-old herder, who had no fear of bears, had grabbed his battered .30/40 Krag when he heard the bear among the beeded sheep, and run out in the darkness of the cloudy night to kill it, leaving his two dogs in the wagon.

The grizzly was feeding on a sheep it had brained when Josif rounded a willow thicket and faced it at twenty feet. He fired one shot from the Krag but missed. Before he could bolt a second shell into the chamber the bear was on him. It tore most of his scalp away and broke his skull with a forepaw. Next it dragged him into a tangle of brush and raked leaves and rubbish over him as if it intended to return and feed.

Sometime after the bear left him the herder regained consciousness and staggered into a tumbledown homesteader's shack about a hundred feet away. He rested there, smearing the floor and bunk with blood, then made it up the bluff to his wagon. There he rested again, probably until the blood from his wounds clotted and dried.

Then he started the terrible journey to the nearest ranch house, a mile and a half away. He covered a mile before he fell unconscious. The rancher found him by accident. He did not speak a coherent word after that, and he died in a

Great Falls hospital ten days later. Every effort was made to track down and kill the bear, but Dick Mosher did not believe that happened.

After a couple of days Dick took me up into the Sun River country for an afternoon with Bruce Neal, who had investigated the killing of the herder. The old game warden had some good stories to tell, including one of the time he had set a trap for a prowling bear at his back door and caught his own big yellow tomcat.

"I had him by about two inches of the tip of his tail," Bruce chuckled, "and he was yowling and tearing around like a mountain lion. The trap was made for grizzlies and a man couldn't depress the two springs without the help of setting clamps. Every time I tried to put a clamp on a spring the cat took a swipe at me with both front feet. He gave me more trouble than any grizzly I ever caught, and that trap hasn't been set since."

Our talk turned to bear behavior in general, and it was then that the old warden summed up his opinion of the risk of grizzly attack on humans.

There are two situations in which such trouble is almost certain. One is a chance encounter with a sow that has cubs along. The other, equally dangerous, arises when a man blunders into a feeding bear or one that is guarding a supply of food.

A female bear of any species is extremely touchy where her young are concerned. Given the short temper of the grizzly and the arrogance most of them exhibit toward man, the human who intrudes on a family, even though he has no knowledge that there are bears in the neighborhood, is in deadly danger.

Hunting in British Columbia in 1961, Bob Munger, a sportsman from Charlotte, Michigan, who has taken exceptionally good brown and polar bears, and his partner, Dick Mauch, located a sow grizzly with three cubs. The men had no interest in shooting her, but did stalk her for pictures on two occasions, getting within twenty-five yards of the family before the old bear winded them and ran off. The next time they encountered her she ran in another direction.

They had gone fishing that day with their guide, Bill Love. Neither client was carrying a gun, but the guide had a .270 Winchester slung on his back.

Climbing a steep rocky slope with the guide in the lead, they heard a snarl behind them, followed by the sound of breaking brush. It was the sow grizzly, coming for them full tilt. The rough footing slowed her and Love just had time to whip the rifle off his back before she overtook them. He killed her with one shot at fifteen feet.

In 1968 a British Columbia rancher had the misfortune to meet a sow grizzly with a cub, and lost an eye when she came for him like a thunderbolt.

Then there was the attack a female grizzly made on Steve Rose and a partner and guide, in Alberta's Jasper National Park in May of that same year.

Rose and a friend, Dave Slutker, were on a spring fishing trip, guided by Leonard Jeck. Because they were in the park, they had no guns. They had tied their horses and gone on afoot, in an unfrequented area where there was no trail. In a stand of thick spruce Jeck came face to face with a sow bear with two cubs behind her, running full tilt.

The bear did not stop or even slow down. She grabbed the guide by the upper leg and kept running the way she was headed, taking him along. Next she fell to the ground with him, man and bear rolling over and over as he tried to fend her off with his bare hands.

Rose had scrambled fifteen feet up a scrubby timberline spruce. From his perch in the tree he yelled at the bear, hoping to draw her off the guide. She dropped Jeck and came for Steve instantly. The tree had thick branches all the way to the ground and she ascended them like ladder rungs, disproving once more the common belief that the grizzly never climbs.

When she was high enough she sank her teeth in Steve's leg, let go her hold in the tree and tumbled to the ground, taking him along. He had time to roll over on his belly, in an effort to protect his face. Then she was on top of him, tearing bites of flesh out of his legs, back and shoulders, even ripping away a section of shoulder blade.

Dave Slutker had been hiking on a ridge above timberline, five hundred yards away from the other two men, when the attack began. He now did a very brave thing. He grabbed up a chunk of wood for a club and raced down the ridge to take a hand.

The bear left Rose and ran to meet him. He swung his club without any effect and she knocked him to the ground with a murderous blow from a fore-paw. Either with claws or teeth she tore his face open from between his eyes down through the nose to the upper lip, leaving a jagged hole the size of an orange.

Next she lay down on Slutker, looking back at Rose and growling. But she broke off the fight as abruptly as she had started it, leaping suddenly to her feet and disappearing in the timber.

Horribly mauled and half blinded, the three men fought their way back to their horses, rode to their camp, and then Jeck went on to the nearest ranger station to break in and phone for help. All three were flown out by helicopter and rushed to the nearest hospital. They recovered but they will carry their scars to their graves.

"I can make one promise," Rose said afterward. "I'll never venture into grizzly country again without a gun. If I can't take the gun, I won't go."

The tree had thick branches all the way to the ground and she ascended them like ladder rungs, disproving once more the common belief that the grizzly never climbs.

The second surest way to get into an argument with the humpbacked bear is to come on him when he is feeding, or when he is watching food that he regards as his. It makes no real difference what the meal happens to be. It can be an elk he has bushwhacked on his own, the leavings of a moose you shot and dressed out a couple of days before, or a winter-killed whiteface steer. Once he finds it and lays claim to it he's not going to give it up without a fight and if you trespass he won't wait for you to start the trouble, either.

The first hunter who ever described an encounter of that kind to me was Father Herbert Winterhalter, a Catholic priest from Terre Haute, Indiana.

On a hunt in British Columbia in 1935, he killed a trophy goat and had to leave it in the woods overnight when darkness closed down as he and his guide finished dressing it. The next morning their horse wrangler, an old placer miner who had had considerable dealing with bears, rode out to pack the goat into camp. He came back empty-handed.

"A grizzly has got your goat, Father," he reported, "and as far as I'm concerned he can keep it."

Winterhalter and the guide hurried out to the place where they had left the billy. Tracks showed that a bear had dragged it up over a windfall and into a thicket of young pines. They followed very gingerly.

In the center of the thicket they came to a small opening, with a big log lying along one side. The instant the priest stepped into the clear a huge grizzly heaved up from behind the log fifteen feet away, and came roaring at him.

He drove a shot from his .30/06 into the bear's open mouth. It ranged the length of the body and tore the animal apart inside, killing instantly. But Father Winterhalter didn't wait to see what it had done. He and the guide had crawled and wormed into the pine tangle. They never knew how they got out, except that they made it like greased lightning. They went back the next morning, crept carefully into the thicket and found the grizzly dead three steps from where the shot had been fired.

Forest Young, an Alaskan hunter, suffered one of the worst bear maulings a man ever endured, under like circumstances. He and a partner had killed two moose, packed the meat and one hide to camp and left the second hide cached in a tree, out of the reach of bears. Forest went back alone the next morning to bring it in. He went light, with no gun.

Two grizzlies had claimed the moose entrails, raking moss and grass over them. One of the bears came for him instantly, pulled him out of a birch he tried to climb, and tore him from calf to shoulders, ripping the flesh free of the bones on the inside of his thighs, tearing a rib out and punching a hole into the chest cavity.

The pain was so dreadful that Young made a serious attempt to kill himself. Luckily he failed. His partner found him and went for help. More than twenty-four hours after the bear had grabbed him he went into surgery in a Juneau hospital. The surgeon had little hope he would live, but he left the hospital after two months, minus three ribs and badly scarred. Within a year he was back at his job as a construction worker.

So the record runs of grizzlies that attacked when a food supply was threatened. I could cite a dozen similar cases.

Finally, there are the grizzly attacks that cannot be accounted for, unprovoked and without warning, made for no apparent reason other than the fact that the bear and the man happen to be in the same neighborhood. Often the man is totally unaware of the bear's presence until it strikes.

The tree-climbing grizzly that attacked Napier Shelton, in the incident described in an earlier chapter, was a good example of that. So was the bear that came for a hunter in the Flathead National Forest in northwestern Montana. The man was walking a brush-grown skidding road with two partners when he heard a noise a few feet behind him and turned to see a shaggy boar grizzly bearing down.

It knocked him sprawling and went for his head and face. It was on him less than a minute before his companions killed it, but that was long enough for the hunter to suffer a savage working over.

Olive Fredrickson and her husband John carried on a running feud with a quarrelsome male grizzly that they named White-Ear, the summer they prospected for gold in the far north of British Columbia.

The bear started trouble by breaking into one of their cabins, eating their cache of dried fish and wrecking everything inside. Before it was finally killed at the end of the summer it had repeated that performance a couple of times, had jumped John for no reason when it discovered him panning for gold in a tiny creek, driving him into a nearby lake, went for a trapper it met on the trail, and finally came into the Fredrickson camp at first light one morning, deliberately looking for trouble. John accommodated it in a hurry.

One more unpleasant fact has to be added. The humpback bear not infrequently feeds on its human kill. The role of man-eater comes easily to him. His hate for man lies just below the surface and it takes little to drive him to insane rage. The human who ventures into his domain must take his own chances and accept the consequences, and they are likely to be dreadful in the extreme.

Many writers have made the statement that an adult grizzly cannot climb. They are much like the scientist who is supposed to have made elaborate calculations and announced that the bumblebee can't fly. The only trouble is that neither the bee nor the bear is aware of the rule.

I have never heard of a case where a grizzly climbed a tree that was free of low branches. As is commonly believed, the bear's long front claws, ideal for digging, apparently are too straight to get a grip on the trunk. But if a tree has branches growing close to the ground and a grizzly has reason to climb it, he goes up as surefooted and fast as a man on a ladder.

In the summer of 1961 Napier Shelton, a graduate student at Duke University in North Carolina, was carrying out botanical studies in Alaska's Mt. McKinley National Park when he was attacked by a grizzly. He had no warning the bear was in the neighborhood until it ripped out an angry snarl only a few steps behind him.

Shelton was boring a sample core from a scraggly timberline spruce to determine its age. He went up the tree like a red squirrel, and the bear climbed after him with deadly determination, growling like a dog in a fight and using the branches for ladder rungs. The man was ten feet off the ground when it grabbed him by the calf of one leg. Its teeth tore free and it fell from the tree.

Shelton scrambled higher and the grizzly followed him once more. Fifteen feet up, and almost at the top of the tree, it bit into his thigh, then lost its hold and dropped a second time. It prowled below him, snorting and snarling, but did not try to come up again. Finally it moved into the brush.

Shelton spent five days in a Fairbanks hospital, and was able to resume his normal pursuits in about a month. The surgeon who repaired his wounds summed things up in three words. "You were lucky," he said.

It's exactly as Bruce Neal said. A man is never safe in grizzly country.

However, Al Erickson of the Alaska Department of Fish and Game, one of that state's top authorities on these bears, believes certain precautions can be taken to lessen the danger of attack.

Following his pioneer research on black bears in Michigan, described in an earlier chapter, Erickson moved to Alaska and carried out extensive live-capture and tagging work on grizzlies and browns. In a report published by the Alaska department in 1965, he spelled out his recommendations for avoiding bear trouble.

In bear country campers should burn all garbage or remove it from the camp and trail areas. Bears can also be discouraged from entering a camp by prominently displaying bright objects or hanging a dish towel where it will flap in the wind. It's desirable to leave plenty of human scent around a camp area, and camp should not be made near a used game trail. Above all, never entice bears in by feeding them.

For the man traveling afoot in bear country, Erickson's first rule is basically the one another experienced Alaskan woodsman laid down for me many years ago: Don't surprise the bear if you can help it, and don't let the bear surprise you.

Trouble arises most often when bears are encountered suddenly at close quarters. Unless there is some reason for silence, sing, whistle or talk when moving through dense cover. An even better idea is to stay out of such places if possible. A few pebbles in a can, hung from the belt or carried in the hand or pocket, serve the same purpose.

Finally Erickson warned, as I have done earlier, that grizzlies are very protective of any animal carcass on which they are feeding or have fed. Such carcasses should be strictly avoided unless the bear is being hunted, and then they should be approached with extreme caution. The same degree of caution is a must for a hunter returning to a moose, elk or other big-game animal he has killed, or to the place where such an animal has been dressed out and the entrails left. Grizzlies often take over such leavings.

For the human who encounters a bear in the open by accident, Erickson advocates "aggressive behavior," particularly loud shouting and arm waving.

Such behavior may halt quarrelsome bears. It has even been found effective in driving sows from their cubs. My own experience with browns also indicates that a party of three or four men is less likely to have trouble than one or two. Apparently the bears prefer to have the odds in their favor.

In case of actual attack, the bear can sometimes be turned if struck hard on the nose with a club or some similar weapon, Erickson says. My own opinion is that that is a risky defense, to be tried only as a last resort and in a life-or-death encounter. The bear is far more likely to knock the club out of the man's hands and swarm all over him.

Few bears continue an attack until the victim is dead. Often the attack is broken off suddenly, perhaps when the bear realizes that his adversary is a human. Other attacks are terminated when the victim loses consciousness, but in such cases the bear is likely to attack again if the human moves or moans. This behavior suggests the desirability of feigning death.

Since in fatal attacks the bear usually kills its victim by crushing bites at the base of the skull or by disembowelment, Erickson recommends that the victim protect his head, neck and abdomen as much as possible. He suggests falling to the ground and curling into a tight ball, with the face between the drawn-up legs and with the arms locked across the back of the head and base of the neck. This leaves the top of the head partially exposed, but bear bites there tend to slide off the skull. Better to be scalped than killed.

Perhaps it should be added that Al Erickson is a lithe and agile woodsman of more than ordinary strength and endurance, cool-headed in the extreme. He has also had a great deal of experience in dealing with wild animals. I recall one occasion when he took a fresh coyote track on deep snow, walked the animal down on snowshoes, pinned it, tied its legs, fixed a stick in its mouth to prevent it from biting, and carried it out to his car alive, all single handed. He would have a better chance of surviving a bear attack than almost any other man I know.

And in conclusion it should be noted, too, that he recommends the procedures I have listed here only in cases where the human involved is without an effective firearm. He doesn't say it, but the safest precaution of all, wherever grizzlies are likely to be encountered, is to carry a gun adequate for what it may be called on to do.

SIXTEEN

The Hunter and the Hunted

The hunter who sets his sights on a grizzly is going after a formidable, difficult, and dangerous quarry. This bear's natural equipment is first class, fully as good as that of the black bear, although experienced hunters and guides who know him well are generally agreed that his eyesight is poor. Many say he is nearsighted and not likely to notice objects that do not move. But whatever the limitations of his eyes, his nose and ears more than make up for them. His hearing and sense of smell are unsurpassed.

If he chooses to escape the hunter his craft and cunning rival those of a fox. More than one outdoorsman credits him with intelligence as keen as that possessed by any trophy game animal on this continent.

Like all bears, he is completely unpredictable. One day, under a given set of conditions, he may stand his ground or even carry the fight to his human enemy. The next day his only thought may be to get away.

In the fall of 1963, Doug Robertson, an outfitter and guide in the Kamloops district of British Columbia, had occasion to hunt down a deformed grizzly (although it was an adult animal that weighed around 350 pounds, its hind quarters were sloping and stunted and it was only about two feet tall at the shoulders) that had severely mauled a hunter who blundered into it in thick willow tangles. The bear had been feeding on and guarding the carrion carcass of a cow moose, and had jumped the man without warning at very close range.

Bob McKelvie, the hunter who was mauled, was not hunting the bear and did not know it was in the neighborhood. He was working through willows higher than his head, looking for moose, when, as he put it later, he stepped by accident in the bear's dinner bucket. The grizzly was lying in a muddy bed close to the moose carcass. McKelvie was bent over, forcing his way through a thicket, when it reared up almost under his feet and lunged at him.

It clawed and bit him, and after a minute or two of trying to fight it off he went limp and feigned death. The bear dropped him and he heard it walk away. In terrible pain and blinded by his own blood, he rolled over, got to his feet and tried to run. The bear was on him again in a flash. He screamed for help and his two hunting partners drove the animal off by shooting over the brush.

McKelvie was mutilated beyond recognition. It took two six-hour sessions by a surgeon to clean and sew him up, and twenty-one pints of blood to save his life. His weight dropped forty-one pounds before he was able to leave the hospital.

Robertson and three companions went after the bear and found it under surprising conditions. It was swimming across a bay at the head of Tum Tum Lake, not far from the scene of the attack. At first, seeing only its head and shoulders in the water, they mistook it for a small moose.

The bear reached shore while it was still beyond rifle range, and lunged for thick brush above the beach. Here was a grizzly that had come very close to killing a man three or four days earlier, and as Robertson learned later, had lain in a thicket only the day before and watched him and his partners hunt for it. Yet now its one concern was escape. It was no longer near its food supply, had been caught in the open, and confronted not a single man but a party of four.

It made the mistake of showing itself briefly in an old burn, free of brush, and Robertson killed it with one shot.

When it comes to cautious grizzlies, I knew one case where a guide came face to face with four full-grown ones on a narrow game trail, the nearest only twenty-five yards away. One of those bears was big enough that the night before it had picked up and lugged off bodily a cow elk that dressed three hundred pounds, with her legs touching the snow only now and then. The guide stood still and stared the bears down without getting into anything like an argument. He admitted afterward that he had no choice. With four grizzlies that close, he didn't dare resort to shooting and there was no tree handy big enough to climb.

In another highly unusual encounter, my friend Judge Lou McGregor, a Flint, Michigan, sportsman, followed a fresh wolf track in snow and crawled up to the entrails of a moose his party had killed three weeks before, in the hope of making a picture of the wolf feeding on the leavings. He was within twenty feet when he inched around a thick spruce and stared a big grizzly in the face instead.

Afterward McGregor had only a hazy memory of what happened. He recalled the bear's eyes blazing with rage as they met his, then he turned and ran, yelling at the top of his voice for his guide, his hunting partner, and his gun.

The bear did the most unlikely thing possible under the circumstances. It ran the other way, up the mountain, in thick cover. The hunters did not catch another glimpse of it but moving brush revealed its line of flight.

Grizzly hunting means wilderness hunting, and for the most part it also means mountain wilderness. Outside of Alaska, the bulk of it is done by pack trip. Most hunters who collect the pelt of one of these bears take their trophy in one of two ways.

They spot the grizzly in an open place, often feeding in a berry patch high on a mountainside, or on a bare slope digging for a marmot or ground squirrel. Once the bear is located, it is usually not too difficult to stalk within range, although the hunter is likely to need physical stamina, hunting craft, and some luck.

The second method is to lure the bear in with bait, and the most commonly used bait is a decrepit horse, killed in a place frequented by grizzlies and left to ripen.

Now and then a hunter, often on horseback and even accompanied by a packtrain, encounters a grizzly at close range by accident and dumps him on the spot. Frequently in such cases, the bear gives the man no choice. He comes in a headlong charge the instant the two lay eyes on one another. In the Yukon a few years ago, a father and son hunting team, leaving camp with their guide, rode single file over a rise and came face to face with a big grizzly feeding on a moose. The bear had winded them, knew they were approaching, and was waiting and ready.

He let out a hair-raising roar, came for them on a dead run, threw the horses into panic, and was killed at fifty yards in a ruckus that had lasted only a minute.

Hersch Neighbor, a rancher, outfitter and guide in the British Columbia Rockies, wasn't even hunting when the same thing happened to him. In the end he killed not one grizzly but four, not from choice but from necessity.

Roaring and clicking its teeth, a dark grizzly stormed out of a thicket. The packhorses broke their halters, tore free of the packsaddles, and scattered gear and equipment through the timber for a quarter mile.

Hersch was riding home with a string of packhorses, from a job of packing supplies for a fire-fighting crew. He was a couple of miles from his ranch, riding slack in the saddle, day-dreaming of a hot bath and a woman-cooked supper, when his horse exploded under him, almost bucking him off, wheeled and spooked the pack animals, and took off down the back trail like a streak.

Hersch caught a glimpse of a big dark animal stepping out of the brush, and assumed he had run across a black bear. He got the horses under control and started on, not expecting any more trouble.

But at the same place a dark grizzly stormed out of a thicket, roaring and clicking its teeth. The packhorses broke their halters, tore free of the pack-saddles, and scattered gear and equipment through the timber for a quarter mile. Hersch's saddle horse swiveled around and ran, and because he had no rifle he let it have its head.

When Neighbor finally got home, long after dark, and heard about a horse that had broken its neck and been left in the woods, he knew what had happened. The grizzly had taken over the carcass. And because a small band of Beaver Indians had come along and camped only a mile from the dead horse, not suspecting that either it or the bear was there, he also knew what he had to do. There were children in the Indian camp, and if they wandered near the grizzly tragedy was inevitable.

Hersch and his wife and a helper went after the bear the next day. They were getting close to the dead horse, on foot and moving very cautiously, when they suddenly learned that they were not confronting one grizzly. A big sow and three two-year-old cubs, half grown and just as ready to make trouble, erupted out of the brush, growling and bawling. A young and inexperienced grizzly is often more inclined to be cocky and reckless than an older one that knows more about humans. They are also more curious, and their curiosity can turn to rage in a split second.

When the fracas ended, four dead bears were lying in a half circle around three thoroughly shook-up people. The farthest was eighteen paces away, the nearest six.

One fact has to be faced. Danger is always a part of grizzly hunting. There is even some danger in hunting in grizzly country, whether or not the hunter is after a bear.

I once exchanged letters with a retired army officer who was treed by a grizzly while on a grouse hunt. His bird dog kept the bear busy for an hour or so, then gave up and went home. The hunter spent sixteen hours in the tree, including the long hours of a cold dark night, before the bear wandered off and he dared to climb down.

"I've always wanted grizzlies protected because there aren't many of them left," he told me. "But after that encounter, my protective instincts have cooled off quite a little."

Nobody has spelled out the risk inherent in hunting this bear better than Bill Schneider, editor of *Montana Outdoors*. Schneider admires and respects everything about the grizzly, including its readiness to fight back. He is also fully aware of the deadly quality of its anger.

"No other animal in North America has the first-strike and even the second-strike capability of an aroused grizzly," Bill says.

All who know the bear agree. Even as far back as 1804, when Lewis and Clark penetrated grizzly country above the Mandan villages on their epic journey up the Missouri, the two explorers concluded that they would rather face a dozen hostile Indians than one of these bears.

Many hunters believe that an unwounded grizzly will not deliberately stalk a man, but even that is not true.

I knew of an incident a number of years ago in which a Montana hunter located a grizzly that had appropriated an elk the man had killed. The bear was holed up in a dense thicket, the hunter was carrying a rifle a little light for the job. He made a big circle to get downwind, hoping for a shot in the open. The next news he got from the bear, it let go a full-throated roar just six yards behind him. When the affair was buttoned up, he learned from sign in the snow that it had picked up his track and trailed him exactly as a hound trails a rabbit, creeping onto him unheard until it was eighteen feet away.

Hunting over bait, few guides are willing to put a client closer than a hundred yards. Most of them prefer to be half again that far from the dead horse they are watching. There are two reasons. They want to stay far enough away that there is little chance a bear will wind them. And the guide also wants enough time to take a hand if something goes wrong. Most guides will tell you that it's a lot better to shoot a grizzly at two hundred yards than at fifty.

About the worst thing that can happen to a grizzly hunter is to hit a bear and fail to make a clean kill. Having started the quarrel, he and his guide are under obligation to finish it, and if the bear goes into heavy cover, which is close to a sure bet, the situation is a very sticky one.

More bear hunters have been mauled or killed as a result of wounding a grizzly than for all other reasons put together. The men I know who are the proud owners of grizzly rugs agree on a few basic rules of safety:

1. Don't shoot until you can place your shot.
2. Break the bear down in the shoulders if you can.
3. Keep shooting as long as he moves or twitches.
4. Never approach a bear you have knocked down until you are absolutely sure he is dead.
5. Avoid a gut shot above all. A silvertip with a mushroomed softnose in his belly is as dangerous as any animal on earth. His rage matches his pain, and he is going to even the score before he dies if he can.

Bert Bell, a Wyoming guide, was sitting with a client in a blind 175 yards downwind from a dead horse, on a fall evening in 1967, when a medium-sized grizzly walked arrogantly in to the bait just at dusk. The bear started to feed and the hunter drove a shot from a .264 Magnum into her shoulder. Bell commented later that he thought at the time the .264 was a light caliber for grizzlies, and before the affair ended he was sure he was right.

Although the shot appeared well placed, the bear stood for a second as if stunned, then ran for the timber. Bert had a very firm rule where wounded grizzlies were concerned. He would not follow one at night. Dusk was getting thick in the timber now, and even though there was tracking snow on the ground he had no intention of taking the bear's trail until morning.

Four men rode out from camp right after daylight to hunt her down. Not far from the place where she had been shot, they tied their horses and went ahead on foot. They soon found the bed where she had lain during the night. Blood sign indicated a lung shot, and they expected to overtake her in a short time.

But two sets of bear tracks led away from the bed. She had walked off, then come back, lain down for a time and left again. The hunters split into pairs and took the two tracks.

The blood trail was very fresh. The bear had turned downhill, lurching from side to side as she walked, staggering blindly into and out of thickets. When the men came to a small creek and her tracks led up the far bank, they halted for a look around, fearing that she might backtrack and be lying in wait for them. An ambush of that kind is common with wounded grizzlies.

There was a windfall beyond the creek that looked like a perfect spot for the bear to hide in. Between it and the creek were two trees they could climb for a better look. They splashed across and started for the trees, but never reached them.

All of a sudden Bell smelled the rank scent of grizzly, and then the bear leaped up from behind a log thirty yards away and came in a lightning-fast charge. Bert's rifle was an old Enfield .30/06 that he carried on pack trips because it could take hard use. It failed him now. The safety stuck, and the bear smashed into him, knocking the gun from his hands and carrying him to the ground. She grabbed him in the belly just below the ribs and bit deep. He forced his hands between her jaws and she started to chew on them instead.

Bell's partner, the camp horse wrangler, got in a shot that entered her rump but seemed to have little effect. She sat back on her haunches with her face only a foot or two from Bert's and cocked her uninjured foreleg as if she intended to smash his skull. In that instant the wrangler fired a second time. His bullet blew up in her lungs and heart, and her eyes began to glaze.

Bell struggled to his feet, the wrangler ran in and put a third shot into the bear's head, and she slumped and fell over.

The guide managed to walk a mile to the horses, rode three miles to camp, fretted through a sleepless, pain-haunted night, and then was helped onto his horse for a nine-hour ride out to the nearest lodge. From there he even managed to drive the forty miles to Cody, where doctors and a hospital were waiting. The bear had left him with no internal injuries and no broken bones.

He told me the story a few months after the encounter. By that time he was as good as new. But one of the first things he did after he got out of the hospital was give away the old Enfield with the unreliable safety and replace it with a brand new Winchester Model 70 that he knew he could count on. He did not plan ever to confront a wounded grizzly again but he was determined to be ready, just in case.

156

Then there was Eddie Dixon, a Shuswap Indian guide from the Canim Lake Reservation in British Columbia, two hundred miles north of the U. S. border. Dixon was forty-four in 1963, when he fought his lightning-fast bout with a wounded grizzly. He had had the misfortune to lose his left arm below the elbow in a sawmill accident four years earlier, but a steel hook enabled him to handle a rifle without any difficulty, save that he was a bit slower at reloading than a man with two hands.

He was guiding two moose hunters from Nevada, when another guide brought word into the camp that he had come across a bear he believed was a grizzly, feeding on the decomposed remains of a moose, killed out of season by an unknown hunter and left in the woods to rot.

Dixon's two clients voted to have a try for the bear the next morning. "I'd rather have a grizzly rug than a dozen moose," one said, to which another member of the party retorted, "Who wouldn't?"

The two men and their guide left camp in a snowstorm at daylight. Half a mile from the place where the bear had been seen they tied their horses and went ahead on foot. Ravens circling and croaking in protest, in the sky above a stand of jackpine, revealed to the guide that the bear was on the moose carcass, keeping the birds from feeding.

The men were thirty yards away when they sighted him. He had smelled or heard them coming and was standing broadside, with his front feet on a log, swinging his head and sniffing the air for better clues. There was not the slightest doubt that he was a grizzly.

It's a good bet that if the humpback bear lets a man get as close as ninety feet he intends to stand and fight. There is almost no chance of a human approaching that near without the bear being aware of his presence. If he intends to give way, he will be gone. If he is still there the intruding human can expect trouble.

One of Dixon's hunters put a shot from a .300 Magnum, an entirely adequate rifle, into the bear's shoulder. The animal dropped off the log and spun like an overgrown cat, but the shot was too far back for a kill. He started for the three men the instant he regained his feet, growling and bawling.

In addition to the first hit from the .300, that bear took six more before he closed. Two were in the mouth, one in the throat, two in the chest and one in a foot. The chest hit knocked him back on his haunches, but he was up and coming again in a split second. There is food for thought in that performance, for any hunter who doubts the grizzly's capability to carry lead.

Dixon had had only three shells in his 6.5mm Krag at the outset. He used them all, and there was no time to reload. He realized that he was going into a bear fight with an empty gun.

He did a very brave thing. As the bear came around a small pine no more than arm's length away, he stepped to one side and rammed the stock of his rifle into its face to divert it from his two clients. The grizzly accepted the challenge. It put its teeth into the gun stock, splitting it as if spikes had been driven through, and in the same instant it struck the gun out of the guide's hand and knocked him to the ground with a blow on the shoulder.

Dixon thrust his steel hook into the bear's mouth but the animal bit down on the hard cuff, slapped the hook aside and grabbed Eddie's good arm instead.

He was not sure how long the fight lasted, but almost certainly it was over in less than a minute. The thing Eddie Dixon would remember most clearly afterward was the terrible stench of the bear's breath, foul from its diet of carrion.

"It smelled as if he was rolling me in decayed moose meat, face down," the guide recalled.

The bear let go of his arm and went for his head. Its teeth slipped on his skull but it peeled his scalp away, from one ear to the top of the head, and took part of the ear along. Then the two clients fired almost together, one on either side less than ten feet away, and the bear crumpled and fell on top of its victim. He couldn't get up until the hunters pulled him out from under it.

It took a surgeon more than two hours to scrape the injured man's skull, fix the torn ear, clean his wounds and suture the scalp back in place.

"If I ever have a fight with another grizzly, he'll have to start it," Dixon told me. "That is one bear I will not look for again."

What is the right gun for this hot tempered and deadly bear? Eddie Dixon's experience conveys a very clear idea of how tough and tenacious of life the grizzly is. Even an individual that weighs considerably less than a big black is a harder animal to kill and poses far more of a threat to the hunter who wounds him but fails to do a clean job.

As with the black, a lot of grizzlies have been killed with the .30/30, for the reason that it was the rifle most frequently carried by outdoorsmen two or three generations ago. But it is not a grizzly caliber.

It will kill the biggest bear that ever walked the earth, and kill him in his tracks, if the shot is placed right. Witness what happened in the case of the record-size grizzly that Jack Turner dropped at six feet. But very few hunters shoot at such close range, and not many can put their shot so precisely where it needs to go.

For my own part, I would not be willing to hunt grizzlies with any rifle lighter than the .30/06, or another caliber that at least equals it in ballistics and performance. That list includes the 7mm Remington Magnum, the .300 Magnum, and the .338 Magnum.

The hunter who plans to kill a bear at 300 yards may have some justification for carrying a high-velocity, flat-shooting gun, say the .270, which has accounted for plenty of grizzlies. But the fast-traveling .270 bullet, weighing either 130 or 150 grains in factory loads, is not heavy enough for this bear, in my judgment. And I do not believe the .264 Magnum belongs on a grizzly hunt, despite the fact that its 140-grain softpoint leaves the muzzle traveling 3,200 feet a second and wallops a target 100 yards away with 2,690 foot-pounds of striking force.

Of the grizzly calibers I have named, the 180-grain load from the .30/06 delivers 2,440 foot-pounds of energy at 100 yards; the 180-grain from the .300 Magnum, 3,250 foot-pounds; the 200-grain messenger from the .338 Magnum arrives 100 yards out with a force of 3,210 foot-pounds; and the 7mm Reming-

Dixon thrust his steel hook into the bear's mouth but the animal bit down on the hard cuff, slapped the hook aside and grabbed Eddie's good arm instead.

ton Magnum with 2,940. The 150-grain softpoint from the last named caliber is light for grizzly work, however.

If the hunter can handle the gun and take the recoil, even the .375 Magnum is not out of place on a hunt for the silvertip. It's a lot of rifle, but he is a lot of bear.

One problem arises in choosing the best rifle for grizzlies. They are often hunted and killed in connection with, or as a bonus to, hunts for elk, moose, caribou, or sheep. The gun that is ideal for the bear may be too heavy or otherwise not right for softer-skinned game that is easier to finish off. But the hunter going into grizzly country and hoping to bring home the makings of a bear rug needs to carry a gun that will see him through in a pinch.

Such advice is not unlike that sometimes given to teenagers: What you date, you marry. The rifle that rides in your saddle boot is the one you will have to use if you come over a rise of ground and confront a bear walking to meet you, close enough that you can see his frost-tipped pelt ripple in the sun. You need equipment that will deal with him then and there. He won't give you time to change guns.

When it comes to bowhunting, much of what I said earlier about the black bear applies equally to the grizzly. A bow with a draw weight of fifty to sixty pounds that will drive a razorhead arrow all the way through the lungs of a full-grown black will do the same for a grizzly, and kill just as quickly. In both cases the key is arrow placement, and the target area on the one is no bigger than on the other, taking the size of the bears themselves into account. The place to put an arrow, assuming the ideal shot is possible, is just behind the shoulder, at such an angle that it will range forward into the heart and lung area.

I have known of two cases where a sixty-pound bow drove a razorhead through the lungs or heart of a grizzly, and the bear ran only twenty feet before it fell stone dead.

Speaking of bow weights for big and dangerous game, Fred Bear killed his African elephant with one arrow from a seventy-pound bow.

There is one important point of difference for the bowhunter between the grizzly and black. The danger of a charge from a wounded bear is far greater with the former. He may be lung shot and bleeding to death inside as he runs, but he is not likely to take the pain and shock of the arrow without fighting back, assuming he locates the hunter. And if he can run far enough to reach the object of his rage he is able to inflict dreadful injuries or even kill in the minute or two it takes him to die.

There probably are bowhunters willing to tackle a grizzly without the backing of a reliable rifleman, but I do not happen to know any, and it's a risk I would not advise any man to take.

SEVENTEEN

The Man Who Tamed Grizzlies

I can think of no better way to conclude an account of the humpbacked bear and his ways than by relating the wonderful story of Grizzly Adams. Almost certainly it has no counterpart in the records of North American wildlife.

Prior to 1975, almost no one of this generation, apart from a handful of wildlife writers, had heard of Grizzly Adams. That year a widely promoted movie carrying his name and based on his life brought him briefly to public attention. What is the real story behind this legendary old hunter who has been dead more than a hundred years?

According to his own account of his adventures, "written by himself," he says, and published in New York in 1860 (the year he died) as a ten-cent paperback of only fifty-three pages, the man who has come down to us as Grizzly Adams was born James Capen Adams, in May of 1805. His version of his birth is that it occurred "under a pine tree" in the wilds of Maine, where his father was building a log cabin for a wife and the expected baby.

Another book, appearing the same year but written for Adams by a ghost writer, places his birth in the town of Medford, Massachusetts, and the year as 1807.

Whichever version is true, Adams apparently spent his early years as a hunter in Maine, New Hampshire, and Vermont, capturing panthers, wolves, and wildcats alive for exhibition.

In 1848 he caught gold fever and the following year he headed for California, going overland by way of Mexico and arriving in the fall of 1849. For the next few years he mined, kept store, and ran a boardinghouse. But he had bad luck financially, and when he ended up with only two oxen, a worn-out wagon, and a good Kentucky rifle, he turned his back on the gold fields in disgust and headed for the Sierra Nevada mountains with a partner and two Indian boys. Fifty miles beyond the sound of other human voices, the little party built a cabin and settled down to a life of hunting and trapping.

They trapped four grizzlies the first year. Adams reported that they kept the bears alive and "subdued" them, but he gave no details.

His next move was north to Oregon with his three companions. They reached the Columbia River, and very shortly Adams shot and killed a sow grizzly that was accompanied by two year-and-a-half old cubs that weighed around 150 pounds apiece. He lassoed one of the cubs, a female, tied her jaws so she couldn't bite, trussed her feet and skidded her back to camp on a green moose hide. There he put a collar and chain on her and named her Lady Washington. That was the beginning of one of the most remarkable man-animal relationships ever recorded.

Adams summed it up in these words: "From that day to this she has always been with me. Often she has shared my dangers and privations, borne my burdens and partaken of my meals. Many times I have nestled up between her and the fire to keep both sides warm under the frosty skies of the mountains. The grizzly bear possesses a nature which, if taken in time and carefully improved, may be made the perfection of animal goodness."

No one, not even among today's animal-loving extremists, has ever exceeded that glowing tribute to the humpbacked bear's potential for friendship with man.

Next Adams killed what he called a hyena black bear, evidently considering it a kind apart from the usual run. It was a female with two small cubs, and he took them back to camp alive.

The next bear encounter happened to his partner, a man named Saxey. Again they ran across a sow with two cubs, and again Adams described her as the kind he called a hyena black bear.

Saxey shot and wounded her and she charged headlong. The description of that encounter certainly loses nothing in the telling, as Adams related it. "The bear rose on her legs," he said, "opened her forepaws to embrace Saxey in a mortal hug, gave a terrific roar that showed a frightful set of teeth, and glared at him like a fiend dressed up in fur." All this action gave Adams time to kill her at the last second with a shot through the heart.

The friendship between Adams and the young grizzly, Lady Washington, was anything but smooth sailing in the beginning. Of the several bears, blacks and grizzlies, that he caught alive and kept chained at his camps, she was by far the most cantankerous, lunging and snapping at him whenever he came near.

In the meantime, the two black-bear cubs that he had taken shortly after he captured her had become tame enough to follow him like dogs, and he had even taught them to sleep with him, tying them to a stake near his feet and boxing their ears if they disturbed him.

With the young grizzly things were much more difficult. He finally decided to settle accounts with her once and for all. He cut a stout club and trounced the bear into submission. He had little trouble with her from that time on, and soon he was leading her around camp with a chain. His next step was to train her to carry a pack. He started with an old flour bag filled with sand. Lady

162

Washington didn't like the arrangement. She ripped the bag apart with her teeth and the sand ran out. But Adams persisted, and soon he had the bear carrying a pack of two hundred pounds with no show of resentment. Years of incredible companionship between man and grizzly followed.

Later Adams taught another obdurate young grizzly to be led by dragging it around camp behind a mule.

His next scrape came when he found a grizzly den in a cave. He believed there was a sow inside with cubs. He lay in wait, the old bear came out half an hour before sunset, and he shot her. She dropped, but when he undertook to stab her in the throat to make sure she was dead she grabbed him by the legs, mangling him badly in the fight that followed.

He finally killed her, "bound up" his wounds as best he could, and crawled into the cave with a fat-pine torch. He found two young cubs, still without teeth and having very little hair. Adams fixes the time as autumn, but in view of the size of the little bears it must have been sometime in the winter instead.

With bears that young, Adams confronted the difficult problem of feeding them through the early weeks of their lives. But he hit on a solution that proved ideal. His dog had just given birth to a litter of pups. He destroyed them and gave the bitch the two grizzly cubs in their place. She accepted them without hesitation.

Adams gave one to his partner Saxey. The other, given the name of Ben Franklin, grew to adulthood and joined Lady Washington as a docile pet and the constant companion of the man who had reared him. In time he even learned to hunt in company with the dog that was his foster mother, and once when a wild grizzly came for Adams Ben Franklin flew at it and drove it off.

There was a lull in Adams' bear hunting the summer after he acquired the two young cubs. Immigrants were coming into California in droves, and he spent the summer hunting deer, elk, and other game for sale to them. But in September he had a chance to capture two more small grizzlies alive. The mother was nowhere in sight, but when one of the cubs squalled she came raging out of the brush. In the bear-man fight that followed Adams was badly mauled and one of the cubs was accidentally killed. He kept the second one for his growing collection of tame bears and, as he tells it, "to please a lively young actress whom I had met in California, I named it Funny Joe."

His final grizzly adventure was the most amazing of all. He came across the tracks of a large adult bear and decided to capture it alive and undertake to tame it, in all likelihood the only time that has been attempted in the long history of this bear.

He set to work with his two young Indian helpers to build an extremely strong log livetrap, fourteen feet long, six wide, and six high. He closed the front end with a heavy drop door of split logs, rigged to a baited trigger inside. He did not describe the trigger in detail, other than calling it a "deadfall arrangement," but in all likelihood it was a variation of the time-honored Figure 4, long used with deadfalls to kill black bears in the Eastern states.

However the trigger worked, that log contraption Grizzly Adams built back in the 1850s was certainly the forerunner of all the bear livetraps that have been used since, including the culvert trap with which Al Erickson began his black-bear research in northern Michigan in 1952.

Adams finished his trap in November and baited it with freshly killed deer, but for many weeks his efforts went for naught. Tracks showed that the bear would come to the door of the trap and stand there, probably sniffing the venison inside, but would not enter. Adams relates that he "wasted" upwards of fifteen deer, rabbits, jackals (probably coyotes), and other game in trying to entice the bear into the trap. He saw it repeatedly and could have shot it many times, but that was not what he wanted.

He offers no explanation for the fact that the grizzly did not den, but it was toward the end of February when he was finally awakened in the night by a terrifying uproar coming from the direction of the trap. He had caught the full-grown grizzly at last.

He found it fighting mad, snarling and bawling. To whip it he went after it with an iron crowbar between the logs of the trap and also intimidated it with firebrands. He says he fought it for days, meanwhile keeping it supplied with food and water. At last it quieted down. "And when they once succumb they succumb forever," Grizzly remarked.

His next step was to build a very stout cage and hire a man with two yoke of oxen and a wagon to take the caged grizzly down to the settlements.

The cage was placed door to door with the trap, and both doors were opened. But a day of whipping the bear and thrusting firebrands at him failed to drive him into the cage. That was finally accomplished by getting a loop of heavy chain around his neck, pulling the other end out through the back of the cage and hitching the four oxen to the chain. Prodded from behind, the reluctant and resentful grizzly was dragged bodily into his new home. Apparently he had never heard of the rule that once subdued he was supposed to stay that way.

Four days later he gave in again, the cage was laboriously loaded onto the wagon and the ox team started for a place called Corral Hollow, where Adams had other wild animals confined. Adams remarks that the expenses left him five hundred "gold dollars" in the red, but he counted himself well satisfied with his bargain.

Named Samson, that bear also became his companion, perhaps the only case on record where a grizzly captured as an adult was converted into an obedient pet.

There, unfortunately, Grizzly Adams ended his story of his bear adventures. The final twenty pages of his little paperback deal with buffalo hunting, catching mountain lions alive, roping bighorn sheep, and severe illness that resulted from eating the meat of a mountain lion that had been poisoned.

In Utah Adams made a hunt for "the Salt Lake screeching bear, a grizzly so called because they have a singular cry that closely resembles a screech." In Salt Lake City, also, he listened to a sermon by Brigham Young, whom he described as "a great, fat, pursy individual."

He says at the end of his book that a second was to follow. By that time he had established the Pacific Museum in San Francisco, with Lady Washington, Ben Franklin, Funny Joe, Samson, black bears, panthers, wolves, and other tame animals around him, and had next moved to New York with at least part of his bears.

He promised that the second book would tell how he shipped his pet grizzlies around the Horn from California to New York, where they were displayed at Barnum's Museum on lower Broadway. The back cover of his book carried an ad for that museum, featuring "a great black sea lion captured in the Pacific by Grizzly Adams." Unfortunately the second book never appeared, probably because Adams died in 1860 before it could be written.

How much of the colorful and amazing story of this old hunter and his bears can be believed? No one is sure. Despite his solemn assurance in the preface of his book that he was telling the truth without exaggeration, it seems certain that he embellished his tale a bit in places. For example, he credits the California grizzly of his day with attaining a weight of two thousand pounds, which it surely did not do. He also says that Samson weighed fifteen hundred pounds, but offers no evidence that the bear was ever put on scales. A zoo keeper who saw Samson many times in New York called him by far the largest grizzly he had ever laid eyes on, however.

In one of his episodes, Adams says that after he had shot a female black bear and taken her two cubs he was attacked by the vengeful father of the cubs while on the way back to camp and had to kill the male bear. And another time, when he crawled into the den of a sow grizzly he had shot, looking for cubs, he fully expected her mate to be lying in wait for him. Which proves that the old hunter,

for all his remarkable dealing with bears, had very little knowledge of their family ways.

Because of these misstatements and minor exaggerations, and also because of his florid style of writing (not uncommon in 1860), over the years his entire story has been questioned more than once by skeptics.

A few essential facts appear to be beyond dispute, however. James Capen Adams did roam the California mountains in the late 1850s with pet grizzlies so docile that they carried pack loads for him, even carried him, shared his campfire beds, hunted with his dog and fought to defend him.

Says Seton, "Of all this there can be no doubt. I have met many men who knew Adams personally in the West and none questioned the truth of his story. And when he came to New York with his big bear Samson in 1860, he and the bear were seen daily by hundreds."

The cage was placed door to door with the trap, and both doors were opened. A heavy chain was looped around the bear's neck, the end pulled through the back of the cage and hitched to four oxen, and the reluctant grizzly was dragged bodily into his new home.

Years later a zoo director from Philadelphia would recall that "Samson, with his owner Grizzly Adams, was the delight of my schoolboy holidays thirty years ago."

Of the basic truth of the almost incredible story of Adams and his pet bears there seems little reason for skepticism, even though it is the most remarkable story of its kind ever told.

While I am on the subject of tame bears, I have always liked a tall tale, one that is not intended to be believed, that is told in Alaska about an old prospector who caught a brown bear cub and raised it as a pet.

He had a mine on a mountain a mile above his cabin, and when the bear was old enough he fitted it with a packsaddle and trained it to carry a light load of ore down to the cabin at the end of each day. As the animal grew he increased the load, until it was packing two hundred pounds at a trip.

When he finished work one evening the bear, which usually stayed nearby, was nowhere to be seen. Looking around for it, he finally spotted it sleeping in a grassy opening across a small stream. He went after it to lead it back and load it, but to his astonishment the bear turned on him for the first time in its life.

Convinced that if he let it get the best of him it would never again be of any use as a pack animal, he cut a club and beat it into submission. At the mine, when he undertook to put the pack saddle on, they fought another hard round but in the end the man triumphed.

Twice more, on the way down the trail to the cabin, the bear rounded on him, grumbling and snarling, and twice more he clubbed it until it gave up.

When he came within sight of the cabin his pet bear was lying near the door, sound asleep.

EIGHTEEN

Twelve in One Afternoon

A full-grown Alaska brown bear is the most impressive wild animal on this continent. The first one I ever saw didn't quite measure up to that description, for the reason that he wasn't full-grown. We figured him for a three-year-old male and he probably weighed around four hundred pounds. I had seen both grizzly and black bears that were bigger.

All the same, there was something about this youngster, his behavior and the setting where we found him, that commanded the ultimate in admiration and respect. Maybe he weighed only four hundred pounds, but he was not a bear that any man in his senses would take liberties with.

Perhaps I imagined it, but it seemed to me that his calm self-assurance said as plainly as words, "I belong to the tribe of the biggest bears on the face of the earth. I'm not in a quarrelsome mood, but I have my dignity. I'll go my way and you can go yours. But don't crowd me."

Every brownie that walks the rockslides, the stream banks, and the alder-thicket bear paths of Alaska telegraphs that same message loud and clear.

I was spending a summer along the coast of what is now the forty-ninth state and in its Aleutian Islands, aboard the U. S. Fish and Wildlife Service patrol ship *Brown Bear,* assigned to protecting the Aleutian Island National Wildlife Refuge. The primary purpose of the patrol was to safeguard the Alaskan sea otter, then just beginning a strong comeback from the very brink of extinction.

I had gone to Alaska under an arrangement with Dr. Ira Gabrielson, one of this century's foremost conservationists and then director of the Fish and Wildlife Service (and his superior, Secretary of Interior Harold Ickes) in the hope of making a record in 16mm color film of the growing sea otter herd. If I succeeded (which I did), the film would be the first of its kind. While I was there, if possible I meant to make color footage of brown bears as well.

It was a great summer, the last before Pearl Harbor and World War II. We cruised at a leisurely pace past the mainland coast and out along the Alaska

Peninsula, filming teeming colonies of seabirds in their cliff cities, sighting now and then a big Steller sea lion or a prowling pack of killer whales — and hunting, always, for brownies.

We were three weeks on the cruise before we laid eyes on one. We walked their trails in the tall rye grass along the beaches, visited streams where salmon were running and where well-trodden bear paths crossed back and forth from bank to bank. We found freshly killed salmon and salmon half eaten, sure proof that there were brown bears nearby.

At the head of Danger Bay on Afognak Island late one afternoon we beached an outboard-powered dory and went ashore to make a spike camp for the night. I picked up a sleeping bag under each arm and started through a belt of rye grass higher than my head, headed for a clump of spruce where we would camp.

Without the slightest warning I stepped into a bear bed bigger than an average dinner table, where the grass was packed as flat and smooth as a golf fairway. Had the brownie left five days before, or two minutes? There was no way to tell.

Whenever he had lain in that bed, he gave me the worst fright I had that summer. I dropped the two bags and bolted for the beach, where Jack Benson, wildlife agent from Kodiak, was unloading the dory, with a .30/06 ready at hand.

Nowhere that summer did we find bear sign more plentiful than along the salmon streams on Afognak, but our hunting luck continued bad. Two days of walking those streams failed to show us a bear.

It was far out to the westward, near the tip of the Alaska Peninsula, that we finally found what we were looking for, and then we saw bears in numbers that were hard to believe.

We tied up for the night at a salmon cannery at False Pass, between the end of the Peninsula and Unimak, first island of the mountainous Aleutian chain that curves twelve hundred miles to the west.

We asked Capt. Don Davis, the cannery superintendent, about bears. He grinned dryly. "I've been here a number of years and I haven't lost any bears that I thought I needed to go looking for," he said. "But if I really wanted to find one or two, I'd go up to the head of Morzhovoi Bay. The Aleuts here at the cannery tell me they're thicker than fleas on a dog between there and Cold Bay. But the Aleuts haven't lost any, either."

The patrol ship's dory put six of us on the beach at the head of Morzhovoi right after breakfast the next morning. We divided into two groups of three and headed inland across a bleak rolling meadow carpeted with moss and sparse grass. The meadow ran up to rocky hills and snowfields at the foot of Frosty Peak, the last mountain on the Alaska Peninsula, six thousand feet high. My companions were Benson, who was in charge of the party, and Frank Beals, a young Alaska game warden who would carry a still camera to leave me free to make movies.

We found plenty of bear sign on the tundra, holes where brownies had dug for ground squirrels, but no bears. We spent three hours stalking a small herd of caribou for pictures, and at noon we were still looking for our first brownie. Any bear hunter knows the feeling.

In the end we didn't find him. He came to us, walking into sight from the mouth of a canyon, following a snow-fed creek that twisted across the rocky meadow.

Something, probably the bear's incredibly good nose, gave us away. Watching through our glasses, we saw him stop and look our way, swivel around and go back into the canyon at a fast walk. He could not have seen us, but all of a sudden he didn't like the neighborhood.

When we got into the canyon we found the bottom filled with snow six to eight feet deep, not melted in mid-June. It formed bridges across the small creek that brawled down the canyon floor, and there in the snow were the tracks of our bear, leading up toward the big snowfields and bare slides on the shoulders of Frosty Peak. We hurried after him.

Beals saw him first. Working across a steep slide a hundred feet above Benson and me, he ducked suddenly behind a rock and signaled us up to him.

"He's out there," Frank said, "and he hasn't heard us."

I was carrying my movie camera mounted on its tripod, ready for use. I eased it off my shoulder and stepped around the rock. The bear was crossing the slide two hundred feet away, unaware there was a man anywhere on the mountain.

He was, as I said in the beginning, not big for a brownie. But he was my first, and my heart was hammering while I leveled the camera and tripped the shutter.

The wind was blowing down from the high snowfields, strong and cold, and it carried the whirring noise away from him. He moved slowly on, nosing among the rocks for roots or the smell of a squirrel. Once he stopped and scratched his back against an overhanging ledge. He passed over the skyline without a backward glance. But he left me half a hundred feet of film, and I was elated.

We overtook him again on the slope of a knife-edged ridge no more than a hundred feet ahead. He was walking slowly, still searching for food, with his back toward us. But we were close enough now that the first buzz of the camera shutter reached him.

He jumped and spun around, and his resentment rumbled out in a low growl. He stood for a few seconds, staring hard, before he made up his mind not to pick a quarrel. He loped off, but every few yards he stopped, turned and stared back in our direction. He was clearing out, but if we insisted on trouble he'd come back and meet us halfway.

When he disappeared over the ridge I was sure we had seen the last of him. He had had a good look at three men no more than thirty yards behind him and he'd keep traveling. Benson didn't agree.

"He wasn't afraid of us," Jack pointed out. "He'll be just as likely to stop on the other side of the ridge and wait to see whether we follow him. We'll have a look."

But when Jack poked his head carefully over the skyline ridge, the young male was out of sight. In his place four brown bears, a big yellowish sow and three young cubs that had been out of their winter den no more than six or eight weeks, were moving across the shoulder of the mountain. They were only two hundred feet away and coming straight at us. Our hunting luck had reversed itself with a vengeance.

Hidden behind a boulder, I got the camera in the clear and started to grind out film. Out of the tail of my eye I saw Benson step a few feet to one side and lean against a breast-high rock. He laid his rifle on top of it, and I heard a soft click as he thumbed the safety off.

We had blundered into a highly dangerous situation. The last thing in the world we wanted was an argument with that sow bear, but there was a fair chance that when she discovered us so close to her cubs she might not give us a choice. Earlier that summer an old bear hunter had warned me, "Never surprise a brownie." Almost certainly, this one was going to be surprised.

Jack let her come sauntering on, with the cubs frisking around her, until she was only fifty yards away. Once I suggested in a low undertone that he let her know we were there.

"Better get all the film you want," he grunted. "You won't see anything like this again this summer."

At fifty yards I spoke a bit louder. "I've got all I want." I said.

He let out a sharp, loud call.

The bear whipped around, her burly head swinging from side to side as she searched the slope and tested the wind, trying to locate the sound, sniffing and snarling. It took her half a minute to spot me, in the open with my camera, and she seemed to rise on tiptoe for a better look.

Hunting an animal of that kind with either camera or gun may scare you half to death, but it also makes you keenly aware you are alive. I think I held my breath while she made up her mind.

We were not quite near enough to put her cubs in danger, and she was not looking for trouble. She turned and walked slowly away with the youngsters at her heels, stopping every few yards to look back and make sure we were not following.

Our score at that point was far better than we had hoped for, but there was more to come.

An hour after that, at the foot of a steep rockslide, we came across a shallow hole that a bear had dug, making himself a level place to lie down on. The ground was still wet where he urinated before leaving. He was somewhere close by.

Benson found him, feeding up a mossy ravine on the side of the mountain eighty feet ahead of us. I put the camera on him, and Benson and Beals dropped prone on either side of me to keep out of the way.

The bear was a big male that would have weighed close to a thousand pounds, and he was a hard and surly looking character. He heard the first whir of camera shutter and spotted me instantly.

He saw one man alone, crouching among the rocks. To his way of thinking I must have been almost on top of him. He stood for three or four seconds, head swinging, a sullen growl rumbling up from his chest. Then he started for me at a deliberate walk.

Did he intend to charge? I never knew. Maybe he was just coming to look me over at short range. But eighty feet is too close to let a bear of that size walk toward you.

I called a sharp warning. Benson heaved to his knees and brought the .30/06 to his shoulder and Beals scrambled erect on the other side of me. Suddenly the odds were more than the bear liked. He swung away and shuffled up the ravine, stopping to look back as the others had done.

Our next contact was with a big blond female and a yearling cub that would have weighed around three hundred pounds. We got close to them, screened by alders along a narrow creek. The cub ran but the sow stood erect on her hind legs three times to look us over. A magnificent subject for the camera. Not until my two partners stepped out of the brush into the open did she clear out. It seemed plain that the brown bear, no matter how big, was more inclined to argue with one man than three, and I have talked with more than one guide who agrees with that belief.

We were ready to leave the mountain when we found yet another bear family. This time it was a medium-sized sow with three cubs no older than the first ones we had seen. Working across a slide where every step started a small avalanche, we topped a ridge and seventy-five feet down the slope the bear was sitting on her haunches giving the cubs an early supper.

The brawling racket of a creek in the bottom of the canyon below her had covered the noise we made, and she had no inkling we were there. I leveled and focused the camera, and then one of the cubs made trouble. She could feed only two at a time and the one that was shut out came scrambling behind her and saw the three of us up on the slide.

He must have sounded a pretty sharp alarm, for the old bear jumped to her feet and stood staring at us, sheltering the three youngsters with her body like an angry mother hen. She snarled and growled at us, and then drove the family ahead of her behind a rock as big as a small house. Next her head came into sight over the middle of the rock, and now she was really raging. She stayed there long enough for me to make the finest wildlife shot I ever put on film, and Benson said quietly, "She means business. When she climbs down she's going to come for us."

The bear went out of sight, and then she rounded the end of the rock, headed up the slope at a lumbering, determined run. I waited for the sound I dreaded, the whiplash report of Jack's rifle.

She was forty feet away and still coming when the cubs broke out of their hiding place with a clatter of loose rocks, slipping and sliding down toward the floor of the canyon. She turned for a look and then followed them, still growling and bawling, driving them ahead of her around a bend in the creek and out of sight.

We saw that family once more an hour later, so high on the snowfields that they were hidden at times in gray patches of cloud, climbing toward some valley

The bear was forty feet away and still coming when the cubs broke out of their hiding place, slipping and sliding down toward the floor of the canyon. She turned for a look and then followed them.

in the high country where the mother reasoned rightly we would not follow. She was climbing faster than the cubs, but every three or four minutes she stopped and waited patiently for them to catch up.

On the way back to the beach later in the afternoon we saw another bear, a lone individual that walked into an alder patch, a place where none but the most foolhardy would follow. And then, just at dusk, two more came into sight on a hill three hundred yards away. They were full-grown bears, about the same size, and they were playing a rough game of tag, chasing one another, romping and wrestling. The month was June, and in all likelihood they were a honeymooning pair. Great camera subjects, but the light was too poor.

That had been the most remarkable afternoon in all my years of camera hunting. Between noon and evening we had put twelve brown bears on film, five adults, a half-grown cub and six very young ones, all at incredibly close range. Best of all, we had accomplished it without firing a shot.

Frank Dufresne, who was then executive officer of the Alaska Game Commission and who knew the wildlife of the Territory as well as any man living, called the film we made that day the most beautiful of the brown bear that had ever come out of Alaska. He based his acclaim on the fact that all the footage was shot in bleak mountain country above timber, rather than along salmon streams where the bears congregated and were comparatively easy to stalk.

In 1947 one of those sequences won the first-place medal of the Boone and Crockett Club, in the first and only big-game photographic competition the club ever sponsored. I would not trade that film for the biggest bear pelt that ever hung on a wall. I prize it for another reason, too. As long as I live it will remind me of one of the most excitement-packed days I have ever had.

When we were back abroad the patrol ship that evening, relaxing over a drink before dinner, Benson turned to me and said quietly, "You paid me quite a compliment today."

I didn't remember that I had paid anybody a compliment, and I said so.

"Your life has been in my hands since noon," he told me.

NINETEEN

The More-so Bear

Most scientists are in agreement today that the Alaska brown and the grizzly are no more than geographic races of the same species of bear. As recently as 1918 Dr. C. Hart Merriam, a highly respected scientist, listed by name a total of eighty-six species and subspecies of grizzlies and brown bears. Their correct classification has been a bone of no little contention ever since, but the majority opinion now is that they are all one species, to which the brown bear of northern Europe and Asia also belongs. The Alaska Department of Fish and Game has accepted this opinion and speaks of its big bears as grizzly/browns.

But because the brown differs from the grizzly in a number of ways, in size, food habits, choice of habitat, and most of all in its rating by hunters as a trophy, I have chosen to treat them here as different bears. I have some support, too. The Boone and Crockett Club has long kept score on North American big-game trophies and from time to time published a book, *Records of North American Big Game,* that is the bible of trophy hunters. (In recent years the compiling and publishing of the records has become a joint venture between the Club and the National Rifle Association; a new edition of the record book is due to come out late in 1977, the first since 1971.) Boone and Crockett recognizes the brown and grizzly in separate categories for scoring purposes.

There is little question that on the average the brown bear is the biggest land carnivore left on earth. An occasional very large male polar bear may equal for weight his counterpart among the browns. There are even those who believe that the ice bear is the heavier of the two. But if a hundred full-grown browns picked at random were weighed and their weight measured against an equal number of polar bears, it seems very likely that the browns would be found to average heavier.

One thing is certain. The brown is a giant among bears, so much so that the initial reaction of a hunter or any other human seeing a big one for the first time is likely to be stunned disbelief. Standing erect on his hind legs, which is something they frequently do, such a bear would have to scrooch to walk through an eight-foot doorway. Stretched to full height, he can leave claw marks on a tree twelve feet above the ground. It is hard to accept the fact that such an animal exists.

Here is a description of a big one, exactly as I had it from the hunter who made the kill:

"An Alaskan researcher who was staying in camp with us went back to the carcass the next morning. He took along a set of scales with a capacity of 100 pounds, sectioned the carcass and weighed it. With an empty stomach (the time was May and the bear was just out of winter quarters) it weighed 1,120 pounds. The researcher thought that its fall weight, fat and ready to den up, would have been around 1,450. The rear feet were 13¾ inches long, and the hide and head, as we packed 'em back to camp, weighed 155 pounds."

That bear was far from a record-breaker, too. It stood a long way down on the Boone and Crockett list.

"Anything you can say about the grizzly is true of the brown, only more so," an Alaskan guide told me. That was well put. In every sense, the brownie is a more so bear, North America's biggest and most impressive predator, one of the world's most dangerous game animals, a splendid wild beast living in fearless independence in the wildest of wild country.

Just what weight does this giant attain? There has been a great deal of wild guessing, and it has to be admitted at the outset that hunters are likely to estimate any bear they kill as far heavier than it really is. But an honest weight of 1,000 to 1,500 pounds is not uncommon for big males, and the heaviest ever recorded tipped the scales at 1,656. That is a lot of bear. If you doubt it, ask any hunter who has taken a big one.

Most hunters judge the size of a brown bear by the squared measurement of the pelt. There is only one honest way to take that measurement. Lay the fresh pelt out flat on the ground, flesh side up, and not pegged or stretched. Measure the length from tip of nose to end of tail, and the width between the front paws. The skin probably will be wider than it is long. Add those measurements together and divide by two to determine what the bear squares. For example, a brownie pelt nine feet long and ten feet wide would square nine and a half.

Mostly because of heavy hunting pressure, browns that square ten feet are shot far less frequently today than they were thirty or forty years ago. Most hunters now consider a nine-footer very good, and many settle for a bear that squares eight or less. In the old days an occasional bear squared as much as eleven feet, and now and then you heard of twelve- or thirteen-footers. But honest guides were firm in saying that those last records were set only by dishonest stretching of the bearskin.

By the Boone and Crockett system, neither weight nor pelt size counts in judging how big a bear is. Skull measurements are the only yardstick. I have never thought that a really fair system, for two reasons. First, it's the pelt of the bear, not the skull, that is sought as a trophy. And second, as my friend Jack

O'Connor has pointed out a number of times, a small bear may have a big head and a giant may carry a skull on the small side. The heads of bears vary as do the heads of men, and very often their size does not reflect accurately the bulk and weight of the animal that carried them.

But one thing skull measurements do prove. The brown is a much bigger bear than the grizzly, bigger of skeleton as well as heavier.

In the Boone and Crockett 1971 book of records, the No. 1 skull on the brown bear list measures $17^{15}/_{16}$ inches long by $12^{13}/_{16}$ wide, for a score of 30 and $^{12}/_{16}$. The best grizzly in the book had a skull $17^{6}/_{16}$ inches long by $9^{12}/_{16}$ wide, adding up to a score of $27^{2}/_{16}$. That No. 1 grizzly falls far short of even being eligible for entry in the brown bear list, where the minimum score has to be 28 inches to qualify.

The question of classifying the two bears for trophy purposes has been a troublesome one for a long time. When Boone and Crockett published its first edition of *Records of North American Big Game,* in 1932, the book listed as its five top bears in the grizzly category animals that had been shot in brown-bear country. Hunters who had taken good grizzlies in the interior of Alaska found themselves hopelessly outclassed, and were naturally resentful.

The second edition of the book came out in 1939, and because by that time scientific authorities were in sharp disagreement as to what was a brown bear and what was a grizzly, all the bears of Alaska except polars and blacks were lumped in one category. Again all the top places continued to be taken by browns from Kodiak Island and the Alaska Peninsula, and grizzly hunters were left out in the cold.

In 1952 the late Grancel Fitz, who had been instrumental in devising a new scoring system for the Club, urged that the brown bears of coastal Alaska be considered separately from the grizzlies of the interior. The plan was adopted, and the line separating the ranges of the two bears was set as approximately seventy miles inland from tidewater, running from southeastern Alaska to Unimak Island at the tip of the Alaska Peninsula. Any bear killed west and south of that line was to be considered a brown, any taken to the east and north a grizzly.

Nine years later, in 1961, Boone and Crockett officials created sharp controversy in hunting circles once more, when they announced that because all the bears of Alaska apparently belonged to a single highly variable species, they were returning to a single category for purposes of record keeping. The Club's Records Committee was flooded with angry complaints, chiefly from hunters who had taken big grizzlies but were not even eligible to enter the big-game competitions.

In 1963 the Club backtracked again, reestablishing separate classifications for the two bears, defining their ranges and setting up a clear line of demarcation between them. The new dividing line ran in general about eighty-five miles from the coast.

It started at the southernmost point of Alaska, below Ketchikan, followed the British Columbia border to Mt. St. Elias and ran north to Mt. Natazaht; thence northwest, following the divide of the Wrangell Mountains to the end of that range; thence north along the 144th meridian of longitude to the most easterly point of the Alaska Range, and westerly on the divide of that range to Houston Pass; thence west along the 62nd parallel of latitude to the Bering Sea.

The country between that line and the sea is the home range of the brown giant. It is a wild and beautiful land of rugged mountains, rock slides, snowfields, forests of spruce and hemlock so dense that the sun barely penetrates, alder thickets, tide flats, beaches bordered by tall rye grass and strewn with kelp, brawling salmon rivers that tumble between banks where devil's club makes an impenetrable tangle. It is a land where man is an alien and unwelcome intruder and he enters it at the cost of great effort.

The rule of bear classification adopted by Boone and Crockett in 1963 has continued unchanged, and Club officials with whom I discussed the matter in the spring of 1976 saw little chance that it will be revised in the future. They stress that the division of Alaska's big bears into two classes is a sport-hunting and not a scientific division, but they are convinced that no other system is fair to bear hunters.

The fact is that if on the borders of their respective ranges a brown male finds a receptive female grizzly, the two mate and produce hybrid offspring. And if it chances to be a grizzly boar and a brown sow the same thing is likely to happen.

More than one hunter has killed an exceptionally large bear on the fringes of the grizzly country, especially along a stream that leads down to the coast, and come to the conclusion, probably rightly, that he had taken a grizzly-brown hybrid.

The biggest of the browns have regularly come from Kodiak, Afognak, and the Alaska Peninsula. Of the top fifteen on the current Boone and Crockett list, thirteen were taken on Kodiak, two on the Peninsula. All but three were killed more than fifteen years ago. There are brown bears on the islands of Southeastern Alaska that do not average much bigger than grizzlies.

Like all land bears, the brown displays a wide variety of color, ranging from almost black to pale straw-yellow. Of the six adults and one half-grown youngster that we filmed on the Alaska Peninsula in a single afternoon (talked about in an earlier chapter), four were rich dark brown, one was yellowish, and two, the youngster and its mother, were blond.

I have seen the statement in print at least once that the guard hairs of the brownie's thick pelt are sometimes tipped or frosted with silver, like those of the grizzly. But I have never seen a brown bear of that type or known a hunter who killed one.

The strength of the brown giant is in keeping with his size. He is very powerfully built, a heavy skeleton overlaid with thick layers of muscle as strong as rawhide rope. He can hook his long, grizzly-like front claws under a slab of rock that three grown men could not lift, and flip it over almost effortlessly if he has reason to believe there is a ground squirrel underneath.

Range of the Brown Bear

Jack Benson told me of a brown on Kodiak Island that took a thousand-pound steer a half mile up an almost vertical mountain, much of the way through alder tangles with trunks three or four inches thick. As often as his burden became snagged the bear bit off the alder and went on.

To appreciate that feat of strength and determination, you have to know what an Alaskan alder patch is like. I have seen nothing to match them, anywhere on this continent. Heavy snow packs the young shoots flat to the ground the first winter of their lives, and they stay that way permanently, growing into thick horizontal trunks, no more than a foot off the ground. But as soon as they

THE GRIZZLY AND BROWN BEARS

$4\frac{1}{2}'$

$3\frac{1}{2}'$

8' –9'

6' –7'

The relative sizes of the grizzly and the brown are shown in the drawing above. The average grizzly weighs 450 to 800 pounds, the brown 800 to 1200, with occasional bears going up to 1500 pounds or more. The grizzly has a more pronounced shoulder hump and a shorter, dished face, but the skulls are almost identical. The newborn cubs of the brown bear are smaller in relation to their mother than the young of any other mammal, measuring barely 9 inches long and weighing about $1\frac{1}{2}$ pounds. The drawing below shows relative sizes of a newborn bear, a 6-month cub, and a yearling—all in proportion to the bear above.

NEWBORN

6 MONTHS

1 YEAR

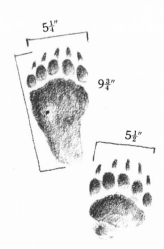

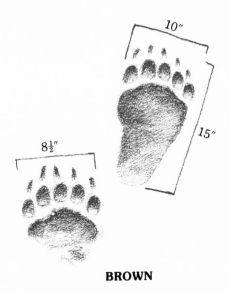

BROWN

GRIZZLY

The tracks of the black, brown, and grizzly bears are similar, differing only in size and geographical location. Where the ranges of the black and the grizzly overlap, larger tracks would probably belong to a grizzly. The ranges of the coastal brown and the inland grizzly don't overlap, so identification would be made on the basis of locale. The grizzly does have longer forefoot claws (right), which often show in the tracks.

183

get big enough to withstand the weight of the snow they turn up and finish their growth vertically, reaching a height of eight to ten feet. They also send up vertical branches. The result is an interlaced thicket about as hard to get through as a barbwire entanglement. It's hard to believe that even a brown bear could take half a ton of beef through such a place as that, but it happened.

Speaking of his strength, I have often wondered what the outcome would be if a really big brown were to clash in mortal combat with an African lion. The bear would weigh upwards of a thousand pounds, the lion not more than five hundred. For all the legendary agility of the big cats, the bear can move about as fast. He also has a far heavier bone structure, a thick pelt that even a lion would have difficulty clawing through, and far thicker layers of extremely tough muscle protecting his vital organs. My hunch is that he would take one swipe at the king of beasts with a forepaw and either crush its skull or break its neck. With luck he might all but decapitate it. A brown bear can strike a blow powerful enough to knock the head half off any cat that walks on this earth. It is interesting to speculate whether something of that sort may have happened, back in the time when the giant cave bear and the saber-toothed tiger shared the wild places of this continent, long before man appeared.

One of the most puzzling things about the brown is how an animal of his size manages to scrounge enough food to live on, in the bleak unforested country where many of his kind are found. The explanation is that, like all bears, he eats whatever is at hand and thrives on it.

When he comes out of winter quarters, early in the Alaskan spring, he relies heavily on grass and sedges, grazing like a steer. I have seen photos of a big brown with his mouth stuffed full of grass, stems sticking out at all angles like the mustache bristles of a walrus.

If he lives near the coast he wanders down to the beach and eats kelp. If he finds a dead or stranded seal, sea lion or even a whale, he lives high for many days in more senses of the word than one. He searches tirelessly for winter-shriveled berries on the bare slopes where the snow has melted, and digs for roots and for every ground squirrel he comes across.

With the arrival of summer, the streams of the Alaskan islands and coastal country teem with incredible runs of salmon. It is a common sight to see a gravel-bottom pool thirty or forty feet across so crowded with fish that no glimpse of the bottom can be caught. Alaskans will tell you (with a wink) that a man can walk across such a stream on the backs of salmon without getting his feet wet.

The big bear turns then to a diet of salmon, and for the remainder of his time out of hibernation he does not know the meaning of hunger. Of all the bears, he is the most able and persistent fisherman.

More than one wildlife artist, striving to turn out a dramatic illustration for an outdoor magazine but handicapped by the fact that he had never seen a brownie on a salmon stream, has depicted the bear flipping fish out of the water with a forepaw.

I have never seen one fish in that manner, and Alaskan outdoorsmen tell me they do it rarely if at all. Their stock method is to pick a stretch of shallow water where the stream runs over gravel or rocks, often at a rapids or low falls. There the bear stands watch until a salmon comes within reach. He pounces like a huge cat, sending water flying in every direction, pinning the fish on the bottom with a forepaw. Next he ducks his head under, grabs his prey in his jaws, crunches or shakes it to break its spine, carries it ashore and feeds, stripping off big slabs of flesh from both sides. Rarely does he eat his fish completely. Salmon abundance makes that unnecessary. The leavings are fare for foxes, ravens, and gulls that hang around in the neighborhood of the fish-hunting brown, tolerated so long as they do not come too close or attempt to rob him of his catch.

No four-footed fisherman is more expert than one of these big, clumsy-looking bears once he is full grown. Youngsters are often inept, and have a hard time catching salmon for themselves when they first leave their mother to go on their own.

Cannibalism among brown bears has been reported a number of times. The most interesting case I have ever heard of was described to me by Lee Miller, a biologist with the Alaska Department of Fish and Game who has carried on extensive research on both browns and polar bears. Lee's story even ends on a note of mystery.

Studying the feeding habits of browns on the Alaska Peninsula in the summer of 1961, he received instructions to collect a female and cub for use in a study of bear reproduction.

He selected the two he wanted from a group of a dozen or so feeding along a salmon stream, followed them five hundred yards away from the others when they left, and shot them. He took a complete series of body measurements and then started to skin the sow. He was standing over the partly skinned carcass when he heard a loud snort behind him and turned to see a second brownie, a four-year-old boar, only ten feet away and coming fast.

Miller jumped aside and grabbed for his rifle, which was leaning against a nearby alder. Expecting an attack, he brought the gun up, ready to shoot. But the intruder swerved away from him, grabbed the dead sow instead and shook her until her entrails started to come out, whereupon he began eating them.

Miller had moved off fifty feet by that time. His first thought was to shoot the cannibal. Then he decided to scare it off instead. He yelled and threw a stick, fired a shot in the air, but the bear went on feeding. Next he hit it with a rock. That brought a false charge in his direction, but the bear broke off the charge and went back to its meal. Not wanting to kill it needlessly, Lee backed away and started for his camp, a hike of more than a mile. He would go back early the next morning and retrieve the equipment he was leaving behind. It included a packboard, binoculars, set of scales, coat, knife, and notebook.

He returned to the area shortly after daylight. When he was still fifty yards away he spotted the bear, lying on top of a big mound of fresh earth. At the

*The bear pounces like a huge cat, sending water
flying in every direction, and pins the fish on the
bottom with a forepaw. Then he grabs the prey
in his jaws and carries it ashore.*

same time he saw a second bear approaching from another direction. The male
on the mound went for the newcomer in a headlong charge and drove it into
the brush, and Miller realized he was going to have trouble getting his gear back.

The cannibal went back to his mound at once. Lee inched in to fifty feet and
tried throwing stones. The bear was far more quarrelsome now than he had
been the afternoon before. When Miller scored a hit he leaped off the heap of
dirt, growling, and came for the man. The charge was not completed but the
bear was only three or four jumps away when he halted, turned and retreated
to his mound of dirt again. It was clear now that Miller would have to kill him
in order to get his equipment back. A shot in the head took care of things.

When Lee got up to the heap of earth, he found it was shaped like a big
beaver house, twelve to sixteen feet in diameter and eight or nine feet high.
The bear had buried the sow and cub and all of Miller's gear.

Lee had no shovel. He managed to free the cub, which had been partly
devoured, and a few items of equipment. There was no way to get the rest without tools, and because he was supposed to fly out that day and his plane was
due, he gave up and headed back to camp.

He went back to the area a year later and, hoping to find the large bones of
the bear intact and take their measurements, he hiked in to the scene of the
encounter. To his astonishment the mound of earth had disappeared and the
ground was as smooth as a green on a golf course. There was not a bone or
other object in sight to hint that anything out of the ordinary had ever taken
place here.

Two inches under the surface of the ground Lee found the knife with which
he had been skinning the sow when the male interrupted him. That was the
only article of any kind he could find.

What had happened? He still doesn't know, of course, but it seems logical
to think that other bears had leveled the mound and made off with the three
carcasses and the missing equipment.

TWENTY

Of Cubs and 'Copters

I have never forgotten a brown-bear skull that Frank Dufresne showed me in his office in Juneau in 1941, when I was on my way out to the Aleutians. A slab of heavy bone the size of a man's palm, carrying one of the big canine teeth, had been splintered off the bear's upper jaw, and the injury had never healed. The chip of bone had floated free in a pad of cartilage, with the tooth pointing out to the front rather than down. At the salmon cannery where he was shot the bear was known as the Grumbler, from the muttering growl that rumbled endlessly up out of his chest. He must have suffered a permanent king-size toothache.

Almost certainly the accident had happened during a fight between two boars for possession of a female. Such encounters and the injuries that result are far from rare. I knew of another big brown that had had a chunk of flesh and skin the size of a man's two hands torn out of his back in a brawl of that kind. The wound had not yet healed when the bear was shot in October.

Brown-bear cubs are born in the winter den in January or February, and the sow takes them back into her den for the first winter of their lives. To accommodate herself to that arrangement she breeds only every second or third year.

As with all bears, the little brown comes into the world a scantily furred midget. The mother may weigh as much as six hundred to eight hundred pounds; the newborn cub will hardly exceed a pound and a half.

When they come out of their birthplace in spring, the infant browns are among the most attractive of young bears, prettily marked with a pale yellow collar around the neck. They are also as playful and mischievous as all bear cubs, cavorting around their mother, bedeviling her, coaxing for a snack of milk between mealtimes, trying her patience in endless ways. She is a devoted and affectionate mother, but now and then a cub pushes things too far and gets cuffed into abject submission.

Lee Miller, the Alaska game biologist referred to in an earlier chapter, tells a fascinating anecdote about a female brown that adopted the cubs of another sow without permission, in a curious mixup of families.

Lee was camped with three companions at the McNeil River Falls, the foremost gathering place in Alaska for salmon-hungry browns, studying their fishing behavior. In midafternoon a big sway-backed sow, already known to the research party from frequent sightings, showed up on the fishing grounds with her three six-month-old cubs. Thirteen other bears were catching salmon at the same place.

Shortly a smaller sow, also with three young-of-the-year cubs, appeared on the bluff overlooking the river and entered the water only a few yards from Big Mama, leaving her youngsters ashore. The two families of cubs promptly mingled, and as all six were the same size and color the men who were watching could not tell which was which. Apparently the mother bears had the same problem.

The smaller sow soon caught a salmon, carried it ashore and went out of sight. At this point Big Mama seemingly realized that something was amiss with her family. She waded ashore and inspected the six cubs, sniffing uneasily, probably wondering what had happened.

She headed downstream, following the shore of the river, and all six little bears trailed along. She swam across with them, came back upstream 150 yards, reentered the water from the opposite side and resumed her fishing. A few minutes later the sow that had lost her cubs came back to the bluff, obviously upset. She found where the two families had merged and took the track, trailing all seven bears downstream as a hound trails a rabbit. She passed in plain sight and within one hundred feet of the six cubs and Big Mama, across the river, but paid no attention to them.

She swam the river where they had crossed it, and followed the tracks back upstream until she reached the cubs. Her own three made no move to accept her, and she was still sniffing and examining them when Big Mama came barreling out of the water and went for her.

The fight was brief. It was interrupted when one of the cubs fell into the river and was swept downstream by the swift current. Both sows dived after it instantly. The smaller one reached it first, helped it ashore on the far side of the river and disappeared in the alders with it. Big Mama went back to the five remaining cubs and led them away.

The biologists kept her and her enlarged family under observation for almost two weeks. They were seen repeatedly, and it was plain that the adoption was a permanent arrangement. A sow with one cub also was seen a number of times, but the men could not be sure she was the one whose two youngsters had been "bear-napped."

A family of five proved to be more than the big sow was up to raising, however. She was seen at the same place a year later, unaccompanied by a single cub.

The den of the brown is identically like that of the grizzly save that it is somewhat larger, to accommodate the greater bulk of the occupant. Examination of dens on Kodiak Island and the Alaska Peninsula has shown the main chamber to be six or seven feet across and as much as nine feet high, the entrance tunnel as long as twenty feet where the digging was good.

The den site is most frequently on a hillside, sometimes above timber on a mountain slope, more often sheltered in an alder thicket lower down.

Studies in Alaska have revealed one amazing thing about the locations chosen by the brown bear for its den. In general the den sites are in places that have deep snow cover, perhaps, as game researchers speculate, because the snow affords insulation and protection against the cold of winter. And the bear is also finicky about the direction in which the den slope faces.

On Kodiak Island, of eighty dens examined most were on north-facing slopes. On the Alaska Peninsula east-facing slopes were chosen most often.

Does this mean that the bear deliberately picks a location where he will have the most favorable snow conditions, the preferred amount of drifting, the melting time he likes best in spring? To assume that is to give him credit for a high degree of intelligence, even reasoning power. Wildlife researchers make no claim to knowing his reasons, but it is an interesting thing to speculate about.

The bear begins the preparation of its winter den in late summer, usually by the end of August. With the coming of cold weather it retires into the den and falls into the light sleep of bear hibernation. The time when it emerges in spring depends on weather and other factors, but in general females with young cubs spend a longer period in winter quarters than do males.

A great deal of scientific research on brown bears has been carried out by the Alaska Department of Fish and Game since the late 1950s. Al Erickson, the biologist who pioneered black-bear research in Michigan, moved to Alaska around 1956 and began the same kind of work with the big browns, capturing them alive, recording their weights and measurements, fitting them with radio collars to keep track of their movements, and learn the size of their home range and the extent of their travels. Leland Glenn, Lee Miller, Jack Lentfer, and other Alaska researchers have continued the work down to the present time. More than five hundred browns have been tagged on the Alaska Peninsula alone.

So much of it has been done that it has become almost routine. "There was adventure in capturing brown bears with snares along fish streams," comments Don McKnight, chief of game research for the Alaska department, "but the excitement has gone out of bear tagging as we do most of it nowadays. Our recent projects have involved the use of dart guns shot from helicopters, in rather open terrain, such as the Alaska Peninsula."

McKnight is certainly right about the element of adventure in the early days of research. Leland Glenn, the Alaska game biologist who has carried on bear research for nine years, and who completed in 1976 a six-year study on the Alaska Peninsula in which over five hundred browns were caught and marked, tells of a couple of captures that were anything but routine.

The first one happened to him in the summer of 1970. He had immobilized a female bear with a drug dart from a helicopter. Her cub, weighing around

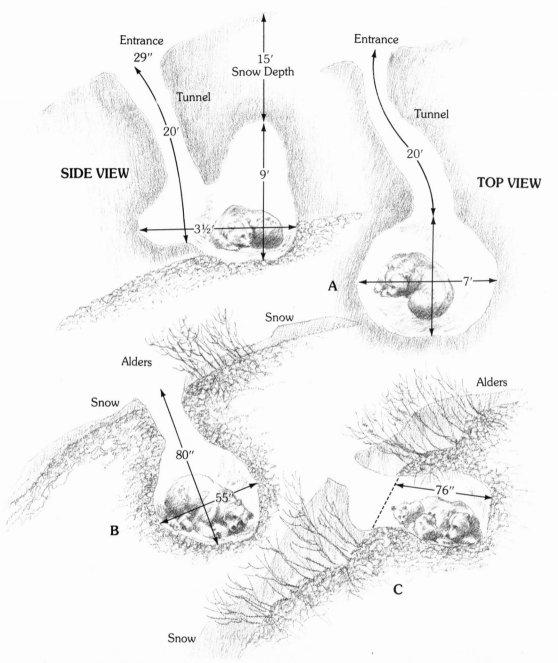

SIDE VIEW

Entrance
29"

Tunnel

20'

15'
Snow Depth

9'

3½'

TOP VIEW

Entrance

Tunnel

20'

7'

A

Snow

Alders

Snow

80"

55"

B

Snow

Alders

76"

C

Three types of dens used by brown bears. (A) Snow den used by a mature bear; (B) natal den used by a female and three cubs; (C) den used by a female and two yearlings. The dimensions given are of specific dens in Alaska that were examined and measured by scientists.

fifty pounds, took to its heels. The 'copter pilot landed, and Glenn undertook to run the cub down and capture it by hand. That was standard procedure at that time.

As Glenn describes it, "We landed a man as quickly as possible near the running cub or cubs. The man would run flat out and if he was lucky make a flying tackle and pin the cub to the ground. If he failed he was usually too winded to make a second try. In that case he would hide and let the helicopter pilot herd the young bear close enough for him to catch it in a short dash.

"The fun really started when you grabbed a bawling bundle of fur that weighed forty to sixty pounds and was all muscle, teeth, and claws. The trick was to hang onto the nape of its neck as tight as you could and keep the rest of it away from your body."

If a sow had more than one cub, and the research crews have captured females with as many as four young, the difficulties were multiplied accordingly.

"Once you got a cub into a 'copter you could pin it on the floor and hope you had enough energy left to keep it there while the pilot made the short flight back to the immobilized sow," Glenn explains. "We always processed the cubs and released them before we began work on her."

This time he succeeded in running down the cub he was after, but the chase took place in a flooded muskeg and the biologist was completely winded. He managed to get the cub into the helicopter but, as he tells the story, it outwrestled him on the back seat after the chopper was airborne.

"I yelled at the pilot to land quick," Glenn says. "Unless he did I was leaving the ship, airborne or not. By then the cub was halfway over the front seat and I was holding him by the hind legs. When we hit the ground I lost my grip and he gained yardage fast, with all ten front claws sunk in the front seat cushion. He was bellowing and threatening to chew an ear off the pilot, and you can imagine what a good time that individual was having, with the cub all to himself in the front seat while he endeavored to set down the chopper. I'd have tried for an action shot with my camera, but I didn't figure the pilot would last that long."

Glenn got a fresh grip on the young bear, the party took to the air once more and made it back to the immobilized sow.

"We later refined our techniques for capturing cubs," Glenn says dryly.

In 1972, before the techniques were "refined," a geological survey team working in the same area as Glenn and his bear-tagging crew reported sighting from their helicopter a sow brown with two six-month-old cubs in tow. They directed the airborne biologists to the location and it was an easy matter to dart-drug the old bear. Glenn's party was waiting out the eight to ten-minute period required for the drug to take effect. The geologists were hovering nearby, and over their aircraft radio they asked whether they could be of help, adding that they'd like to land once the bear was immobilized, take pictures and watch the measuring and tagging close up.

Glenn accepted the offer of help. The sow was moving toward an alder patch and he was unwilling to let her out of his sight while he and his helpers

"The cub was bellowing and threatening to chew an ear off the pilot, and you can imagine what a good time that individual was having, with the cub all to himself in the front seat while he endeavored to shut down the chopper."

landed and chased down her two cubs, which would skedaddle. He asked the geologists to land and catch the cubs.

"It would save us time," he says, poker-faced, "and I also thought it would be a memorable experience for them."

It was all of that. Thirty minutes elapsed and the job of tagging the female bear was about finished, when the crew heard the geologists' chopper lift off and saw it heading toward them. But something was wrong. The helicopter gained about 150 feet of altitude, then descended abruptly. It rose and dipped several times, at the same time changing direction. Remembering his own experience two years earlier, Glenn had a pretty good idea what was going on.

When the two geologists and their pilot finally landed near the tagging crew and climbed out of their aircraft, all three looked as if they had tangled with a buzzsaw, which was close to the case. They were wet and muddy from head to toe, their shirts were bloody and shredded into strips.

"Here are your damned cubs," one of them growled, and they handed over two bedraggled little bears that looked about as worn out as the men.

Glenn made an innocent remark about how cute and docile the youngsters were, and then asked casually whether the geologists would mind giving a hand again if he had occasion to capture another family group in that same area. One of the team put his thumb to his nose in an eloquent gesture, and the three turned back to their chopper and headed for their camp. The bear taggers got no further tips from them.

In recent years, as better immobilizing drugs have become available, cubs are caught by hand but immobilized before they are put into a helicopter. As Don McKnight comments, that has taken much of the excitement out of bear tagging. But it was excitement the researchers can do without.

The studies have shown that male browns roam far more widely than females, some of them traveling a home range close to fifty miles across, in quest of either food or a female willing to be courted.

Of all the results that have come out of the bear research program, none is more dramatic than the discovery that both browns and grizzlies have a mysterious homing instinct as strong as that I described in the black bear in an earlier chapter.

In personal correspondence, Don McKnight listed for me two of the most spectacular examples.

A young male grizzly, captured at the Sagwon dump in the North Slope oil fields, was immobilized, airlifted, and released sixty-seven miles away. It took him just fourteen days to get back.

But the bear that holds the homing record in McKnight's opinion was a three- or four-year-old male brownie drugged in a culvert trap five miles from Cordova on the Copper River highway. He was trucked to Cordova, put aboard a vessel and taken to Montague Island in Prince William Sound, almost seventy miles from home.

Drugged and seasick, he was pushed overboard about 150 feet from the shore of the island. At first he swam in circles as if hopelessly confused, but finally he made it to shore.

He was captured on September 17. In less than a month, on October 15, he was killed within one hundred yards of his original capture site. To get there, he had swum at least seven miles across Hinchenbrook Entrance to the mainland, battling strong tidal currents, and then walked and swum sixty miles home.

There is much that goes on in the brain of a bear that no human will ever understand.

TWENTY-ONE

What Lies Ahead?

What does the future hold for the biggest of the bears? The answer to that would seem to depend in large degree on the use to which the vast acreage of wild and presently unpeopled land in the bear's range is put.

At the present time Alaska is unique among the fifty states in having as Governor a registered Master Guide, in the person of Jay Hammond. Because of his long-established reputation as one of the top guides of the state, and also because of his great interest in wildlife management and conservation, I asked Governor Hammond what he believes the future of Alaska's brown and grizzly bears will be.

In a letter in May of 1976 he replied: "The future of these bears and of hunting them is tied directly to one thing, maintenance of bear habitat. The big bears are rarely compatible with humans unfamiliar with wilderness. When the two meet, often enough the outcome is conflict—which in some cases results in a dead human but much more frequently in a dead bear.

"As long as Alaska has substantial acreages that aren't crowded with people, whether they be preservationists, hunters or industrialists, these bears will make out just fine. Trophy hunting is not likely to decimate their populations.

"Fortunately, most of Alaska is inhospitable to man for much of the year. This factor, coupled with the immensity of our state, results in relatively few ultimate conflicts annually. I can comfortably predict a very solid future for the brown/grizzly bears in Alaska."

Nowhere has the brown come into as much angry conflict with cattle interests as on Kodiak Island. The bear war waged there by cattlemen with varying intensity has gone on for more than forty years, ever since a dozen or so cattle and sheep ranches were established in the Chiniak Cape section of the island. That had been prime bear range and conflict was inevitable. It was intensified when the Kodiak Bear Refuge was established, adjoining the cattle country.

The controversy mounted to a peak in the early 1960s. For years the ranchers had killed any bear they came across, using traps, snares, guns, dogs, and poison. They finally took to hunting the browns from the air, with the gunner shooting from the rear seat of a two-place light plane. Twenty-two bears were killed that way in a single year.

Then, in 1963, a brand-new and very effective piece of bear-control equipment made its appearance. It consisted of a .30 caliber M-1 Garand semiautomatic rifle mounted on top of a Piper aircraft so that it shot four inches above the prop. It was fired electrically with a button on the control stick, could get off its eight rounds so fast they blurred, and the clip could be replaced in flight through a sliding door in the ceiling of the plane. Equipped with a Nydar sight, this ingenious little replica of a fighter aircraft could throw its lead inside a three-foot circle at 150 yards. In a fairly short time at least 35 bears were done in with this deadly contraption.

The whole operation was carried out with the approval and close cooperation of the Alaska Department of Fish and Game. The plane belonged to a rancher, the pilot was president of the Kodiak Stock Growers Association, but the aircraft had been converted for bear hunting at the request of the State of Alaska, under a law providing that game may be killed in defense of life or property. Cattlemen put heavy pressure on state politicians and the politicians gave them what they wanted in those early years of Alaskan statehood.

The bear killing was carried out in such complete secrecy that it was close to impossible for any outsider to learn what was going on. But inevitably there were leaks, and early in 1964 a group of outraged guides on Kodiak Island sent a telegram to Bill Rae, then editor of *Outdoor Life,* asking the magazine to present the facts to the public.

The result was publication, in August of that year, of an article by Jim Rearden, Alaska sportsman and outdoor writer, that blew the lid off. The resulting uproar reached far beyond the borders of Alaska. Angry letters came to *Outdoor Life* from every part of the country. The Alaska Sportsmen's Council, made up of twelve of the state's leading conservation organizations, protested strongly, pointing out that the cattle ranches were located on publicly owned land leased from the Bureau of Land Management. The National Wildlife Federation, made up of sportsmen's groups from every state in the country, went so far as to call ranching on Kodiak a mistake and suggest that bears should be put ahead of cattle.

The converted Piper was grounded, and although the bear war still simmers it has not again reached such a heated level.

"The Kodiak situation peaked out about 1970," an official of the Fish and Game Department told me. "We took the stand that bears were more valuable to the Kodiak people than cattle, and we would no longer assist the ranchers with their problems. Cattle ranching on Kodiak was a marginal venture at best, and the whole thing has more or less faded away as a problem."

Jim Rearden, now a member of the Alaska Board of Game, is one of the best known outdoor writers in the state and knows as much about the bear situation as anyone does. He told me this: "The bear-cattle conflict has been quiet for some years. Bears still kill cattle now and again, the cattlemen have the right to protect their stock and usually they do so, but without any fuss. The cattle industry is not as aggressive as it was in the 1960s. But there will be conflict as long as there are brown bears and cattle on the same range, and I expect it to flare up now and then.

"A significant part of the Kodiak National Wildlife Refuge (intended primarily for the benefit of the bears) will pass into native ownership under the Alaska Native Land Claims Settlement Act. At this time no one can say just what use those lands will be put to, but a spokesman for the natives recently told me that recreation, including bear hunting and concessions sold to guides, will have high priority."

Another land-use threat hangs over some of the best of the brown-bear range. Big chunks of the Alaska Peninsula also have been claimed as native lands, and the Fish and Game Department believes that reindeer and sheep ranching will follow. If that happens, a conflict similar to the one on Kodiak seems inevitable.

In the past, applications for grazing leases on the Peninsula have been turned down by the Bureau of Land Management, in the belief that the best possible use for that land is raising brown bears. Whether the new native owners will adhere to that policy, no one can predict.

Jim Rearden summed up today's situation for me in these words: "At the moment Alaska's big bears, browns and grizzlies, are abundant and increasing. The total population is probably as high as it has been for half a century or more.

"In some areas hunting cut into the population rather too heavily in the late 1960s, but curtailed seasons, with lower kills, have turned that around. The population has increased and the average size of trophies has improved.

"Today's hunting regulations are aimed squarely at safeguarding the bears. Seasons vary in length in the different game management units, from more than nine months to as little as two weeks. The limit is one bear per hunter every four years. Taking cubs or sows with cubs is prohibited, as is hunting with planes. No hunter may hunt on the same day he is airborne, and nonresidents must be accompanied by a licensed guide. The annual average kill of browns and grizzlies is now about eight hundred.

"The future is anybody's guess, but as long as the habitat holds out there will be bears. (Alaska's human population is up fifty thousand in the last couple of years because of oil development.)

"We're getting new roads and hunting is increasing, but any time the bear kill goes too high the season can be cut back or closed altogether. We know a lot more about browns and grizzlies than we did twenty years ago, and we know what is happening to them. A total of more than five hundred browns have been captured, measured, weighed, and tagged on the Alaska Peninsula since 1970. Those studies have yielded a great deal of valuable information.

"I'd say that for the foreseeable future our bears will provide good hunting and their populations will remain stable—unless major changes occur in their habitat."

A detailed analysis of the situation was supplied me in a letter from Stan Frost, president of the Alaska Professional Hunters Association, a group of high-level and strictly ethical guides and outfitters pledged to fair chase, organized some years ago to deal with unsportsmanlike hunting practices in pursuit of trophy game.

"One of the major factors working against both the interior grizzly and the coastal brown is Alaska's increased human population," Frost told me.

"The resident pressure on the brown bear has increased tremendously in the last few years, as a result of the influx of so many people to work on the pipeline and related projects. The requirement for a resident hunting license is one year of residence in the state. Many newcomers hunt brown bears after a year, with no knowledge of the bears. Many browns are shot at ranges of three hundred to four hundred yards, and get away to die in the brush.

"Another factor in the coastal areas of Southeastern Alaska, Prince William Sound and other places accessible only by boat is the indiscriminate plinking at brown bears by commercial fishermen and other boat operators who consider the bear a threat to salmon. Many browns are wounded in this fashion and left to die.

"Finally, the big old boars are an important threat to smaller bears and cubs. On a hunt in Southeastern Alaska in the spring of 1976 I heard of two cases in which a mature boar was shot while actually feeding on cubs.

"The guided hunt, required in the case of nonresidents, is also a factor that has to be taken into consideration. But such hunts, directed by an experienced guide, result in fewer bears being wounded. The guide will not allow shots to be taken at extreme range.

"The operations of unethical guides and their hunters are no longer a threat, as they may have been in the past. Since the creation of Alaska's Guide Licensing and Control Board the penalties for violation of guiding laws are so severe that very few guides will take a chance. The board has revoked the licenses of many guides convicted of violations, and aircraft used in connection with a violation have been confiscated. The penalties jeopardize the lawless guide's very livelihood. It's too great a risk to run.

"In general, the brown bear population in Southeastern Alaska, Prince William Sound, Kodiak Island and the Alaska Peninsula is in very good shape. The guided hunter has about an 80 percent chance of taking a good trophy. By good trophy I mean a well furred bear of reasonable size that he can be proud to hang on his wall. The day of the ten-foot bear is past. We still have a few of them, but they are killed far less frequently than in the past.

"Alaska's interior grizzly population is also in very good shape and is increasing in many areas, although success on guided grizzly hunts probably runs only 30 to 50 percent. This is not due to lack of bears, but to the difficulty of hunting and stalking the grizzly. The grizzly population is not as great as that of the brown bear, and they are wide-ranging animals.

"With the prohibition against hunting on any day the hunter is airborne, both populations should remain stable for many years to come.

"There is, however, one unpredictable factor that could be detrimental to the grizzly. That would be opening to the public the present haul road along the pipeline to Prudhoe Bay. That haul road goes through some of the best grizzly country in Alaska, and I believe that ease of access by autombile and other means of transportation may be the key to the grizzly's future. He is a true wilderness creature, and the more roads Alaska pushes over the tundra, the smaller the area where he can live undisturbed, and the more human pressure he must endure.

"Alaska is still the greatest place in the Union in which to hunt, a place that offers a genuine wilderness experience. But true wilderness cannot tolerate roads or access by thousands of people. When that happens it is no longer wilderness. The pipeline haul road may be the beginning of a road system throughout northern Alaska—and the end of Alaska as we have known it."

TWENTY-TWO

Brown Dynamite, Short Fuse

Just before darkness fell that hot August night, Harry Lance spread his blanket on the moss, rolled in it with his .30/40 Krag beside him, fought mosquitoes for a time and drifted off to sleep. The Saaok River tumbled and chuckled only a few yards away.

Lance would not know it until afterward, but he had bedded down in a place where two of the most heavily used brown-bear trails on Chicagof Island crossed. It was a mistake an old Alaska hand would never have made, but he was not an old hand.

A young biologist just out of school, he was in Alaska for the summer, doing collecting and taxidermy work for an expedition sent out by the Philadelphia Academy of Sciences.

As far back as he could remember he had harbored a dream of photographing brownies. The big bears tugged at his imagination and he had concluded that hunting them with camera would be the ultimate in adventure.

His chance came when the expedition reached Chicagof. They found the beach meadows and river banks trampled by brown bears. Breathtakingly big tracks crisscrossed the tide flats, bear paths followed the streams, half-eaten salmon littered the river bars, and at frequent intervals the bears had flattened the beach grass in beds half the size of a livingroom rug. This was bear country at its best.

But as often happens, finding abundant bear sign and getting sight of the bears proved two different things. For almost a week nobody laid eyes on a brown. Finally Lance won reluctant permission from the expedition leader to hike inland and spend a night beside a salmon stream, where he would be on hand to photograph any bear that came to feed at daybreak.

He was dropped off on the beach in late afternoon, at the mouth of the Saaok, carrying a rifle and his pack with a blanket and camera gear.

He found it far more difficult to follow the river inland than he had anticipated. Thick tangles of devil's club, the terrible Alaskan shrub that grows higher than a man's head and is armed with long needle-sharp spines from top to bottom, made it impossible to walk the river bank. Lance pulled up the hip boots he was wearing and took to the stream itself, wading against the strong current.

Two miles from the beach he came to an opening that gave him a clear view up and down the river, and decided to bed down for the night. He debated in his mind the need of a fire for safety, but decided against it, fearing it would scare off any bear that came along.

There was still enough twilight in the sky for him to see what was going on around him when a commotion in the river thirty yards away attracted his attention. A solitary bear, that looked to Lance as if it weighed a ton, was fishing slowly downstream toward him. It caught sight of him, sniffed, swung its head and finally made him out. It gave him a long, hard stare, ten paces away, but finally resumed its fishing. He had been right not to build a fire, Lance told himself. All the same, the bear had come close enough to give him a bad scare. He gave some thought to leaving and going back to the beach, but decided against it. He had come for pictures and he'd stick it out.

He awoke out of sound sleep around midnight, his heart pounding, not knowing the reason for his fright but sure there was some animal nearby. The night was very dark and he could see nothing. Then sticks broke on either side of him and he was more afraid than ever. He kicked his blanket aside and got to his feet, gripping the Krag—and something warm and furry brushed against his right foot.

He jumped away, and the squalls of two bear cubs ripped into the stillness of the windless night, one on the right, the other on the left. The answer came instantly, a bellow of rage from the she bear, fishing in the river.

She splashed out of the stream and up the bank, growling and roaring. Lance could not see her but he knew flight was useless, so he stood his ground, pointing the rifle in the direction of the sound.

The shot exploded in the night, and the gun went sailing out of his hands. He felt a forepaw on his shoulder smashing him to the ground, and then the bear was standing over him . . .

205

He let her crash into the muzzle before he pulled the trigger. The shot exploded loud in the night, and the gun went sailing out of his hands. He felt a forepaw on his shoulder smashing him to the ground, and then the bear was standing over him, holding him down, grumbling and growling, and her blood was streaming into his face like warm water poured from a pitcher. She started to cough, and Lance concluded in a quick flash of thought that she was lung shot and would die. Would he die first? He wasn't sure.

He was not aware that the bear had left him until he heard her thrashing and grunting in the brush a few feet away. He rolled to his feet and groped frantically on the ground for the Krag. He found it about fifteen feet away, but the bolt seemed to be jammed. Then he realized that the rifle was okay. The bear had bitten through his right hand and he lacked the strength to work the bolt.

He finally got a fresh cartridge into the chamber with his left hand, searched for and found his boots, drew them on and backed into the river. The bear was still snarling and coughing in the brush.

He didn't bother to look for his pants, didn't even think of them at the time, and so had nothing to hold the boots up. The two miles of wading down to the beach was a nightmare. He climbed over windfalls, slipped and stumbled, fell countless times. His boots dropped down around his knees and filled with water. When he finally reached the beach the masthead light of the expedition ship lying offshore was the most welcome sight he had ever seen. He fired the Krag and yelled until a dory came ashore to pick him up.

Lance did not go back to the scene of the bear attack. He had no wish to see it again. Other members of the party went up the river the next morning and retrieved the gear he had left. They found the old bear dead, but the cubs had disappeared. Lance brought the female's pelt home to remember her by.

He had had the bad luck to blunder by accident into one of the most dangerous situations in the woods of North America. He had made his bed in a place frequented by a female brown bear with young cubs. By the time she discovered him she was too close to back off. When the cubs sounded their alarm squall, trouble was inevitable.

It is a brand of misfortune that has happened too many times to count. Another wildlife photographer was killed at Cold Bay on the Alaska Peninsula in 1974 under almost identical circumstances. Given the size (more than twice that of an African lion) and the hair-trigger temper of this bear, and its terrible power to maul and kill, the human who gets close to a family group whether by accident or intent is in deadly peril.

Nor is the sow-and-cub combination the only one to beware in brown-bear country. The late Frank Dufresne, then chief executive officer of the Alaska Game Commission, once warned me never to surprise a brownie—and never let one surprise me. The trouble is, that is advice that can't always be followed.

Most of the time, the brown giant prefers peace to trouble. The chances are better than ten to one that he will let you alone if you let him alone. You can meet him on a bear path or in a treeless mountain meadow, and if you don't

crowd him too close, corner, threaten or injure him, the odds are good he will go his way and let you go yours without any argument. There is one thing you should understand about him, however. The chances are very slim that he will be afraid of you.

If you meet face to face he may lumber off, and your first thought will be that he has been bluffed out. But before he has gone many times his own length the chances are he'll stop, swivel around and look you over with a long hard stare to see what your intentions are. After that he may walk off again, but every few yards he will halt for another deliberate look. Everything about him says plainly enough that if you want to make something of the encounter he'll meet you halfway. And I know of very few things more sure to make human hair stand on end than a bear that stands eight feet tall on his hind feet, turning to face you in that fashion, maybe only thirty yards away.

Every once in a while you are almost certain to encounter a brown that will not yield an inch of the trail to you or any other living thing he meets. When that happens you must be ready to take care of yourself, and taking care of yourself means carrying a rifle adequate for the job and having the ability to use it on split-second notice and place your shot where it will leave nothing to chance.

Only the foolhardy go into the woods in brown-bear country without a rifle, whatever their errand may be. Those who know this giant well enough to respect him do not go unarmed, whether berry picking, hiking, backpacking, or fishing on the streams where he fishes.

They have another very sensible rule, too. They don't go for walks at night.

Jack Benson, the Kodiak wildlife agent who guided and backed me the summer I hunted brownies with a camera, warned me at the outset. "They are brown dynamite," he told me, "and they are timed with a very short fuse."

Individual bears vary in temperament as widely as humans do. One may run at scent of a man, the next may carry a perpetual chip on his shoulder. A few years back, for example out of a concentration of more than fifty browns at the McNeil River Falls fishing ground (where they gather in extraordinary numbers each summer) there was one female that stood head and shoulders above all the rest for aggressiveness. She ran off anything and anybody who came near, while the others were content to mind their own business so long as they were not threatened.

Not many browns will charge unprovoked, although what may look like provocation to the bear may not appear that way to human eyes. And every now and then a genuinely quarrelsome one comes along. Maybe he has reason. Perhaps he has been shot and crippled at some time in the past, and harbors a grudge against humans as a result. Maybe he has recently been in a fight with another bear and is feeling surly toward the world in general. Maybe he just naturally has a bad temper. Whatever the reason, he is literally brown dynamite, short fused.

Nobody has put it better than Stewart Edward White, the widely known outdoorsman and novelist of the early years of this century. White spent a great deal of time in brown bear country, cruising along the coast in his yacht, prowling ashore to hunt bears with a camera. He finally summed up his conclusions this way: Not more than one brownie in twenty will start trouble unprovoked — but they do not come in mathematical order. The dangerous bear may be the first one you encounter, not the twentieth.

It has to be admitted that many victims mauled by this bear bring their misfortune down on their own heads, either by accident, by carelessness or because they underestimate the danger of attack. A trout fisherman runs into trouble when he rounds a bend in a stream and comes on a brownie fishing in the next pool. A hiker following a bear path along a salmon river sees a freshly killed fish in the path ahead and overlooks the fact that almost certainly the bear is watching in the brush only a few steps away and will not give up its kill without a fight. He walks on for a closer look at the salmon. If he escapes with his life he is lucky.

Frank Dufresne had a story of that kind to tell. Hiking back to the beach from an errand along a salmon stream, in an area where the cover was so dense that he was forced to follow bear paths through the devil's club, Frank rounded a turn in the trail and saw a freshly caught salmon only a few yards away.

He was unarmed and he knew enough of bear ways that his skin crawled. "Right then I'd have given a year of my life to know how long that fish had been there," he told me. He didn't have to wait long to find out. While he watched, the salmon flopped.

Dufresne knew then what he had to expect. He did the wisest thing possible. He backed away, moving one foot very slowly behind the other. When he was out of sight he turned and ran.

He waited until the afternoon was almost gone. Then, because he did not dare to spend the night where he was, he crept back down the bear path. The bear had carried the salmon away. Frank tiptoed past the place where it had lain and hot-footed for the beach and the safety of his boat.

"I never saw that bear," he finished the anecdote, "but of the many I have looked at none ever scared me the way it did."

Jack O'Connor once told me that he did not think attacks on humans by brown bears happened as often as attacks by grizzlies, in part because contact between people and the browns was less frequent. There are no statistics to rely on, but I'm not sure I agree. Certainly the brown is fully as short-tempered, unpredictable, and dangerous as the grizzly, equally quick to resent the near presence of a man, any threat to cubs, or interference with food that he considers belongs to him.

Many sportsmen rate good photos or motion picture film of this bear a trophy fully as desirable as his pelt, or even more so. As I said earlier, I for one would not trade my 16mm color footage of this magnificent animal for the biggest and most beautiful bearskin rug ever taken.

The risk involved in hunting browns with a camera is at least as great as in gun hunting. Usually it is greater. Most of the pictures are made at far less than rifle range, and the excitement matches the situation. It is hardly to be wondered at that the brown giant is considered the wildlife photographer's dream trophy.

Plenty of mishaps have occurred as a result of trying to photograph a bear at too close range. An animal of the size and temper of the brownie is bound to regard as a threat any living creature that trespasses in his immediate vicinity, and his response is likely to be to carry the fight to the enemy and drive off or kill whatever it may be. He does that regularly with another bear, and often the same deeply bedded instinct overcomes any caution he may feel where man is concerned.

To meet the widespread demand for a place where brown-bear pictures are a sure bet, and also to protect both the photographers and the bears, the Alaska legislature in 1967 set aside the McNeil River State Game Sanctuary, "for non-consumptive use of Alaskan brown bears," with hunting prohibited.

The sanctuary area is unique. About half a mile above its mouth on Cook Inlet, some two hundred miles southwest of Anchorage, the McNeil River drops over a stretch of big rocks to form a series of low tumbling falls that hinder or in times of low water even block the upstream spawning migration of thousands of salmon. Salmon trying to negotiate the fast water or leap the falls are easy prey for fish-loving brownies, and for years the bears have been drawn to this productive fishing ground in extraordinary numbers.

There are countless salmon streams in Alaska where browns gather for a summer of fishing, but no other place where they are found in such numbers as at the McNeil Falls. It is not unusual for as many as seventy-five to frequent that one section of river in July and August, when the salmon runs are at their peak. Often up to thirty are in sight at one time. The bulk of the brown-bear pictures that come out of Alaska nowadays are taken there.

It was hardly a wonder that wildlife photographers flocked to this bonanza. By 1970 there were days when human visitors, most of them professional or semiprofessional photographers, outnumbered bears. The brownies started to raid camps, a few photographers were guilty of reckless behavior, and trouble developed. In two cases female bears with cubs were killed "in defense of human life," an action allowed under Alaskan game laws.

In 1973 the Alaska Board of Fish and Game found it necessary to resort to a permit system to control the number of visitors. A maximum of ten permits are now distributed for each day, each permit covering an individual visitor. Six of the ten cover a period up to five consecutive days. The remaining four are good for one day only. If applications exceed the number of permits available the successful applicants are chosen by drawing.

The refuge still gets very heavy use, a total of 345 man-days by 79 visitors in 1975, but rules have been drafted to keep bear-man conflicts at a minimum and the situation between the bears and the photographers is much better than it was.

Early in 1976, *Outdoor Life* published a remarkable series of color photos of Alaska browns, taken by a guide who hunts big game with a camera in his off season. The pictures were taken at McNeil River Falls.

The accompanying story told of approaching bears to within twenty-five feet, by slow stalking and not letting them get scent of the photographer, for dramatic closeups made without a telephoto lens. It also told of a regrettable encounter in which a female brown was killed with a Magnum handgun at twenty feet, when she came for the cameraman in a determined charge.

I wrote a box insert for use with that story, in which I conceded that the author had had far more dealing with brown bears than I, but added that in my opinion he was taking unwarranted risks in sneaking to within twenty-five or thirty feet of a full-grown bear for the sake of getting a portrait photograph. Virtually all of the Alaska guides I have known would agree. I then went on to list a few rules of safety for any camera hunter stalking the brown giant. They were:

1. Let the bear know you are there while you are still far enough away that he can clear out if he wants to. If necessary, make a noise to attract his attention at a distance.

2. Keep out of alder patches, tall grass, thick brush or any other place where the bear can wait in ambush.

3. Never crowd him. He has no natural enemies and is lord of the country he roams. If you approach too closely he is likely to decide you are looking for trouble, and he may not wait for you to start it.

4. Carry a firearm powerful enough for the animal you are stalking. In my opinion that means a rifle, not a handgun. If the law bans firearms in the area where you are taking pictures, avoid bears.

5. For the outsider not familiar with the areas and brown bear behavior in general, it's best to be backed by a guide who carries an adequate rifle and can

be relied on to use it in a hurry if the need arises. A guide has one further advantage. The bear is less likely to charge two men than one, and three are in less danger than two.

That story and the photos that accompanied it brought letters from a number of readers severely critical of what they termed recklessness on the part of the photographer, blaming him for the death of the bear he had to kill.

One who wrote was R. A. Rausch, director of the Division of Game of the Alaska Fish and Game Department.

"We strongly concur with your comment that the photographer in this case took too many chances," Rausch said. "Approaching a brown bear as closely as he does not only endangers the man but is also a threat to the bear. The purpose of a telephoto lens is to provide closeup pictures without crowding the animal. This man's attitude clearly indicates a lack of respect for the bears and a willingness to destroy one to accomplish his own goals.

"The permit system presently in effect at McNeil River has two objectives, only one of which is to limit the number of persons present. Equally important is the control of their activities. Such behavior as this man described would now result in his permit being revoked and a possible citation to court.

"Unfortunately, when a human is attacked by a wild animal the general public seldom considers the possibility that the injured person may have been at fault."

James W. Brooks, commissioner of the Alaska Department of Fish and Game, expressed the same feelings in a personal letter to me.

"We remind all visitors to the McNeil River State Game Sanctuary of the potential danger in being around wild bears," he wrote. "The brown bear can be unpredictable and aggressive. We suggest that each party carry a rifle, but we strongly urge that human visitors consider themselves intruders in the domain of the bears. At all times they should show the browns respect and use every discretion."

That last rule cannot be overemphasized. If you are going into the brown giant's home country, unless you are hunting him and mean to kill or be killed, walk warily and do your damnedest not to light his fuse!

TWENTY-THREE

Terrible in Rage

Bob Munger, who formerly owned a hardware and sporting goods store at Charlotte in south-central Michigan and who was also an enthusiastic big-game hunter, has two life-size mounts that are among the most beautiful I have ever seen in any trophy room.

One is a brown bear whose pelt squared ten feet and whose weight, spring-lean, Bob's guide estimated at close to twelve hundred pounds. The other is a polar bear of almost exactly the same size. Both pelts are thick and heavy. Both animals are mounted erect. On low pedestals they stand close to eight feet tall and they are a magnificent pair, the brown looking burly and powerful, the white bear sinuous and graceful by comparison.

It is easy to understand why many hunters have long considered those two bears the most splendid trophies that could be taken on this continent, and among the most beautiful in the world. Both are huge, impressive, and hard to come by. They speak of pristine wilderness, of hunting patience and craft and some luck. Also of some danger. They are wonderful reminders of a hunt that, once experienced, no sportsman can ever forget.

The polar bear cannot be hunted in this country at the present time, but the brown can, and for most hunters a big one remains the most coveted trophy in North America.

Even the track of such an animal, printed deep in snow or sand, is an awesome thing to look at. Beside it, the track of a man's boot looks like the footprint of a pigmy.

In general the brown is hunted about as the grizzly is. The hunter spots his bear, sometimes on the beach, sometimes along a salmon stream, or again in a berry patch or other open place on a mountain, and makes his stalk on foot.

Most of the brown bear country is remote and roadless, accessible only by plane or boat. The Alaskan outfitter and guide may fly his bear-hunting clients to a camp in a promising location in the interior, glass the surrounding mountains as for sheep, and spot a bear of trophy size if luck is with the party. I have never heard of a packhorse hunt for browns, although there are places where I suspect it could be done if the horses were available.

Or, because the bears frequent the beach and the lower reaches of salmon streams, the hunting may be done from a boat anchored in a sheltered bay or from an outboard-powered skiff scouting quietly along shore.

Finding a good bear can be difficult. But most of the time the stalk is the really hard part of the hunt.

The brown bear's vision is not the best, although he seems to make out anything that moves, even at a distance, and no animal in the woods has keener ears or a better nose. The hunter's only hope of getting close enough for a shot is to keep the wind in his favor, and in mountain country where the air currents are forever shifting that can be hard to do.

It's the rugged terrain and thick cover that pose the chief problems for the hunter. A sportsman just back from an Alaskan hunt once told me, "From the air the mountains of Kodiak Island do not look especially formidable, but to a man at the foot of one, wading creeks fed by melting snow, toiling up like an ant through grass and alders and across rock slides and snowfields, they look different. Part of the time the hunter crosses slopes so steep that he has to go on all fours. Now and then he slides on the seat of his pants. In soft snow on a spring hunt he may lie flat, dig his fingers in and belly his way along."

An acquaintance of mine who hunted on Afognak a few years back said afterward that when he first saw the heavily timbered shore from his outfitter's boat he didn't think there was any chance of taking a bear there.

"There were no high mountains such as I had seen on the Alaska Peninsula and even on Kodiak on earlier hunts," he said. "No places where you could glass half-bare slopes from your boat and spot a bear three miles away. There was just a narrow strip of rocks for a beach, fringed with grass and driftwood, and then scrub spruce and underbrush so thick you couldn't see into it.

"One thing I was sure of. I wasn't going into that timber after a bear. It looked about like the cedar swamps where I hunt deer back in Michigan, and I couldn't see myself shadowing a half ton of brownie in that kind of stuff."

My friend was lucky. A good bear came out of the timber to the beach to dig for sand fleas, shrimp-like critters about the size of a cricket, that hide under stones and act like crickets, too. The bears gobble 'em up, pebbles as big as golf balls, sand and all. This bear was so preoccupied with his meal that the hunter and guide wormed their way to a big driftwood log within thirty yards of him. One shot from a .375 Magnum ended the affair. With good luck, hunting from a boat can be like that.

I knew another hunter who, hunting from an outboard-powered dory, lost his balance when the dory lurched in rough water and grabbed the anchor rope with both hands to save himself from going overboard. He was holding his rifle in one hand at the time. He heard a splash, and you can guess the rest.

"That's how come a fine .348 Winchester lies today on the bottom of Deadmans Bay, in water sixty feet deep," he finished his story. With bad luck, hunting from a boat can be like that, too.

Usually in thick cover, such as alder patches and tangles of devil's club (every stem and twig of that terrible shrub bristles with needle-sharp thorns an inch long), the bears themselves leave heavily traveled paths that a man can follow. But not many guides, and even fewer hunters, are willing to walk a bear trail in such stuff as that.

As one hunter put it, "There were places in there where you could step on a bear before you saw him. I don't think I'm a coward but I'm no hero either, and I just don't have the stomach for that kind of thing."

But if hunting the brown giant is a tough and even dangerous sport, and it is, the rewards are also great. I once heard a hunter who came into camp after dark describe it this way: "I can't tell you how I felt right at that minute. I had killed a brown bear, a big one with a fine unrubbed pelt. His color was rich brown tipped with golden yellow, darker on the legs and belly, shading into paler yellow and blond around the ruff and head, and the fur was five or six inches long and very thick. I wanted to sing or dance, or whoop like a painted Indian. I wanted to call my wife and tell her I had killed a bear. I wanted to get back to camp and buy everybody a drink."

Many hunters have felt the same way.

Brown-bear hunting calls for a couple of special items of equipment in addition to a gun and good binoculars: hip boots and rain gear. Much of the country where the bear is found is fog-shrouded and rain-swept a fair share of the time, even in the mountains. More than one nonresident, flying to camp with dazzling sunshine glinting off the snow peaks and telling himself that nobody needed hip boots in such weather, has awakened the next morning to find the snowfields blotted out by fog and the world socked in with cold and misty rain.

What rifle should the brown-bear hunter carry? Save for the polar bear, which at least matches him, the brown is the most dangerous game animal on the North American continent and among the most dangerous in the world. Many experienced hunters rate him more to be feared than the lion, tiger, or leopard. He is a heavyweight, terrible in rage, and the rifle that is used to bring him down needs to be in the heavyweight class. I can offer no better proof of that than the story of Russ Smith and Hosea Sarber and the bear they killed on Admiralty Island.

When I met Dr. Russell Smith, in the 1940s, he was a physician and surgeon at Barron in northwest Wisconsin, with a busy practice in that prosperous dairy country. He was also a zealous gun collector, with cabinets full of the finest lot of rifles I have ever seen. Every one of them was usable, and Russ had spent enough time on the target range to become a crack shot.

A few years later he moved to Alaska and struck up a close friendship with Sarber, a game warden stationed at Petersburg and also a crack rifle shot. Hosea knew as much about brown bears as any man in Alaska. He was credited with the classic observation that the angry bawl of a big one at close range would take ten years off any man's life. He later died under mysterious circumstances. His empty boat was found floating in a bay where he had gone on patrol, but his body was never recovered and to this day no one knows whether his death was a case of accidental drowning or whether poachers killed him.

He and Dr. Smith started hunting bears together, and Russ killed his first seven, four blacks and three browns, in their tracks with seven shots, using a .300 or .375 Magnum rifle.

"I came to the conclusion that a competent rifleman armed with an adequate gun was more than a match for any bear that ever walked on four legs," he told me.

It took his fourth brown to show him the error of his thinking.

On a spring hunt, he and Sarber went ashore in Gambier Bay on Admiralty. The hunt had been a very productive one. In fifteen days they had seen a total of thirty bears, about half blacks and half browns.

Russ had dropped an 800-pound brown with a shoulder shot from a .375, and the bear went down stone dead. The law then allowed two of the big bears, and three days later he went after another. A big one, with an unusual silvery pelt, walked out of the woods onto the open beach, and Russ and Hosea stalked him to within a hundred yards. Russ put his shot in the chest and the bear went over backward like an upset bowling pin. But in the same motion he bounded back on his feet and ran for the timber. He had only three or four jumps to go and was out of sight before the doctor could get off another shot.

Smith and Sarber confronted the unwelcome and highly dangerous chore of following a wounded brownie into thick cover.

They waited an hour. "There are tombstones all over Alaska that were put up for men who were in too much of a hurry in a case like this," Hosea commented. When Russ, blaming himself for failing to make a clean kill, wondered aloud whether he was using enough rifle, Sarber reassured him.

"There's none better for this business," he said. "But you could wallop one of these bears with a bazooka and if you didn't hit him in just the right place he'd travel half a mile and take his time about dying."

At the end of the hour the game warden pulled himself up from the log where they had been sitting. "He should be cooled off by now," he said. "Let's go see."

They followed the blood trail into a tangle of spruce and undergrowth so thick that they had to walk on bear paths, taking a careful half step at a time. They came finally to an open place fifty yards across and separated to circle the edge of it. Russ took only a dozen steps when he saw a pair of big brown ears above the top of an alder clump. The bear came roaring for him instantly.

Hosea's .375 Magnum blasted while Russ was filling his scope with bear. His shot was so close behind that they sounded almost like one. The two heavy bullets belted the brown off his feet but he bounced up like a huge football and came on as if nothing had happened, bawling to make the ground shake.

He was ten paces from Smith when the men poured their second pair of shots into him. Again he went down as if struck by lightning — and again he was up and coming as they worked their rifle bolts.

"He was the most murderous looking thing I had ever seen," Russ told me afterward, "and his roaring was like no noise I had ever listened to."

He fired his last shot when the bear was so close that it was like shooting at the side of a barn, and Hosea's came with it. Smith didn't even hear the game warden's rifle go off. The bear was dead when he hit the ground.

Dr. Smith waited until he was sure. Then he took four steps and laid his hand on the furry shoulder.

"That was too damned close," Hosea summed it up quietly.

The brown had taken seven shots in all, four from Russ, three from Sarber. The game warden had a reputation as one of the best riflemen in Alaska and he had lived up to it. His shots were in the front half of the bear, so close together that the palm of a hand covered them.

"As a surgeon I know something about anatomy," Russ told me afterward. "I wouldn't have believed that any living creature could have withstood such terrible destruction and stayed on its feet. I wish that every sportsman who plans to hunt brown bears could have seen the inside of that one when we finished skinning him and laid him open."

Not only is the brown the biggest and one of the two most dangerous animals on this continent. He is also extremely hard to kill.

The .30/06 has accounted for a lot of his kind. In fact, thirty or forty years ago it was probably the caliber most commonly used on the big bears. Capt. Charles Madsen of Kodiak, in his day one of the best-known guides in Alaska, carried one for years and considered it adequate in the hands of any hunter who knew how to handle it.

But the first rule of brown-bear hunting should be to use enough gun. Most riflemen today rate the .375 Magnum the ideal caliber, and few advocate anything below the .300 Magnum. The .338 Magnum turns in a performance much like that of the .375 and is probably as good. Both calibers have a muzzle energy of 4,000 foot-pounds or more, depending on loads. At 100 yards the .338, loaded with the 250-grain Silvertip bullet, delivers a wallop of 3,280 foot-pounds. The .375's 270-grain softpoint arrives 100 yards out with a striking force of 3,620 foot-pounds. Not a great deal of difference, and both calibers have terrific shocking and killing power. There is almost certainly nothing better for brown bears.

When it comes to using a bow for this hunting, there are not too many men who want to face up to the brown giant. Fred Bear is one who did. He had a hair-raising encounter with a surprise ending, but he took a bear that went into first place on the record list of the Pope and Young Club, which keeps score on bowhunters.

Fred began his hunt on Kodiak Island, guided and backed by Ed Bilderback. Bilderback was fond of saying that a gallon of outboard gas will get a fire going much quicker than a quart, and he followed that same rule when it came to picking a rifle for brown bears. He carried a .375 Magnum, sawed off for faster handling in thick brush. He was an expert rifle shot, cool and dependable, and he was also an enthusiastic bowhunter, fond of calling crows into a tree over his head and picking them off with blunt arrows. He had bowhunted for years and was completely familiar with the requirements of that method. Fred couldn't have had a better man behind him.

Fred himself was fully aware of the risk involved in trying to take a brown with the bow. For use in an emergency, he was carrying a .44 Magnum Smith and Wesson handgun in a shoulder holster, his standard precaution when hunting dangerous game. But he was hoping that he wouldn't need to use it and that there would be no reason for the guide to intervene with the .375.

The hunting party was living aboard Bilderback's fifty-seven-foot salmon boat. When three days of hunting on Kodiak failed to turn up a bear they moved across Shelikof Strait and anchored in a small cove on the bleak and treeless Alaska Peninsula. There, in five days of hunting, they spotted four brown bears, including one that left a track in wet snow fourteen inches long. But Fred was not able to get within bow range of any of the four.

They went two days then without seeing a bear, partly because the wind blew a gale both days. But the time was May and the browns were coming down to the beach to feed, and once the wind dropped a big one walked out of a patch of alders a couple of miles away in late afternoon.

The stalk was an easy one. Piled-up driftwood lay above the high-tide line, and back of it was a belt of tall grass a hundred yards wide. A quarter mile from the bear the grass gave way to alders. There was good cover all the way and the brown was in the open, feeding on the beach. The low sun was behind the hunters, the wind was in their faces and surf was breaking along the shore to cover any small noise they made. They followed a bear path through the alders the last quarter mile and got to within fifty yards of the brown without any difficulty. He was pawing at a pile of kelp, completely unaware that he was being hunted.

When the bear, looming huge and blocky against the sun-reddened sea, turned broadside he brought the bow to full draw and let the string slip off his fingers.

Fred and Bilderback took a few seconds to size things up, but they didn't waste much time. "I learned a long while ago that hunting with a bow means waiting to admire the trophy when it is dead," Fred said afterward.

"What do you want to do?" Ed asked in an undertone.

"Get closer."

Actually, he didn't want to get any closer to that bear. He was already too close for comfort. But he had made this hunt in the hope of taking a brownie, and for a bowhunter twenty-five yards is more than twice as good as fifty. He slid the handgun out of its holster and stuck it in his belt where it would be easier to draw, and crept ahead.

When he stopped behind a pile of driftwood he was just twenty yards from the bear. He discovered at that point that he was on the trail it had used to get to the beach. In all likelihood, when he drove an arrow in it would follow that same trail back to the alders. But he had no thought of backing out at that point.

He was carrying a 65-pound Kodiak model bow, made by his own company, and razorhead arrows. When the bear, looming huge and blocky against the sun-reddened sea, turned broadside he brought the bow to full draw and let the string slip off his fingers. The arrow buried itself to the feathers in the rib cage.

The brownie let go a growling roar and spun round and round, biting at the nock end of the shaft. Then it came head-on. It was not charging, for it did not yet know what had hurt it. But it would go past Fred, crouched beside its path, so close that he could whack it with his bow. It couldn't fail to see him. He whipped the .44 out of his belt, telling himself that he could move a lot of lead in a hurry. Maybe he could move enough.

The bear was thirty feet away and he was starting to squeeze the trigger when Bilderback's voice boomed out behind him.

"Don't shoot! He's a big one."

Fred knew what the guide meant. A bowhunter can't claim as a trophy any animal with a bullet in it. If he finished the bear with the .44 his license was filled, his hunt was over and he'd have to go home with nothing to show for it. In a quick flash of thought he remembered Bilderback's saying about a gallon of gas. In the last split second Ed could do a more certain job with the .375. Fred never finished his trigger squeeze.

The bear was five steps away when he saw Fred. By all the rules he should have kept coming, but for some reason, maybe because he was a very sick brownie by that time, he swerved suddenly off the path and went crashing into the alders.

He ran two hundred yards with blood pouring out of the arrow wound, and fell dead. He had lived less than a minute after the arrow knifed into him, but it was a minute Fred Bear will never forget.

"If you want the last word in excitement and thrills, take a brown bear with an arrow at sixty feet," he told me later. It was advice I had no intention of following.

PART THREE

THE POLAR BEAR

TWENTY-FOUR

Bear at the Top of the World

The top of the world. A place of bitter cold, of long winter darkness and un-broken summer sun; of endless ice and drifting snow, empty gray sea, bleak shore, and treeless islands. Strangely enough, that desolate and frozen region is the home of one of earth's most magnificent game animals, the polar bear.

He is found throughout the polar world, reaching his greatest abundance along the southern edge of the sea ice, whether that be shore-fast or separated from the land by a broad belt of open water.

Five nations claim him as a resident, Russia, Norway, Denmark, (on the big island of Greenland), Canada, and the United States. He is big and beautiful and dangerous, and as a Canadian wildlife authority has said, few other animals are as symbolic of all that is wild.

As recently as twenty years ago even the foremost zoologists of the countries where he is found did not know a great deal about his way of life. Much that was believed was guesswork. There are still gaps in the story, but modern re-search and the determination and dedication of the researchers are fast closing them.

This bear differs so greatly, both in appearance and habits, from the other bears of this continent that it is hard for a hunter encountering one to think of him as a blood brother to the black, grizzly, or Alaska brown.

Until recent years, even scientists accepted the differences as real, classifying the white bear of the North in a group by himself. The other three belong to the genus *Ursus*, the Latin name for bear. The polar bear once carried the scien-tific name of *Thalarctos*, from Greek words meaning sea bear. At the present time, however, scientists are calling him *Ursus maritimus*, the Latin equivalent of bear of the sea.

The Eskimos have always called him *Nahnook*. Of all his names, I like best the one by which the Crees of James Bay know him, *Wahb'esco*. They accent the first syllable hard, and I have never heard them say it but that excitement came into their voices. They understand the kind of bear he is.

THE POLAR BEAR

3′ –4′

6½′ –8′

The polar bear has longer legs and neck, and a more pointed head, than the other North American bears. In contrast to the dished face of the grizzly, the polar bear's nose bulges at the bridge, as can be seen in the drawing of the skull at left. Average males weigh from 900 to 1000 pounds, but bears have been found that weighed up to 1600.

The polar bear's paws are heavily matted with short, stiff hairs that protect them from the cold and provide traction on slippery ice and snow. The claws are not long but they are sharp and are used for gripping the ice. The tracks of this bear are only seen in regions where they could never be mistaken for those of any other animal.

The differences between *Wahb'esco* and his next of kin are more apparent than real. Proof is found in the fact that, surprising as it may seem, successful breeding between polar bears and Alaska browns is not uncommon in captivity, and the polar has also been successfully crossed with the brown bear of northern Europe. In both cases the hybrid offspring are capable of producing young, too, indicating a close basic kinship between the parents.

Perhaps the greatest difference between the sea bear and the land bears is in his looks. The black, grizzly, and brown are all low-slung, burly animals with short legs, short necks and broad, somewhat square heads. The polar bear, despite a heavy and powerful muscular build, has longer legs, a long slender-looking neck and a longer and more pointed head. Seen broadside, the latter two characteristics give him a slinky, almost reptilian appearance. His ears are small (although his hearing seems keen enough), and in contrast with the dished profile of the grizzly and brown he has a "Roman" nose that shows a slight bulge at the bridge. His canine teeth are longer and heavier in comparison with his own size than those of the other bears, and the molars are smaller, a reflection of the fact that meat makes up the greater share of his diet.

In weight he rivals the giant brown bear of Alaska. Accurate weight records of polar bears are hard to come by, for very few of them are killed where scales are available, but the few records that exist indicate a bear nearly as heavy as the brown.

Seton tells of an exceptionally big male killed in Hudson Strait in 1821, hoisted aboard ship and weighed. It tipped the scales at sixteen hundred pounds, and Seton accepted it as the heaviest on record. That record might be questioned because it was set so long ago, but as recently as 1970 two Canadian researchers drove a bear from his den on the west coast of Hudson Bay, knocked him out with a drug dart, and learned to their considerable surprise that he weighed fourteen hundred and fifty pounds. He was the largest recorded in Canada in modern times. All in all, there is plenty of proof that the polar is close to the brown in weight, although on the average adult males run only about nine hundred to a thousand pounds. Most females weigh from five hundred to seven hundred, but weights above one thousand pounds have been recorded for them.

Judged by skull size, the yardstick the Boone and Crockett Club uses in scoring trophy bears, the polar does not quite equal the brown, for the reason that his more slender head counts against him.

Since 1966, Boone and Crockett has refused to accept polar bears for scoring and entry in the record list of North American big game. The refusal was based on the fact that certain unethical practices in hunting the bears from the air violated the club's rule of fair chase, and also on the fact that the size of their world population was not precisely known and there was some reason to question the wisdom of hunting them at all.

The biggest polar in the Boone and Crockett record book at the present time, killed off Kotzebue, Alaska, in 1963, had a skull that measured $18^8/_{16}$ inches in length by $11^7/_{16}$ wide, for a total score of $29^{15}/_{16}$. It was longer than the No. 1 skull on the brown bear list by $^9/_{16}$ of an inch, but $1^6/_{16}$ narrower, and would fall in only eighteenth place on the record list of big browns.

Starting early in the 1960s, wildlife agencies in both the United States and Canada launched intensive scientific studies of the polar bear, capturing bears alive, immobilizing them with dart guns, measuring, weighing and marking them, and in many cases fitting them with radio tracking collars. Between 1967 and 1972 more than five hundred were studied in this way in Alaska alone, and in the last ten years more than fifteen hundred have been similarly processed in Canada. Much valuable information has resulted, and certain earlier theories about the ice bear have been demolished.

Twenty years and less ago, it was commonly believed that he was completely an international character, that most or all of his population drifted end-

Range of the Polar Bear

lessly around the top of the world in a clockwise direction, with the polar ice pack. This theory held that a bear that was north of Greenland this summer might be in the vicinity of Hudson Bay a year later, off the coast of Alaska in another year, and might ultimately become a resident of Russia or Norway. Research has shown that in general this is not true. Instead, each region of the Arctic appears to have its own population of bears, separate from any others, often tied to large islands or specific sections of coast.

Very rarely has a bear tagged in Canada been found later as a member of an Alaska population. Alaska even has two distinct populations off its arctic coast, one to the north, the other to the west, and the two do not appear to mingle. And in Canada, the bears of James Bay do not mix with those of Hudson Bay, despite the ease with which they could pass back and forth.

"The polar bear has a home range, and knows where he is and where he is going at all times," Canadian researcher Ian Stirling assured me. "His home range is far larger than that of the land bears and he is more of a traveler. Where he is found at any given time of year depends largely on ice conditions and his food supply. But you can be sure he knows where home is and how to get back there. The individual bear may be carried fifty miles by drifting ice but he walks or swims back, and a local population drifts hardly at all."

Stirling believes that even females that den and have their young out on the sea ice make their way back to their home territory and remain members of such local populations.

Jack Lentfer, one of the top bear researchers in Alaska, presently working for the U. S. Fish and Wildlife Service out of Anchorage, is inclined to agree.

"In some cases they travel deliberately against the direction of the ice drift in order to maintain their position relative to the land," he says. "Studies indicate that there may be several groups of geographically isolated polar bears."

One of the most amazing things to come out of the tagging studies is the fact that the ice bear, dwelling in a featureless world with few landmarks, has a mysterious homing instinct as strongly developed as that of any land bear. Of four removed from the Churchill area on the west coast of Hudson Bay, where they were rated nuisance animals, and released 150 air miles away, three hundred miles as they were transported along the coast, two made it back to Churchill in about two weeks.

At all times the ice bear is an inveterate and tireless traveler, both on land and in the sea. Hunters using aircraft have followed a bear track across snow-covered ice for seventy-five miles without overtaking the bear. He has been found swimming as far as seventy-five or eighty miles from the nearest land, and now and then he has been known to wander more than a hundred miles from saltwater, up a big river and its delta. Explorers have encountered him less than 150 miles from the pole. In fact it was on the endless, empty ice in the highest latitudes that they met him most often and shot him for food in the early days of arctic exploration.

Andre, the Swedish balloonist who attempted to drift to the pole in a free balloon in 1897 with two companions, was forced down on the ice some five hundred miles short of his goal. In the long and terrible march the three men made south between mid-July until early October the polar bears they shot were their chief source of food. They finally reached land on White Island to the northeast of Spitzbergen and died there, probably of cold. Not until 1930 were their last camp and their bodies discovered, entirely by accident. Their diaries revealed that at the end they had enough bear meat on hand to last them through the winter, and at that time they were less than eight hundred miles from the pole. The white bear is a denizen of the *far* North.

Not infrequently, however, he strays far south of his normal range. Polar bears have been seen a number of times on Charleton Island and at Moose Factory, at the southern end of James Bay only five hundred miles from Ottawa.

Apart from man, this bear has no enemies of consequence to reckon with, and despite all the years of hunting he is not greatly inclined to be afraid of man.

Occasionally he is killed by a herd of walrus, probably as a result of an ill-advised attack on them, a plain case of biting off more than he can chew. I know of no one who has witnessed a battle between a swimming bear and a hunting pack of killer whales, but I doubt the bear would stand a chance.

One other enemy young polar bears and females have to fear. That is the big males of their own kind. Cannibalism is anything but rare among these bears, and there are many records of boars killing sows smaller than themselves, as well as young.

When it comes to food habits, the polar bear is more of a meat eater than the other bears and consequently more of a predator. Luckily, he preys for the most part on animals that are not of major importance to man.

Hair seals are his staff of life. In fact, so long as he is on the ice not much else is available. In the spring the bears kill large numbers of young seals by breaking into seal dens in the snow. Later they hunt the adults, by lying in wait at a hole where the seal comes up to breathe and crawl out on the ice, by stealthy stalking, hiding behind ice hummocks, sliding toward the basking seal on their bellies, or by pouncing from the water onto a seal lying on a small ice pan.

Now and then the white bear kills a walrus, although there is risk in that, or a white whale. Very rarely they succeed in taking a caribou or muskox, so infrequently that their predation on those species is of no significance. On land they catch lemmings and prey to some extent on waterfowl and other birds and on their eggs and young. Years ago they made it a summer practice to catch and feed on salmon in the streams of Labrador, much as browns do in Alaska, the only recorded case of the ice bear becoming a confirmed fisherman.

Like all bears, they turn to a vegetable diet when it is available. They eat grass, sedges, lichens, moss, berries, and even seaweed. The stomach of a four-hundred-pound male that invaded and attacked a geological survey camp in the far north of Canada in the summer of 1975 was filled with the latter, and it seemed logical to believe that the bear was drawn into the camp by hunger for meat or some other food.

The sea bear shares with his land kinsmen a marked fondness for carrion. In late summer he frequently patrols beaches in a search for stranded walrus or

whale carcasses. As many as twenty of his kind have been seen around the carcass of a single whale, probably drawn for long distances by the incredibly keen
sense of smell possessed by all polar bears.

Although the opportunities are limited in the Arctic, if a garbage dump becomes available they are as quick as any bear to find it and rely on it for a food
supply. There are two garbage dumps at the towns of Churchill and Fort
Churchill on the west shore of Hudson Bay. Polar bears gather in extraordinary
numbers in the Cape Churchill area thirty-five miles to the east. Canadian researchers have seen thirty-six adults there in an area the size of a football field,
and have counted more than 250 in four hours of flying along the coast. It is
doubtful that the white bears, normally solitary animals, congregate in such
numbers anywhere else in the world. It is only natural that the nearby garbage
dumps should attract from forty to seventy every fall. They are a major attraction for residents and visitors alike, but they are also dangerous neighbors.

Polar bear meat itself can be excellent eating, apart from the liver, which is
so rich in vitamin A that it has caused serious illness and death. The Eskimos
consider it taboo and are careful to keep it away from their dogs. The flesh of
the ice bear has saved many explorers from hunger or actual starvation.

There is, however, one risk in eating it. The sea bear, like the land-dwelling
members of his family, frequently harbors trichinae, the parasite that begets
trichinosis in humans. The hunter who wants to feed on polar bear meat should
make sure that it is thoroughly cooked.

In September or October the pregnant females of the polar bear population
that were courted and bred back in the spring retire into dens, in most cases
caves dug deep in hard-packed, drifted snow either along the coast or on the
shorefast ice in the vicinity of pressure ridges.

So far as researchers know, there is only one place where the white bears
den regularly in ground caves, excavated in the sand of cut banks or along the
shores of rivers. That is in Hudson Bay. It is believed the bears dig these dens
to shelter them from the summer heat, but when autumn comes females that
are expecting utilize them for winter use. (*Text continued on page 235.*)

*The bear often pounces from the water onto a
seal lying on a small ice pan.*

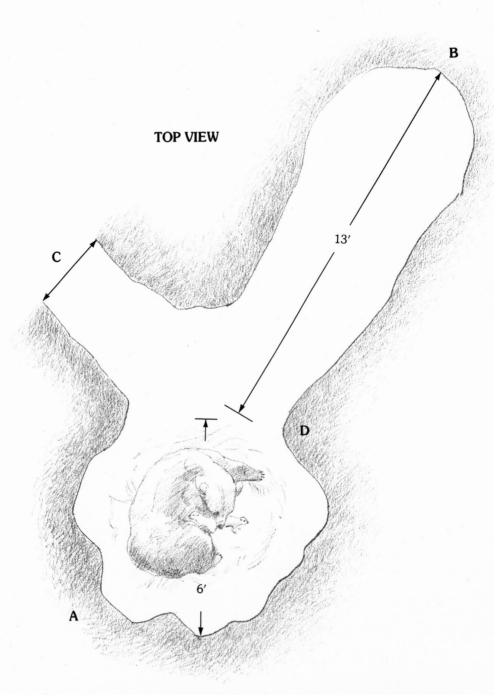

TOP VIEW

B

13'

C

D

A

6'

*A maternity den used by a polar bear on Southhampton Island, N.W.T.
The den, occupied by a female and two young cubs, consisted of an upper
and lower room, and a ventilation hole at right angles to the entrance*

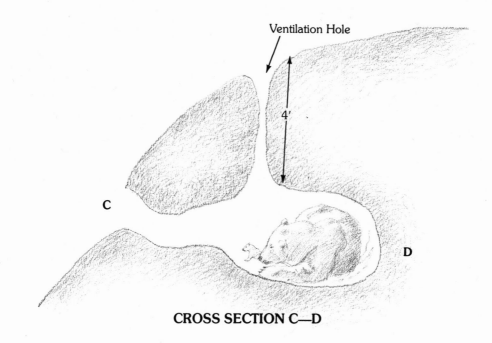

Ventilation Hole

4'

C

D

CROSS SECTION C—D

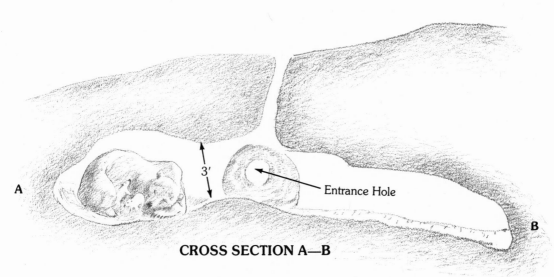

3'

A

Entrance Hole

B

CROSS SECTION A—B

tunnel. Polar bears, like brown bears, den alone, except for mothers with cubs or the cubs themselves after they leave their mother.

Brower baited the sow with a big piece of blubber, luring her far enough away from her cub that he was able to grab it and climb onto his snowmobile. He drove off, the mother in angry pursuit.

This trait of the polar bears was not known to science until modern studies were begun in the 1950s, but our party had encountered an interesting example of it on our trip into lower Hudson Bay in 1937. We found an island off the east coast of the bay that was laced with trails and literally torn up by summering bears. There were dens in every suitable steep bank, some looking newly dug and freshly used, others discarded, with spider webs across the entrances.

The Crees and Eskimos told us these were summer retreats. No one seemed aware at that time that they also served as maternity quarters in winter.

Apart from the females carrying cubs, not a great deal is known with certainty about the winter life of the rest of the bear population. The sun disappears from the sky and the long winter night descends on the ice fields and the desolate polar islands. Apparently the males and non-pregnant females hibernate briefly if at all, perhaps in periods when food is scarce or the weather exceptionally severe. The rest of the time they roam the ice, hunting their favorite food in moonlight or darkness. There are few if any humans abroad in polar bear land then to track them and ferret out their secrets.

Like all bear cubs, the infant polars are born in midwinter, a bit earlier than the land bears. December is birthing time for most of them. They are very tiny in comparison with the size of the mother, weighing no more than a pound and a half.

Because most of them first see the light of day in a snow cave, it would be logical to assume that they are born with a protective coat of fur, but that is not the case. They come into the world almost naked, with a scant covering of short, thin hair, and they shelter in the fur of the mother. They do not open their eyes until they are about six weeks old. But they grow fast.

Today's bear researchers leave nothing to guesswork. They have analyzed and even tasted polar bear milk. Dick Harington, who in 1961 did the first field work carried out by the Canadian Wildlife Service, traveling chiefly on foot and by dog team and lacking immobilizing drugs, describes the milk this way: "It has the appearance and consistency of cow's cream, smells like a seal and tastes like cod-liver oil."

However it smells and tastes, the infant bears thrive on it. The mother leads them forth from the den very early in the arctic spring, in March or April. By that time they weigh a roly-poly twenty to twenty-five pounds. At the end of their first summer they reach 125 or 130. They are usually weaned then, but like young land bears they remain with their mother through the first winter of their lives, and as a result she does not breed more often than every second year.

So far as I know, no member of a research team has been hurt in the course of the polar bear studies, but there have been a few exciting encounters and even a close call now and then.

Ian Stirling and Chuck Jonkel, two of the foremost polar bear authorities in Canada, tell of the night when a member of their team, a native of India studying with the Canadian Wildlife Service, was sitting on an outdoor toilet fashioned from a packing crate when a huge white bear walked up within four feet of him.

The Indian had dealt with tigers in his home country and believed that an unarmed man's best defense in the near presence of a dangerous animal was to stay absolutely motionless. He followed that rule and after a few minutes the bear lumbered away. A 940-pound male was caught in a foot snare nearby the next morning, in all likelihood the same one that had paid the nocturnal visit to the camp latrine.

On another occasion Jonkel and Gene Vinet, a helicopter pilot, landed and approached a drugged bear on the ice. Vinet carried the back-up rifle, unaware there was no shell in the chamber. The bear, not properly drugged, lurched suddenly to its feet and came for him. He pulled the trigger when the animal was four feet away, but the firing pin fell on an empty chamber. At that point Jonkel took a hand, going after the bear with a harpoon and turning it aside.

Jack Lentfer tells of a time when he and Lee Miller, another Alaska bear researcher, shot a drug dart into a female bear on the ice and backed their helicopter off to wait for her to pass out. She lay down after about five minutes, and they landed. Lentfer started toward her with a dart gun, intending to immobilize the yearling cub that was with her. He was close to the sow when she leaped to her feet and charged him. The drug had frozen in the syringe and had had no effect. The bear had lain down because she was tired. Miller fired one shot in front of her and then was forced to kill her as she closed on his partner.

That was one of the very few times, in handling hundreds of bears, when the Alaska team found it necessary to kill one. Lentfer still recalls it as a sad experience. Incidentally, he is the only man I know who has poked his head into a polar bear's den when the rightful owner was at home.

In the spring of 1973 Jack and Chuck Evans of the University of Alaska were searching along the Arctic coast for dens. It was April, the time when female bears with young cubs emerge from their winter quarters, and the two men were using a light plane to look for holes where bears had left their dens or for tracks that could be followed back to a deserted den. The dens were located in deeply drifted snow, either on the land or on shore ice.

About twenty-five miles inland from Oliktok Point the two men spotted an exit hole in the snow and were able to land nearby. They found the tracks of an adult bear and small cub all over the place, and concluded that the sow had led her youngster off toward the sea, although they could not be entirely sure because the snow was packed so hard that in places the bears had left no tracks.

The den had an entrance tunnel about twenty-five feet long, and Lentfer knew there would be a roomy chamber at the end of the tunnel. He wanted to measure and examine the den, but discarded the idea of crawling the length of the tunnel, knowing the den chamber would be in almost total darkness. Instead the two men decided to dig down through the snow and open a shaft near the chamber to let in light.

They dug through four or five feet of hard-packed snow and reached the tunnel close to the chamber. Lentfer let himself down into the shaft head first.

A blast of hot air and very strong bear smell hit him in the face, and the she bear ripped out an angry growl from the den chamber, only a few feet away.

"I got out of there in a hurry, and we jumped into our plane and left," Jack says. He learned later that it's a common practice of female polar bears to take their young cub out of a den and back in for several days after they leave. Do they do it to let the cub grow accustomed to outside temperatures before they are taken permanently from the shelter of the den? No one can say.

Lentfer and Evans kept that den under observation for a few days, until the sow and cub cleared out for good. Then they went back and Jack got the measurements he wanted.

Not long after that they found another den on Flaxman Island. Again there was no way to be sure whether the bear and her cubs had left the area, but Lentfer had learned his lesson.

"I spent a long time listening at the entrance hole before we did any digging," he told me. "Finally I heard what I was listening for, bears at the far end of the tunnel. We postponed examining that den chamber until we were sure they were no longer in it."

Lentfer also told me about Harry Brower, a fox trapper from Barrow, another Alaskan who had an interesting experience with a female polar bear and her cub.

He found a den in March, and tracks showed that the old bear was leading her offspring in and out of it repeatedly. Harry was worried that the cub would get caught in one of his fox traps. He didn't want to kill either it or the mother, and finally he hit on a bold solution.

He baited the sow with a big piece of blubber, luring her far enough away from her cub that he was able to grab it and climb onto his snowmobile. He then drove off with the mother in angry pursuit, keeping just out of her reach, and she followed the snow machine until it was far enough from Brower's trapline that the bear family would be safe. At that point he freed the little bear, speeded up and went out of her sight.

TWENTY-FIVE

Last Shell in the Rifle

I have never heard it said better than by Captain Peter Freuchen, the re-nowned Danish adventurer and explorer who married an Eskimo girl and lived many years in Arctic Greenland.

"No more beautiful animal walks on four feet," he told me once when we were talking about the polar bear.

No matter how long I live, I'm sure I shall never forget the first one I saw outside a zoo. He was standing on a rocky headland, at the top of a cliff that rose vertically from a boulder-littered beach, staring out over a gray and empty reach of sea. A gale was sweeping down from the northwest, savage surf was smoking along the beach, and the sky was black with the clouds of a violent rain squall. Save for the handful of us aboard the schooner, the bear could well have been the only living thing in that wild, storm-swept world.

He was as magnificent an animal as I shall ever lay eyes on. His white pelt was faintly tinged with yellow, and standing motionless at the top of the cliff, he could have been a bear carved out of old ivory. Yet there was about him something wonderfully alive, too, something that proclaimed his rightful place in that desolate, lonely seascape.

It was the summer of 1937. An Ontario man who had hopes of setting him-self up in the guiding and outfitting business, taking clients into remote and rarely visited places in the far north, had organized a trip that summer along the east shore of James Bay and into the lower end of Hudson Bay.

He chartered the Venture, a weather-beaten forty-three-foot schooner, aux-iliary powered with an old Diesel engine, owned and skippered by Jack Palm-quist, then the only free trader competing with the Hudson's Bay Company on James Bay.

Palmquist's crew consisted of a Cree deckhand and a good-humored Eskimo who tended the ancient Diesel as a mother tends a child. Neither spoke English, but the skipper, married to a pretty mission-educated Cree girl, was fluent in her language. The Eskimo also spoke Cree, so there was always a way around the language barrier.

The bear was standing on a rocky headland, at the top of a cliff that rose vertically from a boulder-littered beach. Save for the handful of us aboard the schooner, he could well have been the only living thing in that wild, storm-swept world.

At the trading post and summer camp of the Crees at Eastmain, Palmquist also took aboard a leather-faced Indian pilot to see us through the bleak island-sheltered channels along the coast we would travel. No charts of those waters existed then, and only a Cree who knew them from a lifetime of canoe travel and remembered each island, each headland, each clump of stunted spruce trees could follow the maze of channels and avoid the reefs.

The outfitter had hired three guides and a cook and there were nine clients in the party. I was one of them. We were the first sportsmen to penetrate that wild and roadless country. It was a region that only an occasional roving prospector, the Mounties, missionaries, and the men of the HBC had ever seen. Apart from them it belonged to the Crees and a handful of coastal Eskimos.

Incidentally, the outfitter's plans fell through after one summer, so for many years we were the last as well as the first party of guided sportsmen to travel that coast.

I have roamed the back country of this continent for fifty years, from the

Great Smokies and the diamondback-infested flatwoods of Florida to Maine, from the Texas desert to the Aleutian Islands of Alaska, but that treeless and lonely country that I call the land of midnight twilight was the most fascinating place I have ever seen.

The land was untouched, the people primitive, living by the trapline, the fishnet and the gun. We saw steel traps set on low driftwood posts to catch owls for the cooking pots of the Crees; we heard loons called to the gun and shot for the same purpose. At the trading posts we saw summer camps of as many as five hundred nomad Cree trappers, living in roomy wigwams as they had before the whites came.

We fished the virgin pools of whitewater streams where three-pound speckled trout rose to flies, spinners — or even small strips torn from a red bandanna. It was an easy matter for two or three rods to take in a couple of hours all the trout the party could eat at three meals. We had no way to keep fresh meat aboard the Venture, so we lived for many days on a diet of trout and learned to our surprise that it palled rather quickly.

For ten days we camped beyond the sight of trees, carrying our tent poles along and relying on driftwood for our cooking fires. We tramped mossy barrens where ptarmigan were far more plentiful than ruffed grouse back home. When autumn came those treeless barrens would also be alive with geese, beginning their fall flight from summer homes still farther in the north.

Seals followed our schooner, and at night white whales blew close enough to awaken us. The half-wild sled dogs of a dozen Indian and Eskimo camps howled us to sleep time and again. Every minute of the trip was pure adventure.

There was no hunting. The Quebec government was keeping the wildlife, from waterfowl to seals and polar bears, in trust for the Crees and Eskimos, who needed it. But Howard Cooper, a hunting partner of mine from Kalamazoo, Michigan, and I carried collecting permits obtained by two museums back home, authorizing us to take for scientific purposes any birds or animals we chose.

Toward the end of July, the Venture dropped anchor off Long Island. Not the Long Island you have heard about all your life. This one is a rocky sliver of land three or four miles offshore near the southern end of Hudson Bay. We had come now to polar bear country. We left most of the party camped on the island, and Palmquist and his crew took Cooper and myself on a bear hunt.

It was a strange place to look for polar bears. We headed for a small group of treeless islands, not shown on any map we had, lying thirty or forty miles off the coast. We were farther south than the latitude of Juneau, Alaska. Yet the HBC post managers, the Crees and our skipper had all assured us that we would find bears summering on those islands. At the Fort George post a Cree had even shown us the pelts of three, a female and two cubs, that he had killed only that spring on the adjoining mainland.

We found the island we were looking for but it had no shelter for a boat, and raging seas, driven by a gale screaming down from the ice fields five hundred miles to the north, kept us from going ashore. We found a sheltered harbor on a smaller island half a mile away and landed without difficulty. It was from there that I saw my first polar bear, looking out to sea from his rocky headland.

We watched him for hours through binoculars and spotting scope. In late afternoon the storm subsided and we got a freight canoe ashore on the beach below the cliffs.

Cooper and I and Tommy Lameboy, our old Cree pilot, landed in the canoe. Lameboy had no rifle. Cooper and I were each carrying Model 99 Savages in .300 caliber. At the time I thought them adequate. I would not think so today.

The island was about two miles long and half as wide, rising in vertical cliffs at one end, sloping down to submerged reefs at the other. The top was a rolling expanse of low hills and ravines, all rock and moss, with no vegetation taller than clumps of arctic willow that did not reach to a man's knee. But there were plenty of places for a bear to hide, and ours had disappeared. He had watched our boat as it neared the island, and taken to his heels.

We separated; Cooper and Lameboy headed for the far side of the island, I set out to search the broken sea cliffs. The job was on the hairy side, for there were places where I could round a big rock and meet the bear only three or four steps away. I was moving slowly and carefully when I heard a shot rap out from the direction Cooper had taken, followed almost at once by another. I scrambled to the top of the cliff for a look.

I made out the small figure of my hunting partner, three-quarters of a mile away, but I could see nothing of the bear. While I watched, Howard fired a third shot, and to my astonishment I heard the 180-grain softpoint go whining angrily over my head as a ricochet.

If Cooper was firing toward me the bear must be somewhere between us. And then I saw him, half a mile away, out of rifle range for Howard, running toward me like a big white dog that I had called. I learned later that Cooper had not really had him in range at any time, but had shot in the hope of sending him back my way. He succeeded better than he expected.

I learned something else later. The bear did not know I was there. The face of the cliff behind me was broken by a ravine that ran all the way down to the beach, and there was a well-used bear trail in the bottom of it. That was, in all likelihood, his customary path to the sea and he was coming to use it.

I was aware of mixed feelings. I wanted him to keep coming, for from the time I planned the trip I had wanted more than anything else to take a polar bear. But at the same time, although I had used a rifle for years, starting with a .22 as a boy, I was no crack shot and this bear was the first game I had ever confronted bigger than a whitetail deer. Could I deal with him? Well, I'd soon find out.

I went down on one knee to escape his attention, and watched him come. He dropped out of sight in a shallow dip but when he came up on my side of it he was still on course, traveling at a lumbering, ground-eating run.

I tried my first two shots while he was still too far away for accurate shooting with iron sights. They were clean misses and he paid them no attention.

The next one scored. He braked to a stop, swinging his head from side to side like a big white snake caught by the tail, biting savagely at the top of both shoulders. When it was all over I learned that my 180-grain softpoint had hit him in the back just behind the neck, too high to do any real damage, and had gone through under the heavy layer of fat that padded him, just deep enough to cut muscle and draw blood. I suppose it must have burned like a branding iron.

From his actions I was sure he would go down in a second or two, and in my lack of experience with dangerous game I made a bad blunder. I scrambled to my feet, ready to move closer and put in a finishing shot.

I never got the chance. The instant I stood up he saw me for the first time. He swerved and came for me in a deadly, businesslike charge, head down, running as a cross dog runs to bark at a passing car.

I shot too fast and threw away one more chance to stop him, and as he closed the distance between us to less than thirty yards I felt cold fear of a kind I have never known before or since.

I had started with one shell in the chamber of the Savage and four in the magazine. I had used four. That meant only one was left. There would be no time for reloading and all my confidence that I could kill the bear had evaporated.

Afterward I could not remember firing the fifth shot but my subconscious, if it took over, did a far better job than I had been doing. I heard the whiplash report of the .300 and the bear collapsed as if lightning had struck him. His head dropped between his front legs, he fell and skidded to a stop, rolled almost in a ball. Not so much as a shudder of movement stirred him anywhere.

I sidled away then while I fed five fresh hulls frantically into the rifle. When that was done I began to feel ready for more trouble if it came. I stood and watched for three or four minutes, waiting for some sign of life in the bear. Then I saw Tommy Lameboy coming across the island at a run, only a hundred yards away. Although unarmed, the old Cree was not running to me. He was running to the bear.

I could not let him arrive until I was sure it was dead. I walked in with the safety off and prodded the big ball of white fur in the neck and ribs. There·was no answering quiver, and I stepped back and waited for Tommy.

Together we rolled the bear over enough to pull his head out from beneath his body. The round hole of my last bullet was trickling blood just above the nose, dead center between the eyes. It had mushroomed in the brain and there was hardly a piece of bone bigger than a silver dollar left intact in the skull from the jaws back.

Before we moved the bear I went back and found the five empty cases I had ejected from the rifle. I wanted to know just how close he had been when I killed him. I stepped it off, seventeen paces. Fifty-one feet. I hardly wonder that I had been frightened or that for many nights afterward I dreamed of his final rush, dreamed he was standing over me ready to finish me off. It was a dream that brought me awake in a cold sweat each time.

We hoisted the bear aboard the schooner and took him back to the camp on Long Island unskinned. There Alagkok, our pleasant little Eskimo engineer, offered to take the pelt off.

Alagkok knew no English and of course could not write. But I have never seen hands more deft with a knife.

Three days later, on a somewhat bigger island thirty or forty miles to the south, Cooper made his bear hunt.

The party found anchorage for the Venture in a small harbor and Howard went ashore with Palmquist, Lameboy, and Roy Maguire, one of our guides. Almost at once they found a line of big bear tracks leading up across the sand of the beach, the footprints still wet with water that had dripped from the bear's legs. He had come in from the sea less than an hour before.

Half a mile farther on Cooper spotted a patch of white behind a tangle of driftwood just above the beach. At first he took it for snow, but when Palmquist put a question to Tommy Lameboy the old Cree replied with a firm "Wahb'-esco!" the name for polar bear in his language.

The hunters were within a hundred yards of the bear when it heard or winded them and sat up on its haunches. Cooper told me afterward that it was

I shot too fast and threw away one more chance to stop him, and as he closed the distance between us to less than thirty yards I felt cold fear of a kind I have never known before or since.

so big it reminded him of a short-legged, burly white horse. He broke its back with his first shot, ran in close and finished it cleanly with a second softpoint in the neck.

Unfortunately, at that time neither Howard nor I was aware of the Boone and Crockett system of measuring and scoring trophies. As a result, the skull of that bear was never measured. But his body measurements, taken with a steel tape before he was skinned, revealed a polar bear of extraordinary size.

He measured 18 inches between the ears, 52 around the neck just behind the head, and 10½ feet from tip of nose to tip of tail. I still believe he would have stood very high on the Boone and Crockett record list.

He was skinned the next morning and the hunters came back to our camp at the mouth of a small river fifty miles south of Cape Jones. Two families of Crees sailed their canoes in behind the Venture, and in return for a sweater, a few pounds of flour, tea, sugar and some canned fruit, the women agreed to flesh the pelt of the big bear.

The scene that evening, lighted by a big driftwood fire behind our camp, is printed indelibly in my memory. Cooper had killed a second bear, to which his collecting permit entitled him, an immature animal that weighed around three hundred pounds, and brought it back to the mainland unskinned. The Cree women took the pelt off before they went to work on the big one, and we gave them a big kettle of the meat.

While they worked by firelight on the bear pelts, their men got two wigwams up and baked bannock for supper. In the dim twilight of that subarctic midnight a grease-rimmed kettle of bear stew was bubbling on the fire and the whole party of Crees was hunched in an eager, grinning circle around it.

The last sound we heard in our sleeping bags that night was the wild and doleful howling of a gaunt, ill-fed Indian sled dog, staked on a babiche leash beside one of the wigwams. His nose was full of the scent of bear short ribs but such feasts, alas, were not for him, and he sang his hunger song long after silence had settled over the camp.

The rest of the smaller bear Cooper gave to Tommy Lameboy, and when we reached the Fort George trading post, where the old Cree was camped for the summer, we witnessed a strange and ancient Indian ritual. The bear carcass was ferried ashore in one of our freight canoes, and a group of Crees picked the big canoe up bodily with the bear in it, six or eight men on either side. They lifted it to their shoulders and carried it ceremoniously through the camp of some five hundred Indians to Tommy's wigwam. There it was cut up and divided among many families, in keeping with Cree custom when a big animal is killed.

One of the most surprising things about that long-ago bear hunt was the fact that it happened only about a hundred miles farther, as a crow flies, from Sault Ste. Marie in my home state of Michigan than the distance from that same city south to Detroit. The white bear of the North is not always an animal of the arctic ice.

TWENTY-SIX

Today's Restrictions, Tomorrow's Outlook

A great many big-game hunters consider the polar bear the most beautiful and desirable trophy animal in the world. The pelt of a big male will measure more than ten feet long, the fur is thick and lustrous, and the yellowish-white color, set off in a life mount by the black lips, tongue, nose and eyes, is regal and attractive in a unique way.

Seton said of the pelt in his day, "A favorite floor rug for the palaces of the great, and sought by priests in the north as a carpet in front of the altar."

But the white bear is a trophy almost impossible for a hunter to take anywhere in the world today. So strict are the regulations protecting him that sport hunters probably kill fewer than half a dozen a year, and polar bear pelts are close to a forgotten item in the fur trade. (A few years ago the best ones were bringing $3,000 apiece.)

Three factors combined to bring this about: Sincere and worldwide concern for the bear among conservationists; resentment resulting from the unsportsmanlike use of aircraft and snowmobiles by some American hunters in Alaska and the equally unsportsmanlike practice known as safari hunting in Norway; and demands by organizations opposed to all hunting.

In 1972, under the Marine Mammals Protection Act, the U. S. Fish and Wildlife Service took jurisdiction over these bears away from Alaska. The present regulations ban all sport hunting of polar bears in Alaska. They also forbid an American citizen to hunt the bears in another country. As a matter of fact, there is only one place in the world, the Northwest Territories of Canada, where he could hunt even if United States law permitted. The hunting there is extremely restricted and costly, and no American could bring his trophy home across the border.

When I began work on this chapter I contacted the Fish and Wildlife Service's Office of Endangered Species in Washington, the agency presently responsible for meshing this country's polar bear management policies with the international program, to learn whether sport hunting of the bears is permitted by Norway, Denmark, and Canada; if so, under what rules; and how many bears are harvested annually.

Incredibly, I found no one in the agency who could answer my questions. At the suggestion of the Fish and Wildlife Service itself, I went instead to Ian Stirling, top polar bear authority of the Canadian Wildlife Service, for the information I needed. He had it at his fingertips.

I can only conclude that although the F&WS has able and well-informed field researchers, there is no one in Washington who knows enough about the worldwide polar bear situation to formulate a sound management program for this country. The future of the United States polar bear population would be more secure if jurisdiction over the bears were returned to Alaska.

Here is the international situation, as it stood in the summer of 1976:

Canadian law allows polar bear hunting only by Eskimos or Indians who have traditionally hunted the bears, and the kill is presently limited to around six hundred a year under a quota system.

In Northwest Territories, however, the natives are permitted to guide a very small number of nonresident hunters, again under strict rules. Any bear killed must come out of the quota of the village contracting for the hunt. If the village has an annual quota of eighteen bears, for example, and a nonresident takes one, the village's quota drops to seventeen. The Game Department at Yellowknife oversees the arrangement and makes sure that the natives are paid.

The use of aircraft or snowmobiles is forbidden, and there is no guarantee of a bear. The cost of a guided hunt up to three weeks in duration is $3,000 to $4,500.

"The hunter is buying not a bear trophy, but the experience of living and traveling for a short time with the Eskimos, sleeping in an igloo and hunting as they hunt," Ian Stirling told me.

Hardly surprisingly, however, very few hunters are interested. In 1975, for example, hunters numbered only four, one from this country, one from Canada and two from Europe.

Apart from this highly restricted hunting, there is no place in the world where a sportsman can kill a polar bear legally. Russia gave the bears complete protection in 1956 and the ban is still in force. Norway had a somewhat shady record of dealing with its polar bear population on the Svalbard Islands, five hundred miles north of the mainland coast. As recently as 1970 the bears were being market-hunted legally for their pelts and the hunters were even allowed to use baited set-guns as well as traps. The kill was running three hundred to four hundred a year.

In addition, Norway also permitted a method known as safari hunting, chiefly by nonresidents. The bears were hunted on the pack ice from ships cruising along its edge, and it was common practice once a bear was sighted to land crew members who then hazed the animal across the ice within rifle range of the hunter on the deck of the ship. A Norwegian consulate official told me in 1971 that the bear had absolutely no chance to escape.

Norway has now gone to the opposite extreme, declaring a complete five-year moratorium on polar bear hunting. It is not legal to kill one of the bears even in self-defense.

Denmark, which claims a polar bear population on the island of Greenland, allows killing by Eskimos but bans hunting by nonresidents outright. The kill is presently running 125 to 150 a year.

In view of the almost nonexistent opportunities for hunting the ice bear, it seems somewhat pointless to talk about hunting methods. But the possibility does exist that Alaska may regain jurisdiction over its bears from the Fish and Wildlife Service and that would mean a return of sport hunting.

Most of the bears taken in the Alaskan arctic in recent years were killed with the help of aircraft. Hunters flew out over the pack ice and searched from the air until they spotted a bear or a fresh track that would lead to one. For the sake of safety, it was close to standard practice to use two light planes, operating as a team.

If the hunter and his guide were ethical, once a shootable bear was found one plane landed on the ice some distance ahead, the other kept watch far enough away not to interfere, and the hunter attempted to intercept and ambush the bear from a hiding place behind an ice hummock or pressure ridge.

It has to be said, however, that the ban on bear hunting off the Alaska coast, imposed by the federal government, was to a considerable extent the result of outrageous abuses by unscrupulous guides and unethical hunters, who did not care how they came by their trophy so long as they took one.

All too often one aircraft of a team landed and the hunter was posted on a stand. The second aircraft then hazed the bear into his lap. The standards of sportsmanship slumped to a point where the hunting came under fire in many quarters. Alaska's own sportsmen-conservationists, honest guides and outdoor writers condemned the abuses bitterly.

In 1970 Joe LaRocca, then resource editor of the Fairbanks *Daily News-Miner,* quoted a ranking official of the Fish and Game Department as admitting that the department had lost all control of polar bear hunting. LaRocca charged that although the 1970 polar bear quota was 225 bears, hunters had taken 311 legally and at least another 100 illegally, the latter with the help of a few guides who flouted the game laws openly.

About that same time, Dan Gross, a staff writer on the Anchorage *Daily News,* exposed a thriving bootleg trade in polar bear permits. Three hundred were available, he pointed out, but three thousand applications had flooded the game department the previous spring, and the coveted permits, although legally nontransferable, were being sold openly at prices up to $1,000 and "going like hot meals in a famine area," Gross reported.

The fault did not lie with the game department. With few exceptions, its men were able, dedicated, and hard-working.

"They are so absorbed in their work that you'd have to hold their heads under water for ten minutes before they realized they were wet," an Alaskan outdoor writer told me. But the department was short-handed and working under the handicap of political interference, and the enormous size of Alaska, more than twice as large as Texas, with huge areas roadless and inaccessible, made it impossible for protection officers to keep the polar bear hunting in hand.

"Most Alaska guides are reliable and honest," a veteran protection officer told me in an angry letter, "but we have a few who would kill the last living thing in the state if they could make a nickel doing it. Their lawless operations are a natural outgrowth of our department's short-handedness and lack of money for enforcement."

As for political domination of the game department, Tom Kimball, executive director of the National Wildlife Federation, said after a study of the situation, "As a method of managing fish and game, a political structure such as the one in Alaska, which gives the governor complete authority over the Fish and Game Department, is a total failure."

Given the situation that had existed in recent years, it was an easy matter for the Fish and Wildlife Service to take away from the state of Alaska the authority to manage its marine mammals. Those who advocate a return to state control do not believe that similar conditions would ever again be allowed to exist, however.

What is the ice bear's future worldwide?

To begin with, Alaska has asked that authority to manage its marine mammals be returned to it, and the request was granted in the case of the Pacific walrus in the spring of 1976. Whether the state will regain jurisdiction over its polar bears remains to be seen. I asked several wildlife officials what they thought the chances were, but found none willing to risk a firm prediction.

Among those to whom I put the question was the Alaska Department of Fish and Game itself. The reply came from Don McKnight, research chief of the department's Division of Game.

"You can get as many different opinions as the number of people to whom you talk," he told me. "There is absolutely no reason why our polar bears shouldn't be hunted by sportsmen. Our studies showed conclusively that taking three hundred bears a year, the quota we had set, had no adverse impact on the population.

"Admittedly we were slow in reacting to public pressure opposed to the use of aircraft in polar bear hunting. But by the time the Marine Mammals Protection Act was passed by Congress in 1972 we had regulations prohibiting the use of aircraft, and a very workable permit system restricting the harvest to about three hundred bears a year. Under those regulations the repugnant aspects of the hunting would have been done away with and the harvest likely would never have exceeded one hundred animals annually.

"Alaska is attempting to regain management authority over beluga whales, polar bears, seals, sea lions, and sea otters. Of all these, my own opinion is that polar bears are the least likely ever to be returned to us for management. The widespread misconception that the species is endangered (it isn't), the tarnished public image of polar bear hunting that resulted from the use of aircraft, and current hostility toward hunting in general will all hurt our chances.

"But with a lot more work and even more luck, I see a chance that in a few more years there may be rigidly controlled polar bear hunting by sportsmen in Alaskan waters."

No one has summed up the situation more accurately than a Canadian official who told me, "The outcome of Alaska's request depends entirely on whether reason or emotion prevails."

Reason calls for allowing Alaska to manage its own wildlife resources. Emotion means using the long but spineless arm of Uncle Sam to prevent any bear hunting. Antihunting forces bitterly oppose the idea of state control, knowing that it would almost certainly mean a return of hunting.

The hunting would be strictly regulated, however. Alaska has proposed a kill not to exceed 250 a year. The use of aircraft would be banned and in all likelihood all snowmobiles would also be forbidden.

Events of recent years have proved that countries having a polar bear population are willing to ban or strictly curb hunting if the need arises. Despite the fact that this bear roams far out on the sea ice, beyond the jurisdiction of any nation, it has been shown that rules can be established and enforced to give him the protection he requires. Taking those things into account, plus today's international concern for the bears, there seems little reason for worry.

In 1965, for the first time, a worldwide effort was begun to learn how many polar bears were left, what the annual kill by hunters totaled, and what steps were needed to insure the safety of this splendid animal.

Representatives of Russia, Norway, Denmark, Canada, and the United States got together in a scientific meeting at Fairbanks, Alaska. Agreement was reached on such matters as the protection of cubs and sows with cubs, and the need for a concerted program of research and management carried out by all the countries concerned.

This conference was later moved to Morges, Switzerland, under the sponsorship of the International Union for Conservation of Nature. It is now held somewhere in Europe every two years. Out of these meetings has come a determined effort to safeguard the world's population of polar bears.

What is the size of that population? Some authorities put it at only eight to ten thousand. But Ian Stirling, who knows as much about the bears as any living man and is in position to make a reliable estimate, believes the figure is twenty thousand plus. He calls the polar bear's future completely secure, apart from the unpredictable threat posed by offshore oil drilling or some other industrial development that may damage the areas where it lives.

"As with the land bears, if we can keep polar bear habitat intact we can keep the bears," Stirling says.

A top official of the Alaska Department of Fish and Game holds that same opinion.

"The future for the polar bear looks excellent," he told me. "His habitat is not attractive to man. There'll never be any sheep ranching or reindeer herding in the places where he is found. Hunting is no threat and never has been. The animals he preys on, mainly seals, are not likely to be affected on a major scale by human activities. The only real threat to his future is oil development and its consequences, and aside from local problems we do not see that as a serious concern. I only wish Alaska's big land bears were as well off."

TWENTY-SEVEN

What It Was Like To Hunt Him

There was high adventure in an honest polar bear hunt, and there was also no little danger to the hunter himself. Not infrequently light planes landing on unsafe ice broke through. A few hunters and pilot-guides lost their lives, and many had close calls.

The experience of Dick Wilson, a retired California businessman, was typical. He was hunting the pack ice off Point Hope on the northwest coast of Alaska with a partner, John Osborne. They were flying together in one light plane.

Their Eskimo pilot, Tommy Richards, spotted a good bear in an area of rough ice and followed it until it reached a place that looked safe for landing.

The men had no warning. The plane coasted to a stop and there was a sudden crunching sound as new ice broke beneath the skis and the Cessna went through into bitterly cold water. The wings, resting on unbroken ice, took the weight and the dive ended. Water swirled up into the cabin and in seconds it was belt deep. The cabin door was blocked by broken ice, but Osborne, a powerfully built 260-pounder, smashed it open far enough for him to inch through.

Wilson had to crawl back over the front seat to reach the door. Halfway over, his left foot wedged. He fought desperately to free it while the water rose to his chin. In the end only three inches of space remained between the water and the roof of the cabin, and Wilson and the pilot, whose escape he was blocking, turned their faces up against the ceiling to gulp the air that was left.

Wilson never knew how he freed himself, but suddenly he and Richards had their weight against the door and wrenched it open. Wilson pitched out first. Osborne, perched precariously on a wing, reached down and helped his partner up beside him. Then the pilot popped to the surface and the two of them pulled him from the water. The three men crawled along the wing to solid ice and climbed down.

They were drenched to the skin. Their sleeping bags and all their gear were lost in the drowned cabin of the Cessna. The temperature was fifteen below zero and a knife-keen wind was sweeping across the ice. They were eight miles from the nearest land, across rough and broken ice seamed with leads and patches of open water. They had five hours before darkness fell.

They started to walk, heading south where the ice was better. Their clothing turned quickly to icy armor. They walked only a short time before it became apparent that there was no hope of reaching land the way they were going. They retraced their steps and trudged away to the north.

At the end of a couple of miles a maze of leads blocked their way again, and they turned back to the plane, still resting on the ice with the wings and top of the cabin showing. There the pilot elected to make one more attempt to reach shore. He left Wilson and Osborne beside the drowned Cessna and went out of sight. Darkness would fall in an hour.

The night was a terrible one. The temperature dropped lower and the wind continued to blow. The two men walked endlessly to keep from freezing to death.

All through the endless night, from time to time they heard ice break as the water-logged plane settled lower in the water. If it plunged to the bottom there was very little chance that rescue aircraft would be able to spot two men in the vast expanse of broken ice.

Their luck held on that score. The morning dawned clear and the red tail of the Cessna was still above water. Shortly after sunrise they heard search planes in the distance. One of the many planes combing the ice for them finally spotted the blob of red and landed fifty yards away.

It was only a ten-minute flight back to Point Hope. There the pilot unloaded them and gunned his plane back off the ice to search for Tommy Richards, who had not made it to shore. He was found marooned on a big ice floe, only a short distance from where he had left the two hunters.

Wilson lost twenty-five pounds and his toenails and fingernails, and one toe had to be amputated. Osborne also lost most of his nails. The Eskimo pilot came through in the best shape, chiefly because he was wearing more protective clothing.

The hunt Tony Sulak, a Seattle manufacturer, made off Point Barrow ended even more tragically.

Sulak and his partner, Bill Niemi, also from Seattle, looked forward to their hunt as the big adventure of their lives.

"The polar bear is the most majestic trophy a hunter can take anywhere in North America," Tony told me when it was all over. "He roams a remote and forbidding world where man is always an intruder. You hunt him in the face of bone-chilling cold, treacherous sea ice, terrible winds and gale-driven snow that turns the air to milk. He has beauty unmatched. Hung on any wall, his white pelt is a breath stopper."

Sulak and Niemi were using two planes for the sake of safety. In two days of hunting they failed to find a bear big enough to qualify as a good trophy. The third afternoon the planes went down on the ice to refuel and Sulak and his pilot, Jack Hovland, broke through. The wings came to rest on the ice and stopped the plunge, but water flooded into the cabin. It was up to their necks by the time they kicked the door out and escaped the death trap of the sinking aircraft.

They climbed up on a wing, Hovland carrying a rolled sleeping bag to use as a life preserver. Sulak counted on his down-filled clothing and parka to help keep him afloat.

Between them and ice that would support a man lay more than 200 feet of unsafe ice, dangerously thin but thick enough that a swimming man might not be able to break his way through it. Niemi and his pilot were waiting on the good ice, powerless to help.

Tony and Hovland slid off the wing and started to battle to safety. Sulak went first.

The ice was half an inch thick and hard. Tony broke it without gloves, smashing a path through, leaving a trail of blood where the sharp edges gashed his bare hands. He did not look back. It took him twenty minutes to reach solid ice. His two companions flipped a canvas motor cover within his reach and he took the end of it between his teeth when he found his frozen and lacerated hands could not hold it. He was pulled out of the water that way.

Hovland had swum a few yards and gone down. The rolled sleeping bag still floated in the water by itself.

In addition to the use of aircraft that had become close to standard practice, there was another method of polar bear hunting off the Alaska coast, one that called for the highest standards of sportsmanship, and in the final years before the moratorium an increasing number of hunters were turning to it in the interests of fair chase.

It consisted of establishing a camp on the ice and using dog teams or snowmobiles to find a bear—but not employing the snow machine to pursue the animal or help in any way with the kill—or of hunting from shore with dogs and Eskimo guides, going after a bear as the Eskimos did before the days of aircraft.

My friend Gleason Taylor, a sportsman from Coshocton, Ohio, took a good polar bear pelt that way back in 1956 and had the hunt of his life doing it. Taylor dreamed of a polar bear hunt for years, but from the time he started planning he was firm on one point. He wouldn't use a plane.

"Not that there's anything wrong with that method if it's done right," he told me afterward, "but that isn't always the case, and the idea of flying out on the ice and knocking over a bear just didn't appeal to me."

He hunted off Point Hope, an Eskimo village and trading post on Alaska's arctic coast about 150 miles northwest of Kotzebue. When he left his home in Ohio in mid-March there were early robins on the lawn. He landed at Point Hope in a howling storm with the thermometer registering twenty-eight degrees below zero.

"Spring comes a little late up there," he commented with a grin.

He and a hunting partner, Bill Payton from New Mexico, headed out on the ice with two Eskimo guides named Kingik and Billy. They planned to camp offshore and stay until they killed two bears. Kingik was driving a team of eleven dogs, Billy had thirteen.

The party made a comfortable camp, pitching their seven-by-seven tent in a hole scooped out of a snowbank. By the next day snow had drifted in around the tent, making it so snug and windproof that they did not need to use a stove for heat.

A blizzard delayed the hunt for a day. Payton killed his bear the following forenoon, hunting without dog teams. Taylor's chance came only a day later.

Driving the dogs out on the ice to bring the meat of Payton's bear to camp, the hunters spotted a big bear lying at the foot of a pressure ridge. Apparently it had come in off the polar ice fields and in all likelihood had never seen men or dogs before, but the two dog teams winded it and made enough commotion to spook it and send it out of sight behind the ridge. Somewhat surprisingly, however, Taylor and Billy caught up with it less than half a mile farther on.

Gleason had hard luck. The dogs saw the bear and went wild, yipping and howling across the ice in frenzied pursuit. Billy stopped the team with an Eskimo ice brake, three heavy iron claws rigged between the sled runners at the back. By throwing all his weight on the brake, the guide made one of the claws bite two or three inches into rock-hard ice and brought the frantic dogs to a halt. But Taylor jumped off while the sled was still in motion and tangled one foot in a rope. He was thrown flat on his back twice before he could free himself. The bear got away and the frustrated and disgusted hunter wrote the hunt off as a total loss.

Astonishingly, he had the great good fortune to find another bear only fifteen minutes later.

This one was half a mile away, approaching at a rolling walk. Both Taylor and the Eskimos had had enough of dog-team hunting by that time. They fastened the dogs with sled anchors, sharpened iron bars driven firmly into the ice, and Billy and Taylor went on foot to meet the bear.

They came to an open lead three hundred yards across. The bear lay down on the far side, and they could not cross to get closer. Because he had no choice, Taylor centered the crosshairs of his .375 Magnum on the bear's shoulder and tried a shot at that range. It knocked the bear over on his back and a second softnose in his chest finished him. He was dead in seconds.

"I took him the hard way," Gleason summed things up, "but I've never cared for a trophy I didn't earn. So far as I'm concerned, the Eskimo way is the only way to hunt the ice bear."

In the old days before they had rifles, the Eskimos followed a method of hunting that put their courage to a severe test.

They spotted a bear on the open ice and turned their sled dogs loose to bring it to bay. That was rarely difficult, and while the bear was fighting the dogs one or more of the Eskimos dodged in and made the kill with a spear or lance.

The scene is easily imagined. The bear on the open ice or on a bleak reach of treeless coast, ringed by dogs almost as wild and savage as himself, growling, roaring, turning this way and that to cuff his tormentors aside; the dogs snapping and snarling, leaping in, dodging out, and the fur-clothed hunter moving closer and closer until he was part of the ring of dogs; the bear, turning its back to lunge at a dog, and then the quick hard thrust of the lance.

At a coastal camp on Hudson Bay in 1937, I talked through an interpreter with an old Eskimo who remembered such hunts by his elders.

Until relatively recent times, most of the ice bears killed by white men were shot by explorers, usually for food. The hunting was easy. The polar bear has never shown much fear of man on the ice, maybe because he encountered humans so infrequently that he did not identify them. It was not uncommon for him to stalk a man, probably in the mistaken belief that he was after a seal.

Either the exploring party traveling on the ice blundered across a bear and shot it if they needed it, or the bear prowled boldly into camp and was done away with. The total kill taken in a year was very light.

Often the explorer used his sled dogs as the primitive Eskimos did, with a rifle taking the place of the lance. The job of the dogs was to hold the bear until the hunter could come up. There was grave danger of losing dogs, however, and some of the men most experienced in arctic exploration advised against resorting to this way of taking a bear if it could be avoided.

When it comes to guns and bows for polar bear hunting, the things I said in an earlier chapter about the brown bear are equally true of his white kinsman. One is roughly as big as the other, fully as hard to kill and equally quick to fight back. The rules can be summed up simply. If you are after an ice bear, go loaded for what you are after.

The bear on the open ice or on a bleak reach of treeless coast, ringed by dogs almost as wild and savage as himself, growling, roaring; the dogs snapping and snarling; the fur-clothed hunter moving closer; and then the quick hard thrust of the lance.

I knew of one case in which a young Eskimo hunter killed a bear with a .22 Hornet, but he admitted it wasn't a very good idea. Hunting seals, he came across the bear by accident and shot it in the neck at very close range. It dived into an open lead and he knew that if he killed it there in the water he could not drag it out onto the ice by himself. So he prodded it with the long spiked pole Eskimo seal hunters carry, until he tormented it into climbing out on the ice under its own power. Then it came for him. Man and bear ran a foot race, the Eskimo whirling around and shooting with one hand. He finally got in a brain shot that did the job.

"But Eskimo boy fall down, no more Eskimo boy," he acknowledged.

TWENTY-EIGHT

Most Dangerous Bear of All?

No hunter gains a closer acquaintance with the game he pursues than the man who uses a bow. First of all, that is true from necessity. If the bowhunter is to make a killing shot on any big game, dangerous or not, he has to narrow the range to a fraction of that at which the rifleman is justified in loosing off.

Take bears, for example. With the exception of those treed or held at bay by dogs, most of the blacks and grizzlies shot in this country and Canada are baited, and most hunters like to keep a respectable distance between themselves and the bait station where they expect the bear to show up. Most of the Western guides I have known prefer to have their hunter something like two hundred yards from the dead horse intended to lure a grizzly in, and I know none who want the distance less than a hundred.

By contrast, the bowhunter is not likely to risk a shot at more than thirty to forty yards, and often he deliberately seeks a situation where he can shoot at that many feet instead.

Apart from the angle of necessity, there is a special challenge in bowhunting, and the men who resort to it are for the most part a special breed who seek to heighten that challenge as much as possible. Many of them get close for the sake of learning how close they can get.

The result is that they see their game as the rifleman never does, have an opportunity to study its behavior and reactions in a special way.

I have known many hunters who have taken polar bears, myself among them. But I have known none who knows more about the temper and behavior of the white bear, threatened or wounded at very close range, than my friend Fred Bear, who ranks high among the ace bowhunters of his generation. All animals are likely to do things at fifteen yards that they wouldn't do at two hundred, and *Wahb'esco* is no exception.

Fred has not hunted with a rifle since 1935, when he went into the business of making archery tackle. His trophies, all taken with bow and displayed in the Fred Bear Museum near his home at Grayling, Michigan, include an African elephant, a cape buffalo, a lion, an Indian tiger, and the three big bears of North America. When he discusses dangerous game, he knows what he is talking about.

In six years, between 1956 and 1962, he killed two grizzlies and three brown bears, and put arrows into two polar bears that proved too much to be handled that way and had to be stopped by a rifle in the hands of the guide. Out of those experiences, Fred came to be firmly of the opinion that the polar bear is the most dangerous game animal on this continent, the one that fears man least and is most ready to fight once his anger is aroused.

"A poll taken among hunters, especially those who have not gone after a polar bear, probably would give the Alaska brown top billing as the most dangerous," he told me once. "He reaches tremendous size, he's short-tempered and unpredictable, slow moving one minute, lightning and fury the next. He has the brute strength to kill a man with one swipe of a paw, and the vindictiveness to maul him as long as he is breathing. I suppose he has maimed or killed more hunters than any other animal Americans encounter. But on the basis of my own experience, I still say the white bear is more to be feared."

Not backed by a rifle, Fred put an arrow into his first grizzly at twenty-five yards, as I related in an earlier chapter. It started for him, snarling and bawling, then swerved, ran off and died.

He came across his second grizzly, a five-hundred-pound boar, fishing in a creek, and stalked to within fifteen yards. His arrow went in too far back for a quick kill, and the bear fought it long enough for Fred to get another on the string. Then the animal turned and ran. Fred was never sure whether it failed to locate him or whether it preferred to avoid a fight. In any case, his second arrow punched a hole in the skull and sliced all the way through the brain. Although it ran forty yards by reflex, the grizzly was dead on its feet.

Fred's first brown was sixty yards away when he drove an arrow into its lungs. It gave him less trouble than black bears he had shot. It turned tail, ran for fifty paces, fell and stayed down.

Brown No. 2 was only eighteen yards away when his razorhead knifed cleanly through its lungs. It ran past him on a used bear trail so close that he could have struck it with his bow. It must have seen him, but did not turn on him. It was dead in less than a minute.

The third brown Fred and his guide spotted on the beach of the Alaska Peninsula, using an outboard-powered skiff to hunt along shore. They shut off the motor, rowed ashore, took cover behind a big rock, and the bear came sauntering to meet them.

"There is no other experience in hunting quite like the last minute or two of waiting while an animal the size of a brown bear walks within bow range," Fred said afterward.

That bear was only twenty-five feet away when he discovered the two men crouching behind the rock. He stopped, swinging his head from side to side, testing the wind for scent. But they had it in their favor and it told him nothing.

They stayed as motionless as two driftwood stumps and when he moved on, broadside and a perfect target, Fred released his arrow. The bear was twenty feet away then.

The arrow sank to the feathers just behind a foreleg. Fred is convinced that the bear knew what had hurt him and where the hunters were. But he chose not to fight. He let go a hair-raising roar, streaked down the beach and tried to climb into the alders above high tide line, but couldn't make it. He rolled free of the brush and died.

When Fred went after his first polar bear the outcome was altogether different. Hidden by the upturned blocks of a pressure ridge on the ice off Barrow, he and his guide inched up within seventeen yards of a good bear. It was facing away from them and Fred could not get into position for a lung shot. On the advice of the guide, he risked driving a shot into the bear's rump.

"Hit him there and he'll turn around to fight the arrow, and you can get in a good one," the guide predicted.

It didn't work out that way. The arrow sliced into heavy muscle and the bear whipped around, but it wasted no time fighting the razorhead. The two men had not realized it knew they were there, but it came for them instantly, bawling its rage. The guide killed it with two shots from his backup rifle, a .300 Magnum. Fred was left with a filled polar bear license, but a trophy that a bowhunter could not claim.

Two years later he tried again, in the same general area off the coast of Alaska. When Fred and his pilot-guide spotted a bear of the size they were looking for, the guide dropped low and buzzed it to see what would happen. Plainly that bear had a chip on its shoulder. As the aircraft slanted down he came raging to meet it.

They landed a long way ahead and hid behind a pressure ridge. The bear came on, at the shuffling walk that can take one of his kind across thirty miles of ice in less than twenty-four hours. When he was abreast of the men, twenty-five yards away, he saw them and turned his head to watch, but did not quicken his pace.

Fred's arrow was a bit too far back. When he saw it bury itself to the feathers in the white fur he knew he had a wounded bear on his hands, but he was given no time to worry about that. The bear didn't even bawl. He swiveled around and charged like a thunderbolt. The guide's 180-grain softpoint smashed into his head at fifteen yards. Fred had two white-bear trophies now that he couldn't claim.

"I'm convinced that the white bear is the one to watch out for," he said after that hunt. "One swallow doesn't make a summer, and maybe my seven encounters with grizzlies, browns, and polars don't make me an expert, but at least they entitle me to an opinion."

He had better luck on his third polar bear hunt. He tried a different method that time, camping on the ice and baiting bears in, dispensing entirely with the use of aircraft. But bad weather interfered, and although the hunting party cooked seal blubber until they concluded that a bear could get scent of it fifteen miles downwind, none were attracted.

By that time the polar bear was the only major trophy in North America that Fred had not taken with bow. "I'll kill one that way one of these days," he told me before he went on the hunt. "When I do I'll consider I have taken the most dangerous animal on this continent."

In the end, after four weeks of fruitless effort, he gave up hunting from the ice and resorted to a light plane to locate a bear. It took only fifteen minutes of flying to find what he was looking for. His guide landed miles ahead of the bear and the men hiked back to meet him. They waited more than an hour but it paid off. The bear came on until he was only fifty yards away. Then the wind shifted a bit and he caught man scent.

He halted, looking straight at the hunters. Fred let his arrow go and saw a red stain spread close to the shoulder. The bear went down, recoiling from the hit and snapping at the arrow, but he didn't stay down long.

Fred's first two white bears had charged like steel springs released. This one rolled to his feet and ran like a rabbit. But he was lung shot and fell dead a hundred yards away.

"No man who goes after a polar bear can ever be sure whether he's going to be the hunter or the hunted," Fred says today.

All the evidence indicates that the ice bear's rage is extremely quick to kindle.

The one I killed in Hudson Bay in 1937 turned on me the instant he made me out.

I know a hunter in the north of Canada who killed a big female that was accompanied by a half-grown cub weighing about three hundred pounds. His

first shot spun the sow around but she did not know the cause of her hurt or where it had come from. She turned on her cub and knocked him flat with one blow, but he was big enough to fight back. He regained his feet and the two bears slugged it out, erect on their hind legs like overgrown human fighters, bawling and growling and tearing at one another. The hunter finally broke it up with a shot that killed the sow.

Seton believed that a female polar will always fight to protect her young, which is not entirely true of either the grizzly or brown. Stefansson, who dealt with a great many polar bears in a lifetime of arctic exploration, called them timid and afraid of man if encountered on land. But out on the limitless ice, where they were familiar with only three living things apart from their own kind, seals, foxes, and gulls, he rated them a different bear, likely to stalk a man and pounce on him as if he were a seal.

Stefansson told of one narrow escape he himself had, when he was hunting a bear among ice hummocks. It turned the tables, sneaked up behind him and gave him just enough time to fire one shot. It had not occurred to him to watch his back trail, he said, and that came close to proving a fatal mistake.

There have been countless instances of the white bear mauling or killing Eskimos, and it has been said many times that such attacks occur because the bear mistakes the man for a seal.

That is probably true in some cases. Certainly many of the bears live out their life on the ice or along desolate and unpeopled shores without ever encountering humans, and it would be easy for such animals not to recognize man for what he is if they finally came onto him. But errors of that kind do not account for all of the unprovoked attacks made by polar bears on people. The

arctic record bristles with reports of those that walked boldly into an Eskimo village or invaded the camp of explorers and attacked without warning. Driven by hunger? No one knows, but it seems likely.

In the last three years two oil workers were killed by white bears in the north of Canada. "Man-bear encounters have been increasing at an alarming rate," says Ian Stirling. "In 1975 alone, ten bears were killed in self-defense. As the number of people and camps in the Arctic continues to increase, the incidence of bear problems will also rise."

In the summer of 1975 a Canadian Wildlife Service research team headed by Stirling drugged and marked a four-hundred-pound male at the tip of the Boothia Peninsula, northernmost point on the mainland of North America.

A month later that bear invaded the camp of a geological survey party on the north shore of Somerset Island, two hundred miles farther north and one of the most desolate places in the Canadian arctic. Whether it had walked, swum, or ridden drifting ice those two hundred miles will never be known.

It came into the camp in the half-light of the northern summer night, about two o'clock in the morning. A young dog was tied outside one of the tents, and it may have enraged the bear by barking. In any case the dog was attacked instantly and injured so badly that it had to be killed later.

In a savage, slashing attack that has to be rated completely unprovoked, and that lasted less than five minutes, the bear tore up two rubber boats, ripped a tent open, put the dog out of action, and severely mauled two men. It was killed as it was dragging one of them out of the camp, apparently intending to make a meal of him.

In October of 1966 a polar bear killed a twelve-year-old boy near Fort Churchill on Hudson Bay, where large numbers of the white bears are attracted to a garbage dump, a highly unusual situation.

A year later another bear attack and mauled two Cree Indians near Churchill, a short distance from Fort Churchill. And in the autumn of 1968 a third bear killed a nineteen-year-old Eskimo youth just outside Fort Churchill.

In a savage, slashing attack that has to be rated completely unprovoked, and that lasted less than five minutes, the bear tore up two rubber boats, ripped a tent open, put the dog out of action, and severely mauled two men.

All three bears, killed by Royal Canadian Mounted Police, were males and none was full grown. Police rated the attacks unprovoked, but Canadian bear biologist Chuck Jonkel, who investigated the three cases, disagreed.

Jonkel found that the bear that figured in the 1966 episode had been shot at and wounded prior to the attack. A rifle bullet some time before had driven one of the animal's canine teeth into a nasal passage, resulting in blindness in one eye. And shortly before the attack, unknown persons had foolishly and wantonly fired .22 caliber bullets into the belly and hind legs of the bear.

"That attack could hardly be classed as unprovoked," Jonkel concluded dryly.

The bear that mauled the two Indians had frequented the Fort Churchill garbage dump for two months and had been photographed, fed, stoned, and chased by dogs and cars, until any natural fear he had felt for humans probably had turned into contempt and even hatred.

The bear that killed the young Eskimo in 1968 did so with less reason but again the human was at least partly to blame. The youth and several companions found bear tracks in the snow, followed them and crowded in on the bear where it had bedded down. It also had garbage in its stomach, and in all likelihood had grown unafraid of men from frequent contact with them. Certainly the fatal accident could have been avoided if the humans involved had used the caution that is due every wild bear.

The Manitoba Wildlife Branch has coined a very sensible slogan that deals with the situation perfectly. It has posted warning signs around the Churchill area, where humans and bears come in contact more frequently than anywhere else in the Arctic and where conflict is all too common. The signs read: "A Safe Polar Bear Is a Distant Polar Bear."

Wildlife authorities have made the statement many times that attacks on man by this bear are extremely rare. The same thing has also been said of the brown and grizzly. Actually, such attacks happen more frequently than many outdoor observers and writers are aware. What happens is that the incidents are usually reported in a very limited way if at all, and few persons learn of them. Unless the circumstances are extraordinarily dramatic or revolting, as in the case of the grizzlies that killed two college girls the same night in totally unrelated incidents in Glacier National Park, an attack on a human by any wild animal, bears included, rarely reaches the pages of newspapers outside the immediate area and almost never beyond the borders of the state involved.

For many years I made a specialty of investigating and verifying the circumstances of such attacks, in my capacity as a field editor on *Outdoor Life*. Often they supplied outstanding story material. There was no dearth of the occurrences. Our problem was to get word of them.

Some years back I made a trip to central British Columbia in quest of outdoor adventure stories. In a period of three weeks I unearthed a hunter who had been attacked by an enraged bull moose, a guide who had been scalped by a grizzly, a homesteader who had killed a charging grizzly at six feet, and three people who had been the victims of unprovoked attacks by cougars. Even the big cat that many hunters call the gutless wonder tries now and then to kill a human. Of those encounters not one had ever been reported outside the neighborhood where they occurred.

So far as I know, no wildlife agency in this country or Canada makes any attempt to keep track of and catalog wild-animal attacks on humans. Consequently, there is no real source of information on how often they happen.

Until a few years ago, the same thing was true of snakebite. Any statement on its frequency was pure guesswork. Then a painstaking study covering more than 5,000 hospitals and 36,000 doctors was carried out by Dr. Henry Parrish of the University of Missouri. It revealed the astonishing fact that between 6,500 and 7,000 persons are struck by venomous snakes in the United States in an average year.

No comparable study has ever been undertaken on animal attacks. I am sure they do not occur in anything like such numbers as snakebite. But I am also convinced that a reliable survey would show them to be more frequent than is commonly believed.

Whether the polar bear is in reality the most dangerous animal on the North American continent, more to be feared than even the grizzly or brown, is a question on which hunters, explorers, researchers, and others who have had dealings with him do not agree. Certainly I make no claim to knowing the answer. As a matter of fact, no one does. But of one thing I am sure. He belongs to a hot-tempered and dangerous clan and lives by its rules. He has killed men in the past, and will again. If you are a hunter compiling for your own safety a list of the trophy animals likely to retaliate, you will do well to put him at the top or close to it.

Index